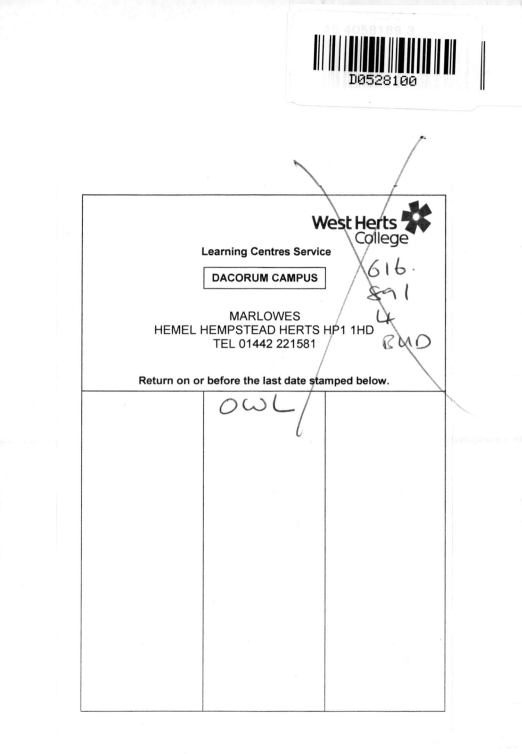

PSYCHOTHERAPY AND THE EVERYDAY LIFE

A Guide for the Puzzled Consumer

Emily Budick and
Rami Aronzon

KARNAC

Published in 2007 by
Karnac Books Ltd
118 Finchley Road
London NW3 5HT

British Library Cataloguing in Publication Data
A C.I.P. for this book is available from the British Library

ISBN-13: 978-1-85575-429-4

Edited, designed, and produced by HL Studios, Long Hanborough, Oxford
Printed and bound in Great Britain by Biddles Ltd., King's Lynn, Norfolk

www.karnacbooks.com

Contents

ABOUT THE AUTHORS   1

INTRODUCTION   2

CHAPTER ONE   11
Resisting therapy; or
every reason in the world not to go into therapy

CHAPTER TWO   25
The dynamic unconscious and the resistance to therapy:
a mini-introduction to Freud's theory of mind

CHAPTER THREE   43
Accepting the gift of therapy: resistance revisited

CHAPTER FOUR   60
The dynamic unconscious speaks

CHAPTER FIVE   74
Speaking your own mind; or
why words matter

CHAPTER SIX   91
Transference; or
the performance of your life, Part I
The clinical experience of psychotherapy:
what it feels like, how it works

CHAPTER SEVEN   116
Transference; or
the performance of your life, Part II

CHAPTER EIGHT   136
The listening cure: the therapist speaks at last

CHAPTER NINE   166
Neurobiology and the "value" of the talking cure

CHAPTER TEN   190
The psychotherapeutic couple: where we are after therapy;
an afterword

**SELECTED READINGS IN PSYCHOTHERAPY,
NEUROBIOLOGY AND RELATED MATTERS**   212

BIBLIOGRAPHY   214

INDEX   216

This book is dedicated to the daughters, our ideal readers:

Rachel Budick Almakies
Ayelet Budick Sharon
Shira Aronzon
Michal Aronzon

About the authors

Emily Budick, PhD, holds the Ann and Joseph Edelman Chair in American Studies at The Hebrew University of Jerusalem, where she is also Chair of the Department and coordinator for English literature studies. She has published and edited eight books and numerous essays in the field of literature and cultural studies. Her recent work includes psychoanalytic readings of Israeli as well as American Holocaust fiction. She is also the co-author (with Dr Judith Besserman) of *The Jerusalem Diet: Guided Imagery and the Personal Path to Weight Control*.

Rami Aronzon, MD, is a practising psychiatrist, psychoanalyst and psychotherapist in Jerusalem, Israel, where he is a member of the Israel Psychoanalytic Society. He teaches and consults at various institutions in Israel, including The Hebrew University and the Hadassah Medical School. For more than two decades he headed outpatient services at Jerusalem's Talbieh Mental Health Centre, while also serving as consultant and supervisory psychiatrist for the *Shaar Hanegev* Mental Health Clinic of the kibbutz movement. He continues to work summers as a general medical officer in northern Norway.

Introduction

*P*sychotherapy and the Everyday Life* is neither a textbook in the theory or practice of psychotherapy, nor is it a self-help manual. It is also not an autobiographical narrative—although it has something in common with all of these genres of writing. This book is primarily, as its subtitle suggests, *A Guide for the Puzzled Consumer*. It is intended to help a variety of individuals with differing relationships to the field of psychotherapy to negotiate its somewhat perplexing and slippery terrain.

First and foremost this book is written to serve as a guide for prospective and beginning patients of psychotherapeutic intervention of the particular kind known as psychoanalytic or psychodynamic psychotherapy. Psychoanalytic psychotherapy (hereafter also referred to simply as psychotherapy) is the kind of therapy that most closely follows Freud's own dynamic model of mind, both in theory and in practice. This is so despite its important differences from Freudian psychoanlysis, which we will also be detailing (the title of our book echoes a famous work by Freud). *Psychotherapy and the Everyday Life* is intended to help individuals who are seeking some sort of psychological help to determine whether psychoanalytic psychotherapy is appropriate for them and why. It is also geared to helping those who have already entered such therapy to understand what the process entails so that they will be better able to stick with it, especially in the early weeks when (as we shall see) the "resistance" to therapy is extremely high. Psychoanalytic psychotherapy is in every way a perplexing business. Its value to its recipients might well be enhanced through certain sorts of clarification concerning both its goals and its processes.

There are therapists who would disagree with this approach. They would argue that psychotherapy is best entered into innocently, precisely because of the centrality of "resistance" to the therapy itself. Yet who of today's consumers enters psychotherapy or any other sort of therapy "innocently"? In the 21st century Freud is a household word, and often a dirty word. Most of us are also familiar with different sorts of psychological interventions and their purported benefits and disadvantages. We therefore decide to enter psychotherapy or not on the basis of partial information, including misinformation, and a good measure of false expectation and misconception. These can be fatal to either initiating psychotherapy or sticking with it. In the same vein, even though psychotherapy of the type we are going describe shares many features with the *ur* therapy psychoanalysis, including the concept of *resistance*, nonetheless psychotherapy is a compromise with the rigours of psychoanalysis proper. It is already an accommodation to the very different demands and expectations of the contemporary patient. By entering psychotherapy knowing something about how it works and what you are likely to gain from it, it may be possible to help augment this shift from some of the premises and structure of psychoanalysis without losing altogether the vital connection of psychotherapy to psychoanalytic theory and practice.

In this way, *Psychotherapy and the Everyday Life* is a guide to the perplexed consumer who is considering or only beginning to experience psychoanalytic psychotherapy. But the book imagines a second audience as well. *Psychotherapy and the Everyday Life* is not a scholarly book. Nonetheless, it does undertake to say things that might well be of value to students of psychotherapy and novice psychotherapists as well, concerning what the process looks and feels like, in particular from the patient's perspective. As a guide to all of these perplexed consumers and practitioners, *Psychotherapy and the Everyday Life* hopes to transform some of the often off-putting difficulties of psychoanalytic psychotherapy into useful frustrations and even fascinations. It also hopes to help sustain them as such.

Psychotherapy of the particular kind we are going to present in this book is about discovering meanings. It is about what we might think of as the meaning-making-ness of our lives. In the psychoanalytic psychotherapeutic view of things, such meaning-making-ness does not refer simply to how our lives—our thoughts, feelings, perceptions, wishes, fears and so on—seem meaningful to us in some ordinary, rational, common-sense kind of way. Rather, psychoanalytic psychotherapy is concerned with how meaningfulness is produced in our lives in sometimes troubling and less than satisfactory ways, and often in ways that we barely grasp. When we examine the production of the meaningfulness of our lives, we discover that (sometimes for the better, sometimes for the worse) it often has very little to do with what we think is meaningful to us, or what we would wish our meanings to be. In large measure, psychoanalytic psychotherapy is concerned with exposing the discrepancy between our rational, intellectual comprehension of our lives and some other way we might have of understanding ourselves. It is also about providing us with tools for mediating the gap between what we mean and what we think we mean or want to mean.

Most of us do not, however, go into therapy in order to discover something so abstract as how our lives make sense. And this is the rub. We go into therapy because we are in psychological distress. We are in pain. What we want is comfort. We want relief. And indeed: because the simple act of talking to another person, whatever the nature of the conversation, often does provide some measure of relief, many people do experience the comfort they seek, at least initially. And then, feeling better, they quit. Or, staying on a bit longer, they discover what psychoanalytic psychotherapy is really about, which is the often frustrating and difficult process of reflecting on those psychological mechanisms by which we are who we are. And then they quit.

A major objective of this book is to help the patient of psychotherapeutic intervention to stay with the therapy beyond both the initial satisfactions and the initial frustrations that the process entails. The perplexing paradox that this book is intended to help unravel is how and why the route provided by psychoanalytic psychotherapy might be a better path to psychological health than other seemingly simpler and more straightforward therapeutic paths, at least in the long run, and at least for some of us. This is so even though the process, as we've begun to suggest, does not initially provide the comfort most of us come into therapy seeking, except in a very superficial way.

In the years since Freud first developed his psychodynamic model of mind, many competing and conflicting theories and practices have entered the field of psychological therapy. Although *Psychotherapy and the Everyday Life* is not a theoretical or scholarly book and is not intended as an introduction to Freudian or other theories of mind, we will, in the course of our discussions, be explaining certain basic Freudian and non-Freudian concepts—for those whose interest in their own minds might also lead them to be interested in theories of mind as such. We will also be specifying some of the important differences between psychoanalysis and psychotherapy, which make a book of the sort we have written a useful tool for patients of psychotherapeutic intervention in particular. We are throughout this book very mindful of the transformations in the fields of psychoanalysis and psychotherapy, some of which began to develop during Freud's own lifetime. Yet *Psychotherapy and the Everyday Life* is an unabashedly Freudian book. In what follows we will suggest why Freud's model of mind, even if we want to reformulate some of his theories, might still be the best way we have of conceptualizing mental process. We will also suggest why, therefore, it might also still be the best guide for developing strategies of psychological intervention.

When all is said and done, what almost all psychological theories of mind give us are verbal "pictures" or descriptions of what are otherwise incomprehensible, inexpressible and largely unimaginable mental activities. This is true of all the contenders in the field, from the behavioural and cognitive therapies to object relations theory and relational psychology to Freudian theory itself. It is the case even with the more scientifically adduced models produced by fields such as neurobiology or neuro-psychoanalysis (about which we will have more to say in the later chapters of this book). The technical vocabularies of the mental sciences almost inevitably fail to capture adequately the concepts they are meant to describe. Nonetheless, the mental activity that forms of the basis of Freudian psychoanalytic theory, as of other contending theories, is not dependent on our ability to name and describe it. Whatever terms particular analysts use to define this or another phenomenon of the psychological life doesn't change the basic fact that we *have* an internal, mental world. Concerning this fact, analysts, therapists, scientists and most of us ordinary folk as well are agreed. Definitions shift; theories change; the human mind persists and begs to be understood. Therefore, another objective of this book is to contribute (even if in a small way) to the project of understanding who and what we human beings are as creatures of consciousness and mind.

The two voices

A final word of introduction before we begin, concerning who is addressing you in this book; for this is a book written in two voices, not one.

One of these voices is the voice that most of us expect to hear in a book like this. This is the voice of the professional psychotherapist, who in this case is also a psychiatrist and a psychoanalyst. This professional person of over thirty years' experience has headed a major department of psychiatry and psychotherapy. He has also maintained a private clinical practice and he is currently active in numerous institutes and institutions involved in psychiatric, psychoanalytic and psychotherapeutic work. Sometimes this expert voice of the professional therapist speaks on its own—especially towards the end of the book. More often, however, it speaks either through or in combination with the less tutored, more anecdotal voice of the non-professional former psychotherapeutic patient—in fact, his own former patient.

This other non-professional voice is the more pervasive and

persistent of the two voices in this text. Be assured: even where this non-professional voice is speaking more or less independently, it has been everywhere informed by extensive reading in the field of Freud, psychoanalysis and psychotherapy. It has also been deepened by the professional expertise of the professional therapist. The professional therapist has acted to ensure that all the statements made in this book are accurate and that the therapist's, as well as the patient's, perspective on psychotherapy is fairly represented. Nonetheless, it is the non-professional voice that dominates this book: her stories and anecdotes, her experience of psychotherapy. Since this non-professional voice is also the voice of a professional literary critic, a feature of psychoanalytic psychotherapy that will emerge very strongly in these pages is its story-telling—story-listening quality. But we get ahead of ourselves.

Most introductions to psychotherapy, whether for the popular or the professional audience, have been written by professional psychotherapists (psychoanalysts, psychiatrists, clinical psychologists, social workers, and so on). These are individuals who are often sufficiently removed from their own early experiences of psychotherapy that they may perhaps no longer remember precisely what it feels like to encounter this strange and bewildering terrain of therapeutic process. They lack the non-professional patient's more basic and immediate experience of therapy. It is this immediacy of experience that we hope to provide in this book. It is our hope that by presenting psychotherapy through the personal experiences of a non-professional patient we will provide access to the processes of psychotherapeutic intervention in a way that makes these processes more comprehensible and (even more importantly, perhaps) more tolerable to the potential or beginning patient. By the same token, even though this book is *not* a handbook or guide for professionals, nonetheless professionals, especially those at the beginning of their careers, may also find here a useful picture of the therapeutic process from within the patient's experience of it. For those who have had the experience of psychotherapy in the past, whether they are now professionals in the field or not, this book might even serve as a useful, friendly reminder of where you've been and what you experienced there.

There are other advantages, we believe, to the non-professional, autobiographical approach. Common to almost all of the professionally authored books on the market (many of which we cite at the end of this book) is that they assume a great amount of familiarity with psychological theory and clinical practice. Often, too, there is a blurring of the lines that differentiate one kind of therapy from another, such that the theory and practice they present do not correspond to the experiences and needs of the ordinary reader. Most of these studies also proceed through multiple case studies taken from the analyst/therapist's own practice. As such, they often deal with individuals whose life crises are more complex and troubled than what many of us experience in our lives. This means that many of us, whose life problems seem to us more mundane and uninteresting, cannot quite find ourselves in the studies presented.

Even though psychoanalytic psychotherapy very often deals with very serious psychological problems (such as chronic depression, borderline personality disorder and any number of psychotic, as opposed to neurotic, conditions), it is also geared to treating the more common and less life-threatening situations that characterize many of our psychological lives. Therefore, even though *Psychotherapy and the Everyday Life* proceeds from a much narrower and less dramatic base than many of the professionally authored studies, it may be more pertinent to most of us seeking professional help with our emotional problems. In staying with the same patient, it can also tell a more continuous, coherent story of the ordinary, individual person confronting the paradoxes of psychotherapy. Psychotherapy puts in the way of the patient hurdles that can be so off-putting as to interfere with the process getting under way. These hurdles are integral to the psychotherapeutic process. Without them, psychodynamic psychotherapy cannot proceed. By presenting a single, non-professional, albeit informed experience of psychotherapy, we hope only to help prospective and beginning patients of psychological intervention to navigate those hurdles with a bit more ease.

As a co-authored book, we will also be opening up to view not only the patient's experience of psychotherapy but the therapist's as well. Even if the cooperation and mutual interaction between the two voices through which this book has been written might seem to imitate the dialogue through which psychotherapy proceeds, it is, as we hope to make clear, very unlike that other conversation. For the most part, we will be presenting the conversation of psychotherapy as the patient experiences it: as having to do with patient's thoughts, feelings, wishes, enactments, and so on. Yet we did not want to lose the special opportunity afforded by the post-therapy relationship between the therapist and the patient to let the patient into the arena of the therapist's mind as well, even though this is precisely not the site of psychotherapy itself. By gaining access to the therapist's inner thoughts and responses (the internal dialogue, as it were, which the therapist does not necessarily bring directly into the clinical setting, and certainly not in so many words) we can, we believe, achieve additional insights into the therapeutic process. These insights can also be of assistance in helping the psychotherapeutic dialogue to proceed, especially in the early stages of therapy.

For the therapist, as for the patient, there are considerable hurdles and paradoxes to confront in the psychotherapeutic conversation. There are feelings of frustration, failure, even irritation and anger, which the therapist needs to negotiate in order to keep himself available to the patient. The psychodynamic component of psychodynamic therapy doesn't have to do with the patient alone. It has to do with the therapist as well. This aspect of the therapist's experience will also be brought to bear on the picture of psychotherapy that this book presents.

In general the therapeutic relationship between the patient and the therapist ends with the end of therapy itself, often to the great consternation of the patient as well as some sadness on the part of the therapist. We will also speak, in our afterword, about this often painful but very important final stage in the therapy. There we will also talk about why this particular therapist, still reluctant despite the gap of many years, finally consented to participate in the writing of this book, and what that has meant for the book as such. Throughout our authorial collaboration we have tried to use the post-therapy exchange between us to reflect on psychotherapy itself from the somewhat unique perspective that our co-authorship provides. Since "post-therapy" is the place most of us come to occupy in our experience of therapy, there is in this final dimension of the exchange between us also some insight into how therapy changes the way we perceive and act in the world.

***

Preserving our ability to remain self-conscious and self-reflective can be one long-range effect of psychotherapy. The same might be said of our ability to maintain our ongoing conversation with ourselves and our world—a conversation that this book itself endeavours to embody. Therefore it is with the conversation that is psychoanalytic psychotherapy that we open this book. Or, more precisely, it is with the *resistance* to that conversation that we begin. Somewhat ironically, perhaps, the resistance to therapy and the many resistances to self-knowledge through which the psychotherapeutic conversation proceeds and on which it will reflect are the fundamental (if highly perplexing) components of this particular brand of psychotherapeutic intervention. Resistance is at the heart of psychotherapy. It is, therefore, the resistance-to-therapy to which we now turn.

CHAPTER ONE

Resisting therapy; or every reason in the world not to go into therapy

E ssentially psychoanalytic psychotherapy is a conversation. It is, however, a conversation of a very special kind. Like an ordinary conversation, it takes place between two people. Two people sit in a room and talk. But unlike our everyday conversations, the psychotherapeutic conversation is not a symmetrical or even a mutual exchange. Rather, the conversation takes place only for the benefit of one of the participants. This person, furthermore, who also does most of the talking, does not engage in conversation for the usual reasons. He does not talk in order simply to inform, or amuse, or otherwise interact with the other individual—even though he might think this is why he's speaking. Rather, the psychotherapeutic patient talks for the very specific purpose of eventually coming to hear his own words in a new and more psychologically pertinent or useful way.[1]

[1] A word concerning the uses of the pronouns *he, she, him, her*: especially in a book on psychoanalytic psychotherapy, where the issue of the gender of the patient and therapist has constituted a topic unto itself, it is very important to achieve gender-neutrality in the use of pronoun referents. Therefore, unless we are referring specifically to a male or female individual (Freud, for example, or to the male co-author psychotherapist or the female co-author former patient), the pronouns referring to the patient and the therapist are arbitrarily male or female. Sometimes the therapist is a *she* and sometimes a *he*. Occasionally we have referred to the patient or therapist as *he or she* or even *they* in order to remind the reader of the rule of gender neutrality. This is now standard practice in scholarly writings. We hope it will not be confusing to the reader less familiar with these new conventions of gender reference.

In many ways the conversation of psychotherapy is more like story-telling and story-listening than conversation as such. This story-telling and story-listening conversation must also be understood to include a number of somewhat unique features. When we say that the patient in psychotherapy tells his story, we don't refer only to the words in which he narrates events or feelings or ideas to his therapist. Rather, the patient's story-telling consists of all the actions and feelings, thoughts and desires through which he enacts himself in his everyday life, that often form the content of the stories he is now, in therapy, telling his therapist. The story may also include elements and components that the patient doesn't mean to include. In fact the story told may have more to do with what the patient is not telling in so many words than with what he chooses to say. In other words, the story told in the psychotherapeutic settings exceeds the intended, edited version that the narrator is putting together for the benefit of his listener. As the therapy proceeds, such story-telling also comes more and more to involve the patient's relationship with the therapist. In the patient's reactions and responses to the therapist and in what stories he chooses to tell or not tell to the therapist and when, the patient is also telling a story. This has to do with what is called *transference* and we will discuss it later.

When we say that psychotherapy is a form of story-telling, then, we mean that it both proceeds through and is concerned with all those life stories that we are telling and living all the time and in many different ways. This is true in terms of both the lives we live and tell in our "real" lives and the stories we tell and enact about those lives in the clinical setting. It also concerns not only the stories told but the story that is itself being told in the when and why of which stories the patient chooses to tell the therapist at any particular moment. Additionally, it has to do with both the conscious features of our story-telling (whether we are telling those stories or enacting them) and, as will occupy us more and more in this book, with its *un*conscious aspects. We will speak in a moment about what it means when we say that something is *un*conscious. It is not in the least obvious what the word *unconscious* means, at least in the psychoanalytic psychotherapeutic context. But when we speak of story-telling in the psychotherapeutic sense, we do not mean only what we rationally, consciously intend our stories to say or mean. Rather, we mean also what in fact they do say and mean in multiple and complex ways.

The purpose and texture of story-telling in the clinical setting is also somewhat different from ordinary story-telling in our everyday lives. Its purpose is not so much to communicate something to someone else (though it may often seem like this is what we are doing in therapy). Rather, its purpose is to produce on the part of the story-teller a certain relationship to her own story—a relationship of introspection, reflection and self-understanding. The story-telling we do in psychotherapy, in other words, is intended to enable the story-teller to hear her own story and "retell" it in new and different terms. This revised re-telling, furthermore, is to occur not only in the verbal narration of her story in the clinical setting, but in the living of that life-story in the world as well.

Therefore the story-listening that accompanies the story-telling in this psychotherapeutic conversation is also quite unique. It is being done not only by the ostensible listener, the therapist, but also by the story-teller herself. Both of the story-listeners in this conversation—that is, the therapist and the patient—are also listening for specific things.

The therapist for his part is largely, though not completely, a silent partner to the story-telling aspect of the psychotherapeutic conversation. At the same time, however, he is an extremely *active* listener; and in the early stages of therapy often a more vocal listener than the patient himself. When the therapist does respond to what the story-teller is saying, it is to call attention to this or that detail or to note a repetition or a pattern or a hesitation or an excess of emotion. The purpose of this active listening is to make the story-teller into an active—focused and insightful— story-listener as well. For, as we've said, that is what the story-telling conversation of psychotherapy is finally for: the story-teller's re-hearing of his story. This re-hearing does not take into account only what the patient thinks he is saying or wants to be saying (on the conscious level). Rather, it takes into account what in fact he *is* saying, in all its multiple, affective, unconscious as well as conscious depths and nuances. It is this re-hearing that may ultimately permit the story-teller to re-tell his story on more useful and satisfying psychological terms, not only in words but, more vitally, in the actual living of his life.

What is essential in psychotherapy is telling and reflecting on *our own* stories. Nonetheless, as we all know, other people's stories can also be of help to us, even in our most personal and private areas of concern. In fact, we are usually better equipped to pay attention to other people's stories than to our own. We grow up listening to such stories, whether in personal conversations, books, newspapers, or movies, and indeed we do learn from them. We are generally less defensive about other people's narratives than we are about our own, more ready to be amused or saddened or enlightened. The former patient is the major protagonist in the stories about to be told in this book because there is no other experience of psychotherapy she knows as well as her own. Hopefully her experience is sufficiently normative to be applicable to others. Insofar as such autobiographical narrative also continues the work of therapy, it may also be taken as an indication of the ways in which, once we have had the experience of psychotherapy, we can continue to make use of it. This is true not only of the particular insights we have gained into ourselves, but also in terms of what psychotherapy can teach us in a more general way about how thinking and feeling may come together in the living of our lives. In the absence of your story (or until you have your own story of psychotherapy to instruct you), our hope is that my story will suffice to make certain useful points about the psychotherapeutic process—including the all-important point that our stories are worth telling and listening to.

So let me begin with the story of my resistance to therapy. A story about the resistance to psychotherapy might seem as odd a way to begin a book advocating such therapy as telling somebody else's story to introduce a process almost wholly predicated on telling your own story. Yet a major feature of the story-telling conversation of psychotherapy, as we've already begun to suggest, is our resistance to reflecting on the stories we tell—both in the narrating of them and, more importantly, in the living of them. No matter how narratively inclined or motivated for therapy we are, most of us do, for the most part, defend against hearing what our stories (including our everyday enactments of our lives) are really saying to and about us.

During therapy itself, it is the therapist's job to find ways of helping you recognize and tackle your resistances. But the resistance to therapy is one of those paradoxes or hurdles that also precede therapy. By putting the subject of resistance up front and making it a part of your conscious knowledge of what psychotherapy entails, we hope only to enable you to enter into the process with just a bit more readiness to meet, grapple with and tolerate this way we all have of defending against and resisting self-understanding.

Without further ado, then, here is the story of my resistance to therapy. I call it:

The gift of the two mugs

I'd been in therapy for a few months when I decided to buy my therapist a gift. I felt grateful for any number of things (including, simply, that I felt better), and giving gifts is one way that I, like many people, have of showing appreciation. My impulse to give him a present seemed as natural and innocent as that.

So I presented him with two very charming brick red coffee mugs with little blue birds on them. He thanked me for them. He asked if I wished to "reflect" on them (whatever *that* might mean). And then those two coffee mugs stayed put on the therapist's desk, unused, stationary like statues, for the next several sessions until, in desperation and anguish (and some measure of wry humour), I said to him: those cups aren't going anywhere, are they? until they are thoroughly analysed! At this point the therapist, with that infuriating calm of the professional therapist (which most of us in psychotherapy come to know all too well), asked me again if I wish to "reflect" on my gift of the two mugs. It was at that point that I blew up at the therapist completely—an odd reaction for me, who tends rarely to express anger, at least not so directly. I was terribly hurt. I felt accused, rejected. I had not gone into therapy to analyse anything so trivial, inconsequential and (in my view of things) rather endearing as my gift-giving tendencies. I wanted my gift to be accepted simply as a gift. Some things, it seemed to me (and I said so), were beyond analysis. (Sometimes a coffee mug is only a coffee mug).

Now in truth I had put some time and thought into the selection of my gift. I felt awkward giving a gift to this person whom I really didn't know that well, and a man at that. I didn't want my gift to be "misinterpreted" in that ordinary way in which sometimes our gestures are, we feel, misunderstood. Also, I already knew enough about psychotherapy, both from my own slight experience of it and from the reading I'd been doing, to know that, like everything else I said or did, the gift could (alas) become an occasion for some sort of "deep interpretation" or other. So I worried whether to give my therapist one cup or two. One cup seemed to me to imply that I thought he was alone in the world, which I actually also knew not to be the case. Two cups might seem to be an invitation for him to invite me to share a cup of coffee with him: one cup for him, one for me. And so, realizing there was no way out of this dilemma of the way in which the coffee mugs might be seen to express some feeling or idea or whatever in my mind, I decided to go with what seemed to me the more generous of the two options: two cups, and analysis be darned! After all a coffee mug in and of itself, I said to myself, is a rather innocuous kind of gift. That is why I'd chosen it (I thought). The two cups, for me at least, expressed my generosity.

Among the many things I didn't really think to ask myself was why I'd wanted to give my therapist a gift in the first place. I didn't, in other words, want to think about why I give gifts in general. Nor did I especially want to consider why I wanted to give *this* gift at *this* time to *this* person in *this* particular, specifically *non-personal*, *clinical* relationship. This was a relationship in which I was already rewarding him in the form of money for being so kind as to listen to me.

I had entered therapy for many of the typical reasons people enter therapy. I was feeling very unhappy. Old satisfactions seemed to have dissolved. I was having trouble adjusting to the new realities of my life: grown-up children, for example, who had, as children do, moved out of the house; and, much more sadly, the death of a child some years earlier. My gift of the two mugs seemed quite beside the point. *All people give gifts,* I reasoned to myself.

Furthermore, generosity is by anyone's standards a *good* thing, not a bad thing. I didn't exactly feel like having my generosity analysed out of existence. It was, I felt (and for that matter still do), one of my better qualities. Let those who don't give gifts, I argued to myself, get themselves examined and condemned.

It was only much later in the process of my therapy that I came to see two crucial elements of the psychotherapeutic experience. Once I could see these things, I would be able to lower my guard enough to seize the opportunity for self-understanding that even two little coffee mugs might afford.

Firstly, everything that we say and do expresses us. These expressions, furthermore, both positive and negative, are all part of the same fabric that constitutes our own unique personality. In other words, the way we hang together as psychological entities (as personalities or selves) is true on every level of our being, from the profoundly serious to the apparently trivial. For this reason, while our major life issues can never be reduced to the little things we say and do (like giving gifts), they can be broached and explored through even these minor enactments of self. Freud's rule of *free association*, which psychotherapy adopts from psychoanalysis and which my own therapist was constantly urging on me, insists that the patient say whatever comes into his mind. This rule makes use of the fact that everything we say or do originates within our own minds. Where else might we imagine such thoughts to originate? Therefore simple utterances and deeds can provide a window into that mind. The mind we are expressing when we say and do things is *our* mind, no one else's. That's not something to fear, it's something to cherish and hold on to.

The second thing I had to come to understand is that self-reflection isn't about finding fault. It is not about blaming anyone, not even one's self. That is why the therapist had asked me to "reflect" on my gift; he didn't ask me to "interpret" it, as if it had a fixed, absolute and very dark, murky meaning. Reflection, *self*-reflection, is about seeing reasons, perceiving depth, and comprehending the circumstances in which we do the things we do, both for better and for worse. It is about seeing for ourselves and putting into our own words how we are unique, coherent psychological entities.

What I wanted when I entered therapy—what I thought therapy was for—was simply to take away the pain I was feeling. And to some degree, in those early months, that is what happened. My simply being able to talk to this other person, who was also outside the immediate circle of people who were a part of my life's tensions and frustrations, did bring a measure of comfort. That is why I wanted to give a gift, or rather, that is why I *thought* I wanted to give a gift. But while diminishing psychological pain is certainly a major goal of psychotherapy, it isn't the only goal. Nor is it necessarily the immediate goal. Just as there are many forms of therapy, so there are variations within the field of psychotherapy itself. Some psychotherapists intervene more than others, some less. My own therapist was very kindly, but he was also very formal and reserved. He intruded as little possible. As I came to understand it later, he was trying to give me as much space as possible to come to my own insights and perceptions. That meant that sympathy and consolation were not always immediately forthcoming.

I couldn't for the life of me see how reflecting on my gift-of-the-two-mugs could possibly be of any benefit in helping me cope with the large life issues that had brought me into therapy. In retrospect is it hard for me to see how I could *not* have seen, at the very least, the connection between feeling lonely because my children were grown and into their own lives and being thankful to and wanting to further my relationship with this person who was sitting there listening to my every complaint and problem.

Part of what therapy had to teach me, in order to open up even this narrow avenue of insight into my inner life, was to see the gift-of-the-mugs from outside myself. In fact I had to come to see it as if from the therapist's perspective. From his point of view the mugs were not simply a gift (though they were that too, which is why he thanked me for them). Rather, they were also—and primarily—an action or event in which I was saying something to him. Indeed, instead of saying this something in words, I was expressing it as an enactment. I was giving him a gift. To make matters even more complicated, this enactment was anything but self-knowing.

I had decided, with all the powers of my conscious mind, to buy him a gift. I had also decided, again with all my faculties of decision-making wholly intact, what gift to buy. I was also convinced I understood why I was doing this. Nonetheless, the giving-of-the-gift was *also*, perhaps even primarily, an enactment of wishes and desires of which I was not in the least conscious. Just as importantly, my giving of the gift was also a censoring of those wishes and desires. For whatever reasons, I could not permit myself to express these wishes and desires directly. I couldn't even acknowledge them to myself. Nor was this gift-giving event taking place somewhere in the past or in the outside world that formed the bases of the many conversations that he and I were having. On the contrary, it was taking place right here and now, with him, in this clinical setting. My therapist was inviting me to reflect on nothing less than all these facets of my giving of the gift-of-the-mugs.

While I was thinking and feeling whatever I was thinking and feeling, and defending against those thoughts and feelings, the therapist was also having thoughts and feelings. He was asking himself, how does it happen that she is giving me a gift, this gift? What might the giving-of-the-gift-of-the-coffee-mugs express, and just now, in the context of these other things we have been talking about? in the context of the reasons she has given me for coming into therapy in the first place? He may not have been *saying* any of these things—for reasons we will get to. And these thoughts and questions may not be as orderly and unperplexed in his mind as this transcription of them on the page makes them seem. For the therapist, psychodynamic therapy is every bit as dynamic as it is for the patient. It is very often frustrating and bewildering, even annoying and irritating. Indeed, as I write these words I can still feel my co-author peering over my shoulder, cautioning me, as I set about describing the therapist's role, not to idealize the therapist: what the therapist does *not* know concerning the patient, he assures me, is far greater than what he does know—as we shall see in greater detail later. And this is a great source of tension for the therapist; also one of the reasons he continually has to return the conversation to the patient, for the patient's active clarification, reflection and narration.

Whatever the therapist was thinking and feeling and whatever he was saying—none of which I understood in any depth—what he did after he ran into my hurt refusal to reflect on the gift-of-the-mugs was to let the issue drop, at least for the time being, and at least as a direct topic of conversation between us. To be sure, even after the issue of the coffee cups was set aside, he was still nonetheless thinking his thoughts and feeling his feelings in relation to the gift, as in relation to the many other things I was saying and doing. And what he was bringing into our conversation, while not expressing these thoughts and feelings directly, were often hints in their direction. He would try to prompt or prod me to reflect on what I was so clearly resisting reflecting on—not the gift itself but the giving of it and the wishes that the giving was expressing. In this way he was holding open a space for me for such time as I might be ready to reflect, if not on this particular event of gift-giving, then on some other incident or item of conversation that might arise in some other context. This other subject, he knew, because of the way we humans are psychologically wired, would probably be some other expression of many of the same wishes being expressed in the gift-of-the-two-mugs.

The therapist already understood what I still had to come to see: that to understand the many things my gift was saying *to me*, *about me*, I had to permit myself to become self-reflective where I least wanted to be. I had to be willing to hear for myself the story—indeed, the many stories—my gift was telling. I had to be willing to reflect on those stories. I also had to be willing to put them into other words: the words not of unconsciously motivated action but of conscious knowledge and reflection. Language is a major tool of psychotherapy. It is how the conversation proceeds. Nonetheless, not any word suffices to clarify what an action or feeling is expressing. Words can be just as un-self-knowing as the actions or feelings they attempt to convey.

In large part psychotherapy is about discovering the larger depths and meanings of the words in which we tell our stories. This means finding still other words through which to narrate our experiences. Such words can begin to clarify and specify with ever increasing precision and depth what *else* our words and actions are saying. These words can do good, useful psychological work for us. They can help us retell and thereby revise our stories, in the living as well as in the telling of them.

Many details pertaining to my gift-giving and my "generosity" emerged later, in the course my therapy, as I began to "work through" the resistance to hearing what my story of the gift-of-the-two-mugs was saying. What working through resistance means is a part of what psychotherapy is all about, and we will have more to say about it in the course of this book. What I want to put up front now, however, is the way in which I initially experienced the gift-of-the-mugs, or, more precisely, what I understood to be its rejection by the therapist. Specifically, I want to illustrate how I resisted reflecting on the mugs. This resistance, in this particular instance, was also a very apt expression of what might be termed *my resistance to therapy* as such.

Resisting therapy

Of course, as I've already indicated, on some level at least I knew that by giving my therapist the mugs I was inviting a discussion of what the gift might mean. Indeed, the word *invitation* even occurred to me, albeit in relation to giving him two mugs rather than one. But rather than take my own word seriously (that giving the two mugs might be construed as an invitation to something), I refused the invitation I myself initiated. That invitation was not simply the invitation I might in some veiled way be expressing when I gave him the two coffee mugs. After all, if I'd given him the single mug I would have been issuing the same invitation, albeit in a different way: if the single mug expressed the thought that he was alone in world, didn't it also express my wish that, by giving him a gift, by entering myself into his world, I might help make him feel less alone? Wasn't the single cup, like the two cups, a projection onto him of my own sense of aloneness and of my desire for conversation over a cup of coffee?

The invitation I was refusing in refusing to reflect on the gift-of-the-two-mugs was not the invitation to drink a cup of coffee. It was, rather, nothing less than the invitation I had issued *to myself* when I entered into therapy. This was the invitation to reflect on who and what and how I am in the world—in every way and in every context, down to the last coffee cup. For that is what psychotherapy is: a story-telling-story-listening conversation in which we are being invited (as much by ourselves as by the therapist; we're the ones who are paying, after all) to reflect on our selves. In refusing to reflect on the gift-of-the-mugs, I was doing nothing less than refusing that invitation to therapy, and I was doing so vehemently and angrily.

Why? Why should I resist what I had chosen for myself and was, indeed, paying to receive? After all, I was the one who had entered therapy. No one was forcing me into it, least of all the therapist. And yet I was resisting doing what therapy, in some large degree, is about.

I had engaged this other individual, a professional in the field of psychotherapy, to do precisely what he was doing: listening attentively, actively to my story and trying to help me reflect on it so that I could learn from it. But I was totally unwilling to let his thoughts, his feelings, his intuitions about what my story might be saying (indeed, that it might be saying anything at all) in any way contradict what I knew, absolutely *knew,* beyond the shadow of any doubt, my actions meant. I was, in short, absolutely unwilling to surrender control over *my* story as I understood it and wanted it told. Among the many things that psychotherapy is about, it is also about letting another person in to the place where our thoughts and feelings happen for us. That is not an easy thing for most of us to do.

Ironically, paradoxically, psychotherapy almost seems to require having already resolved the resistances to self-knowledge which are the objective of psychotherapy to "work through". Entering into therapy while resisting almost any opening up of one's life story expresses a conflict between the wish and need for insight and the tremendous anxiety that such an insight threatens to produce. This is one of those catch-22s (hurdles or paradoxes) of the psychotherapeutic situation, which this discussion of resistance is meant to help soften and negotiate for those who are just entering into the process.

One reason for telling my story (indeed, one reason for writing this book) is that even though the resistance to self-reflection and self-knowledge is inevitable at every stage of the psychotherapeutic process, for me it was also a feature of my not having any clear idea whatsoever what psychotherapy was all about. As I have already said, I knew that I was supposed to talk about anything and everything that came into my mind. My therapist certainly said this to me often enough. What I thought this meant, however, was simply that I got to choose the subjects. I thought it meant merely that it was OK to talk about anything I wanted—even (or especially) subjects one might avoid in one's everyday conversations. It didn't occur to me at all that my conversation with the therapist wasn't going to be so straightforwardly deliberate and consciously motivated. It certainly didn't occur to me that I was going to actively resist saying so much. So what about that?—he might casually interject as I was hurrying through one incident or another; does this bring anything to mind? Any feelings? Associations? And I would be totally bewildered as to what he wanted from me. I thought maybe the problem was linguistic, that I wasn't expressing myself clearly enough, which for a literary critic like me wasn't a good feeling at all. It just made me more jittery, more defensive.

I came into therapy to talk about what I, with all the powers of my reasoning mind, considered to be the large issues of my life and to get advice, sympathy and an explanation from him (who was supposed to be an expert in matters of the mind) as to why I felt the way I did. I didn't come to talk about what a gift of coffee mugs might, in some associative, unconscious way I didn't in the least comprehend, be telling me about those large issues. I certainly wasn't going to be told that my gift might somehow be a more profoundly meaningful expression of what I wished and what I felt about those wishes than what I could rationally and more discursively explain for myself. One of the most disappointing aspects of psychotherapy for the beginning patient is that you don't usually get advice. You are not told why you feel what you feel. You are told instead to reflect on what you feel. You are encouraged to clarify and explain to yourself what it is you want and what prevents you from acting on those desires. Sometimes it's frustrating beyond words.

Of course even if in the early days of my therapy my resistance had something to do with ignorance and misunderstanding, it was also, perhaps primarily, an expression of those defences against self-knowledge and transparency that, we will now see, operate in all of our ordinary everyday lives all the time—often to our great psychological benefit. Psychological distress isn't caused by our defence against self-knowledge or what are known as the defence mechanisms. Rather, it is when these defence mechanisms aren't doing their work well enough that we begin to experience just that anxiety and distress that brings us into therapy. Then we need to interrogate those internal unconscious mechanisms of mind. We need to get them back on track somehow. Our defences, however, are so deeply entrenched and inaccessible to conscious reflection that even now, when we are suffering acute anxiety and distress, we—which is to say our dynamic unconscious processes of mind—still resist and defend against self-knowledge.

But what are those defence mechanisms exactly? And why should psychotherapeutic process in any way influence a set of mental processes that seem not only impervious to the powers of our conscious intellects to change them, but even impenetrable to self-perception? The question really is: what is the *dynamic unconscious*? And how does psychoanalytic psychotherapy work as a therapeutic engagement of the unconscious contents of mind?

The following chapter is an attempt briefly to sketch some features of the dynamic unconscious. Anyone not interested in this theoretical picture can skip this chapter and go on to Chapter Three, where the resistance to the gift-of-the-two-mugs begins to be worked through, only to yield to some even harder and more trenchant resistances.

CHAPTER TWO

The dynamic unconscious and the resistance to therapy: a mini-introduction to Freud's theory of mind

C uriosity about one's own inner life is both a prerequisite of psychotherapy and one of its benefits. The famous psychoanalyst D.W. Winnicott was once asked by a priest during a public lecture how to determine when he should himself listen to his parishioners' complaints and when he should send them for professional help. Winnicott answered, "If a person comes and talks to you and, listening to him, you feel he is *boring* you, then he is sick and needs psychiatric treatment. But if he sustains your interest, no matter how grave his distress or conflict, then you can help him all right."[1] Psychotherapeutic story-telling has to do with recovering and maintaining your interest in yourself, especially when you might be experiencing yourself as the least interesting organism on the planet.

The psychodynamic view of psychological dis-ease

Most of us do *not* go into therapy because we've suddenly developed an overwhelming interest in our life stories. We go into therapy because we are experiencing psychological pain, often quite acutely. We seek therapy (of whatever kind) because of feelings of what we might

---

[1] Cited by M. Masud R. Khan in the Introduction to Winnicott's *Holding and Interpretation* (p. 1).

want to call psychological dis-ease. Psychological dis-ease can be any one of a number of states of mind that make us feel uneasy or unwell: anxiety, depression, sadness, anger, conflicts that seem irresolvable, life situations that seem unbearable, feelings of failure, frustration, helplessness. These dis-eases, like physical diseases, can be chronic or acute. They can be extremely serious, even life-threatening, or they can be rather ordinary and mundane, like the common cold. And as is also the case with diseases of the body, so with these dis-eases of the mind or spirit, we seek help from professionals in order to feel better. But unlike diseases of the body, dis-eases of the spirit cannot usually be treated exclusively through drugs, surgery, plaster casts, braces and other more external, mechanical means. Our thoughts and feelings may well originate in the physiological processes of the body. They may even, as some recent theories suggest (we'll get to these later), be simply another way of viewing those processes. Many emotional conditions can for this reason be treated (at least in part) through medication, as the increasingly popular use of Prozac and other antidepressants more than confirms. Nonetheless, our feelings and emotions are no more identical to the physiological processes of the body than those processes are identical to one another. To sneeze is one thing, to walk is another, and to worry about a job, or sorrow over the death of a friend, or fall in love is something else again.

In the Freud-based, psychodynamic view of mental processes, feelings and emotions are basically intra-psychic phenomena. That is, even if our feelings of dissatisfaction, frustration, sadness or whatever tend to manifest themselves in relation to the concrete and external aspects of our lives—relationships, professional decisions, life crises—they are understood in psychodynamic theory to take place *within* our minds. However much we may want to attribute those things that disturb us to external causes (our parents in the past, our friends, family, employers and co-workers in the present), it is a fairly obvious, observable fact that other people in very similar life circumstances respond quite differently than we do. What depresses us or angers us or makes us happy is *not* what depresses, angers or gladdens someone else.

To put this somewhat differently, in the psychodynamic view, whatever the external circumstances of your life—your relationships with other people, your job, your socio-political world—*you* are the dynamic agent of your life. *You*—and no on else—are the source of everything you say and do. To be sure, there are in all of our lives external conditions, and even some internal ones, which we cannot change. We cannot, for example, usually (and certainly not on a day-to-day basis) change the limitations imposed on us by our bodies or the rules and regulations imposed on us by our societies. Similarly, we cannot change other people's personalities and how they see the world. We may on occasion influence external reality. But we are not, as a rule, going to transform it. By the same token, terrible things happen to human beings, which it would be foolish to deny. Not every problem is going to be solved by psychotherapy or any other means. Yet even here, in relation to tragedies and sadnesses like death and illness, our responses and our reactions belong to us; all of us respond differently and uniquely even to the shared features of our human existence.

This is a fundamental tenet of psychotherapy: that how we perceive, interpret and ultimately respond to the "facts" and conditions of our lives (even those that are most painful) derives solely from *within us*. This is true whether no one agrees with our perceptions, interpretations and responses or whether everybody does. The stress we are feeling in relation to this or that event, or the sadness or anxiety or anger—however legitimate or justified from some distant philosophical perspective—emanates from within us. If you think about it for a minute, where else might our responses come from, if not from within us? We aren't, after all, automatons or puppets. We are thinking, breathing beings of consciousness and feeling.

This focus on the specific, unique internal dynamics of our individual personalities is a fundamental difference between psychodynamic, psychoanalytic psychotherapy and other forms of therapy. It accounts for one major difference between the practice of psychotherapy and that of other therapeutic approaches. The so-called non-dynamic therapies (behavioural therapy, for example) tend to approach emotional problems more externally, as it were, often through the more conscious, reasoning aspects of mind. They aim at remediation of a specific behaviour or symptom, sometimes through behavioural retraining, sometimes more intellectually, through direct appeal to the cognitive processes of mind (as in cognitive therapy).

The objective of psychotherapy is often also to make possible or facilitate a change in behaviour and/or an expansion of the range of our conscious knowledge concerning ourselves and our interactions with others. However, in contradistinction to behavioural-cognitive and other modes of therapy, psychotherapy proceeds through a more or less direct engagement with the affective, unconscious, internal dynamics of our minds. This is the internal place of psychological disequilibrium or imbalance, which, in the psychodynamic view, is what the external expressions of psychological dis-ease are manifesting.

Psychotherapy, then, is a way of treating dis-eases of the mind from within the dynamic processes of that mind. This is especially the case in relation to that province of mind known as the *unconscious* or (more precisely) the *dynamic unconscious*. We will have a good deal to say about the *dynamic unconscious* in the chapters to come. It is one of the most difficult concepts in Freudian theory to comprehend and to accept. It is, therefore, also one of the areas in which psychodynamic psychotherapy is most vulnerable to attack. *Why* and *how* the direct engagement of the dynamic unconscious might yield therapeutic results, and why those results might be even better than those produced by other forms of therapy, are enquiries that stand very much at the centre of this book's undertaking. For the moment, however, what is important is that psychotherapy is a technique deployed in order to help us become more conscious of the unconscious contents of mind. Or rather, more precisely (since, as we shall see in a moment, the unconscious contents of mind always remain just that: unconscious), it is a method designed to assist us in becoming more conscious of the derivatives or expressions of the dynamic unconscious as they manifest themselves in our everyday reactions, feelings and behaviours.

So what is the *dynamic unconscious* and how might it be

understood to function in our everyday lives?

The dynamic unconscious

Before we present a basic definition of psychodynamic terms and processes a note of caution needs to be sounded. Terminologies in the field of psychoanalysis are elusive at best. They slip and slide and are extremely difficult to pin down. To complicate matters even more, many of Freud's original concepts and terms have been contested, revised and even refuted by the generations of analysts who have come after Freud—though truth to tell, when the specific and differently accented vocabularies of more recent theorists are peeled back, a view of mind highly consonant with Freud's is often revealed. To mount an interpretation of the mind we need terms, however imprecise and even metaphorical these terms are. Freud's psychodynamic theory of mind is one very astute and in many ways paradigmatic theory of how the mind works. It is a theory that also has important implications for how dis-eases of the psychological life might be broached.

Freud's basic claim that the major portion of the activities and contents of our mind is unconscious remains generally accepted today. Indeed, this view has received additional confirmation from neurobiological research that it simply wasn't possible to conduct in Freud's own time. Within the realm of these unconscious processes and contents of mind one particular kind of processes and contents was and remains of major importance to most major theorists of mental functioning. This is what Freud variously referred to as *the unconscious* or (our preferred term) the *dynamic unconscious*. What Freud further maintained is that this dynamic unconscious is throughout our lives an active determinant of our everyday functioning. This idea is also still generally accepted today. It too has received reinforcement through neurobiological research. Whether or not psychological dis-ease ought to be approached through a direct address to this dynamic unconscious, and/or how we might imagine this address to take place, are other matters altogether. We will return to those questions later.

The dynamic unconscious in Freudian theory does not refer to what is unconscious per se. Rather, the dynamic unconscious refers to those *contents of mind that are being actively, albeit without our knowing it, rendered unconscious. However, these contents of mind continue to influence and be expressed in our conscious thoughts and behaviours, also without our knowing it.*

The reasons certain materials have been rendered unconscious are many and multi-determined. For the moment, what is important here is that there is, if one subscribes to this theory of mind, always an internal psychological pressure within us for certain materials (ideas, wishes, thoughts, memories and, most especially, the feelings that attach to these ideas, wishes, etc.) to remain outside our conscious awareness. At the same time, there is another pressure (also unconscious) for them to break through to our conscious knowledge. This is especially the case when, for any one of a number of reasons, those wishes, desires and needs that are being kept in the unconscious, because they remain for whatever reasons unacceptable to our conscious minds, are evoked by situations connected to our current lives and come to crave more direct expression and satisfaction.

The dynamic unconscious is not, as in one popular misunderstanding of Freud, things that we are have forgotten. On the contrary, the unconscious contents of mind consist of those memories, feelings, impressions, wishes and desires that are precisely *not* forgotten. They are remembered, albeit unconsciously. They are now *present* in the mind. Indeed, they are always also attempting to push through out of unconsciousness into the conscious mind itself. It is for this reason that they are being actively resisted or denied entrance to the conscious mind. And for this reason these memories, wishes and feelings are nonetheless being dynamically expressed in, sometimes even come to govern, present modes of behaviour and response.

The dynamic unconscious is not to be understood spatially or geographically. It is not a specific place in the brain, even though our descriptions sometimes tend to give this impression. It is certainly not a graveyard where feelings and thoughts and memories are once and for all buried, never again to bother or haunt the conscious mind. Were that to be the case, then we would suffer no internal psychological conflict, no intra-psychic pressure for feelings and thoughts to emerge against some equivalent force that they not emerge.

There is no reason to disparage or despise the dynamic unconscious as if it were the enemy of everything we wish for and strive to be as human beings. The dynamic unconscious is a very efficient storage device we humans possess. It permits us both to keep in mind and yet to keep out of conscious awareness a whole array of useful knowledge, comprehension, memories, skills and the like. These are the residues of our experience that aren't, at any particular moment, necessary or useful. They might even interfere with or derail our other mental activities. But they are nonetheless valuable materials, containing our life's history. The dynamic unconscious is indeed a vital and even vitalizing set of mental activities or processes. It as much enables as inhibits desire and the achievement of our wishes and aspirations. It is as important a part of our mental functioning as are our more rational, cognitive modes of thought. But sometimes the dynamic unconscious can cause us problems.

Psychotherapy is predicated on the idea that with a certain effort of the rational intellect (the more cognitive component of our mind) we can become aware of some of the manifestations or precipitates of unconscious contents and processes in our consciously experienced thoughts and behaviours. As we've already stressed, we cannot become conscious of the unconscious contents and processes themselves. They are, by definition, *un*conscious. We can, however, come to perceive their influences and residues. By this means we can enlarge our conscious, cognitive knowledge of who we are and how and why we act and feel as we do. In other words we can, through reading the *consequences* or *residues* of the unconscious contents of mind in our conscious thoughts and activities, expand the range of our possible responses and behaviours to one or another situation. This is one major goal of psychotherapy. But unlike other modes of therapeutic intervention (cognitive therapy, for example), the route psychotherapy takes towards this enlargement of our conscious knowledge is through a more or less direct, dynamic engagement with the dynamic unconscious itself. This engagement is in the form of the story-telling-story-listening conversation between the patient and the therapist. In our life stories, both as they are enacted in the living of our lives and as they are narrated in the telling about those lives, are often contained evidences of the unconscious contents and structures of our minds, to which we do not have conscious access. Nor are these evidences purely cognitive or rational facts. In powerful ways they contain the emotions and affects that pertain to these unconscious contents. We can read the clues. We can decipher our stories. We can experience affectively our inner realities.

All of us, in our mental lives, have made compromises among various conflicting wishes and desires. Such conflicts may exist on many different levels: from the more archaic and primary forms of oral and anal pleasures which characterized us in early childhood to the more complex forms of erotic and intellectual passion that define adulthood. They pertain to whatever we humans wish and desire. We have also found mechanisms (unconscious ways) not to feel the shame, guilt and anxiety that are attached to some of these wishes and desires. Many of our wishes and desires come to seem to our more mature selves unworthy of us and inappropriate. Indeed, it is often not so much our memory of this or another behaviour or experience that plagues our minds. Rather, it's the embarrassing or compromising emotions attached to them that we would prefer not to revisit. Often the shame, guilt or anxiety that attaches to a particular memory or wish or fantasy goes way back into early childhood. There it may have been a part of even more childish wishes or desires that we couldn't then cope with or even comprehend. Certain feelings we defend against are very old indeed. And if we let ourselves revisit and re-experience them, many of these feelings could now, in our adult lives, be experienced and tolerated without shame or guilt or anxiety.

Sometimes the internal compromises and accommodations arrived at by our unconscious mental apparatus are more successful, sometimes less. Sometimes there is absolutely no reason to address them, our internal mechanisms have done their work so well. Sometimes, however, there is internal dissonance and dis-ease. Sometimes our compromise formations threaten to come apart. They risk permitting the conflicts they were meant to resolve or contain to erupt into conscious awareness. There, in the conscious mind, the feelings of shame, guilt and anxiety associated with those wishes, which the defence mechanisms were supposed to be holding in check, would also erupt. Then we need to do something to dispel our dis-ease and restore equilibrium to our mental processes.

The id, the ego and the superego

Freud's three-part division of the psyche into *id*, *ego* and *superego* is one way of describing both the historical development and the structure of the mental processes that from infancy to adulthood do the work of preserving our psychological balance. It is worth our while staying a few moments in this foray into psychodynamic theory, as a way of establishing what Freudian, psychoanalytic psychotherapy is about.

Like the dynamic unconscious, the concept of the ego is widely misunderstood. The ego is *not* the seat of all human selfishness, vanity and everything else that most woefully defines us—as when we say of someone: he suffers from too much ego. It is also not a specific organ or a particular location in a specific organ (in the brain, for example). Nor is it a single, homogeneous phenomenon. Rather, the ego is a way we have of describing a set of mental processes. These activities of mind have to do with how we "mentalize" experience. They pertain to how our minds convert or translate internal needs and wishes (many of them merely physiological), and the possibilities of fulfilling those needs and wishes (or not), into a mental language that the brain can understand and act on. The ego is a set of dynamic, constantly self-transformational functions and processes. These functions and processes come into being over time, beginning with the moment of our birth into the world as human beings. They come to an end only with the end of our conscious lives as such. As Freud himself put it, "mental life" is "a storehouse for external impressions and a receiving-post for internal excitations."[2] The mind as such, in the Freudian view—and this seems no more than common sense—doesn't exist autonomously and independently of what mind is *for*, namely, the mediation between internal and external realities.

Like other creatures of our Earth, we humans are born with mechanisms geared towards helping us survive. These "instincts" (as they are called in one set of terminologies) are wired in such a way as to issue in behaviours that will yield the satisfaction of our basic needs. The need for food or warmth, for example, cannot be

---

[2] Sigmund Freud, *Transformations of Puberty*. In: *Three Essays on Sexuality*.

satisfied from within us. That is, we cannot manufacture our own food for ourselves or provide ourselves with warmth from within our bodies. Rather, our needs—for food, warmth, even (eventually) for knowledge, companionship and love—can only be satisfied through external objects (including other people) in the world outside. Through our various behaviours we attempt to satisfy these needs.

The needs and the mechanisms we have for satisfying our wants and desires are not necessarily conscious processes. What becomes conscious to us, what may itself be said to constitute consciousness as we know it, is that set of mental processes, including the feelings they arouse, that mediate between the unconscious inner demands and the external world of objects and people through which those demands might, or might not, be satisfied.

The ego functions, we might say, develop as a consequence of this necessity for mediating between the unconscious inner demands and external reality. Ego is that mental mechanism which conceptualizes need. It gives it mental representation. It also evaluates, judges and grants relative value both to innate needs and to the possibilities of their satisfaction, given the limitations of the human body and the intractability of the external world. The ego functions are essentially about maintaining a balance between what we desire and what, practically, we can expect to get. Indeed, what the ego functions are *for* is the enhancement of our possibilities of survival in an often hostile, parsimonious, intransigent reality in which it is not always possible to satisfy all our needs or wishes.

The baby experiences hunger and cries. The body's need for food, in order to be registered by the body as hunger and thereby produce the call for food (crying), needs first to be communicated to the brain. What hunger "looks like" in the brain isn't necessarily a picture (of a breast or a bottle, say)—at least, not in the very small infant. But there is some sort of process of mentalization going on whereby one physiological or chemical process signalling the need for food produces another, very different sort of process: the cry. In order for the baby to survive, this cry (under natural conditions) must produce a response in the outside world. Like many mammals, we humans are equipped such that the baby's cry produces the right response on the part of the parent or caregiver. The caregiver (mother, father, nanny) is what might be thought of as an auxiliary ego. He or she enables the infant's very rudimentary ego to begin to realize its demands on the world—in a double sense. The auxiliary ego enables the demands to be met by the otherwise helpless infant. Over time, that auxiliary ego also helps facilitate the self-conscious perception of those demands on the part of the baby. What our caregivers either promote or hinder is the internal dynamic by which we not only regulate our feelings and sensations—our "affects"— but by which we come to internalize and produce mental images of the affects and their regulation.

As we grow and mature, the representations and the processes of evaluation and judgment by which we negotiate external reality become more sophisticated and complex. Our cerebral representations (or re-representations) increasingly incorporate earlier experiences. They contain earlier processes of evaluation and judgment and the relative success or failure of those decisions. In this way the ego functions permit the efficient use of our mental resources. They enable us to build on our experiences without having to examine every new situation as if for the first time. The older we get, the more efficiently we operate in our engagements with reality through continuously deepening mental pictures of the world and ourselves. These mental pictures incorporate not only our previous experiences of ourselves and of one or another situation *but also* (crucially) the feelings that attach to those experiences.

Because human babies depend for such a long period of time upon the ego functions of other people, there is introduced into the workings of the mature human ego a high level of dependency, complexity and conflict. Not only must the human ego negotiate between instincts and an external, natural world, but it must negotiate as well between those instincts (and their development over time) and a world of other human beings, some of whom have an intimate relationship with us. Infants and children are not only literally dependent on other humans. They also come to love them, and not only because they "need" them. Love may itself be a human faculty or need. That doesn't make it any less biological than if it were only an outgrowth of our other, more concrete needs, like the need for food and care. As many psychoanalysts have begun to stress more and more, for whatever reasons, we humans seem bound to others by love.[3] Love may also be an inherent need. Like many others of our innate needs, it may serve to enhance our possibilities of survival. Whatever the reasons for love, the fact remains that those others whom we love and on whom we depend are also always in the process of the same balancing act of ego functions. Therefore they cannot but, occasionally at least, become sources of frustration as well as pleasure.

In Freud's terminology, *id* consists of the instincts and drives (all of them unconscious) which the ego functions mediate, regulate and express. *Id* can be thought of as the force, the dynamo, the engine that drives ego. It is not itself a tool of expression. That is the job of the ego functions, including those functions stemming from what is called the *superego*. *Superego functions* pertain primarily to our internalization of and, perhaps even more importantly, our compliance with what we perceive to be the norms and values (physical as well as social) governing our lives. Superego influences specifically how we ought to act in the world of other people. Indeed, it often determines how and what we will permit ourselves even to feel in relation to what we wish and desire. Superego isn't conscience exactly. It is not a general moral philosophy arrived at by years of study and contemplation. Rather, it is a private, subjectively arrived at and rather creative self-censorship. Where it is like conscience is in its inhibitory function. Superego inhibits actions, thoughts and emotions that would contradict those inner values (some of them purely biological) that we have acquired over the course of our lifetimes. It is the agency whereby we internalize what we imagine to be other people's and finally our own expectations of ourselves. Like so much else about us humans, superego (unless it becomes overly zealous) is an efficient way of regulating our relation to ourselves, the world, and other people.

Through the ego functions, including the functions of the superego, we achieve that boundary by which we are differentiated from others (perhaps even from that "other" which is our own body). That boundary is also, however, the border through which we communicate with the outer world. Through the borders of ego we let the world and other people into our minds. We also

---

[3] See, for example, Jessica Benjamin's *The Bonds of Love* and the writings of Stephen Mitchell.

communicate with or express ourselves to that external reality. Mental health can be defined as balance or equilibrium. It is about maintaining flexibility around this boundary. All of these words— balance, equilibrium, flexibility—convey an idea of motion. Mental health is anything but stasis. It is rather the capacity to accommodate the different circumstances in which we find ourselves without losing ourselves: without losing our sense that we are selves with discrete, individual identities.

The ego achieves balance, equilibrium and flexibility through various defence and coping mechanisms. These *defence mechanisms,* as they are called, are the instruments by which our minds navigate a world of desires and wishes, frustrations and disappointments, in which the one thing you can't have is everything you want. They are also, and perhaps even more importantly, the set of unconscious processes by which we also preserve ourselves from the feelings of anxiety, shame and guilt that pertain to such wishes and desires as we do *not* (either consciously or unconsciously) permit ourselves.[4]

What is to be stressed about the defence mechanisms is that they are unconscious processes. They also have a double function. Towards the outside world they are coping mechanisms. They are tools of the ego in the service of mental stability. Towards our inner, emotional world they protect us against the feelings of anxiety, shame and guilt that would arise if we were actually to act upon or even become conscious of those drives, wishes, feelings, fantasies, etc. which we have "decided", in that unconscious way such matters are decided for us in our minds, are improper. *Repression* is

---

[4] Technically defined, the defences or defense mechanisms are the "group of operations aimed at the reduction and elimination of any change liable to threaten the integrity or stability of the bio-psychological individual." They are "different types of operations through which defense [against such instability] may be given specific expression." J. LaPlanche and J.-B Pontalis, *The Language of Psychoanalysis*, p. 103 and 109. Some of the basic defence mechanisms are: *denial*, "in which the *ego* avoids becoming aware of some painful aspects of [internally] *reality* "i.e. feeling powerless the the child fantasies being omnipotent: *projection*, "whereby a painful impulse or idea is attributed to the external world," i.e., feelings of anger against someone are transformed into a feeling of being aggresssed against by that person; *reaction formation*, in which a "painful idea or feeling" is replaced in "conscious awareness" by its opposite; i.e., feelings of hatred become expressions of extreme concern for another person's welfare; *displacement*, in which feelings become expressed in relation to a substitute object; i.e., instead of feeling hostility toward the parent, the individual feels hostility toward other authority figures instead (Burness E. Moore and Bernard D. Fine, *A Glossary of Psychoanalytic Terms and Concepts*, pp. 30-31

the most general term used to describe the processes in the mature adult whereby such wishes are rendered and kept unconscious. It is the "prototype" of the other defence mechanisms.[5]

If we were able totally to bury, once and for all, one unacceptable wish or desire (to completely, perfectly repress it) such that some other more useful or profitable wish might wholly takes its place, then we wouldn't have to deal with it any more. Similarly, if we could, once and for all, banish the discomforting emotions of shame, guilt and anxiety that often are associated with those repressed wishes and desires, then we wouldn't need various defence mechanisms to protect the wishes and desires that have "won out" from the other banished wishes and desires. Those substitute wishes and desires are also, it is to be understood, genuine wishes and desires. They also express who we are and what we want.

But repression is an incomplete and imperfect process. The repressed wish or desire will usually find some partial and disguised way of being expressed or represented in our everyday thoughts and behaviours. In other words, such wishes and desires as we now consciously express will generally contain some residue of the wishes or desires that have been displaced. What happens to us, which upsets our psychological balance, is that on occasion something in our lives reactivates the repressed wish. Something occurs to weaken the forces of repression which have been keeping these wishes out of our conscious mind. Then the defence mechanisms need to go to work once again. They need once again to repress undesirable wishes and the feelings that attach to them. Indeed, sometimes they need to go so far as to repress desire itself. Sometimes, when we are feeling especially bland and listless, what we are experiencing is our defending against the possibility of feeling itself.

Under the best of circumstances repression requires a certain amount of on-going mental or psychological energy. When we have to apportion too much of our internal resources to defending ourselves against this or another wish or feeling (or against feeling

---

[5] Most generally defined, repression is the "operation whereby the subject [i.e. the individual] attempts to repel, or to confine to the unconscious, representations (thoughts, images, memories) which are bound to an instinct. Repression occurs when to satisfy an instinct—though likely to be pleasurable in itself—would incur the risk of provoking unpleasure because of other requirements. ... It may be looked upon as a universal mental process in so far as it lies at the root of the constitution of the unconscious as a domain separate from the rest of the psyche." J. LaPlanche and J.-B. Pontalis, *The Language of Psychoanalysis* p.390.

itself), then we have to attend to what is going on. When we have to so fortify our defences that they become rigid and even exaggerated, then the patterns of mind that are regulated by these mechanisms become symptoms rather than comfortable accommodations between and among our different wishes and feelings. We "treat" symptoms.

From the dynamic unconscious to psychotherapy

Most of us do not suffer from symptoms in the full sense of the word. But many of us do experience feelings of psychological discomfort or imbalance or even apathy. Many of us also engage in less-than-useful behaviours (such as needing to make a gift of a set of coffee cups to a virtual stranger rather than talk about what is troubling us to someone who might help). We might, at least now and again, feel the need to investigate and try to comprehend those feelings and behaviours. We human beings seem to be designed to minimize conflict and instability in our lives. What we do through repression is to defend ourselves against conscious awareness of conflict and instability. And our defences do not always work to our best advantage.

Psychotherapy is not intended to rid us of repression and the other defence mechanisms. These mechanisms are inevitable, necessary and even valuable to our human functioning. Rather, psychotherapy helps us confront and reflect on those accommodations that have become too rigid. It assists us in investigating those internal mental processes that have begun to get in the way of the dynamic stability and equilibrium they are meant to protect. Since many of our defence mechanisms and the conflicts they keep at bay originate in childhood, the mature ego, which is at work in therapy, is better able than the immature ego to manage conflict. By becoming more conscious concerning our particular defences, the mature ego may lessen the need for some of them. The force of unnecessary inhibitions can be weakened such that we gain more space and internal energy for our ordinary interactions and pursuits. Then we can achieve perspective. Then we can expand our repertoire of responses.

To serve the needs of human survival on the best terms possible, the ego has to be flexible and permeable in two directions. It has to let the self happen to the world and it has to let the world happen to the self. It also has to be stable. It has to permit this two-way border crossing without losing the sense that it is a self, that it is its *own* self. The ego has lots of very complicated and important work to do. No wonder we humans feel ourselves to be under so much stress so much of the time. No wonder we sometimes have to get some help in order to assist the ego in doing its job.

It is because the ego functions and the dynamic unconscious are ongoing, dynamic processes which have very palpable, felt consequences in our everyday lives that (in the psychodynamic view) we sometimes have to attend to those unconscious features and contents of mind. It is also why we *can* attend to them. It is why they are not totally and irrevocably inaccessible to conscious awareness. The ego functions and the dynamic unconscious have everything to do with our daily and often very conscious experiencing of our lives, for better and for worse. The intention of psychotherapy, we might say, is to help us live on better terms with our dynamic unconscious. It does this by putting us in conscious relation to some of its consequences in our thoughts and feelings and actions. Contrary to popular belief, psychotherapy is *not* about blaming anyone for the internal conflicts we experience or the external problems we face. Nor is it about defining what is wrong with us, as if everything about us is being determined by ugly forces beyond our rational control. Quite the opposite. Psychotherapy is about expanding the range and quality of our acquaintance with and access to dynamic unconscious processes. It is about coming to exercise greater *conscious* control over our lives, without at the same time losing the important affective and emotional bases of who we are and what we desire.

Psychotherapy, in other words, is about helping you to hear the unconscious as well as the conscious features of your stories— not only in the telling of them in the therapist's office but, more importantly, in the enacting of them in the everyday activities of your life. Indeed, as therapy proceeds, the stories told come to have more and more to do with the relationship with the therapist himself. This produces, in the clinical setting, a kind of mini-staging of your life outside in the real world of your everyday relationships and thoughts and feelings. We will have much more to say about this phenomenon known as the *transference* later on. What is pertinent here is that the idea of story-telling in the clinical context (and therefore the transference relationship itself) only makes sense because of the ways in which our lives—all of those interactions, thoughts and feelings which are being narrated in the stories we tell and live—are themselves dramatic enactments. In a very real sense our lives are stories which we are telling over and over again.

Yet strange as it might seem, learning to hear your stories and being willing to stay with them long enough for them to do you some therapeutic good is not easy. Indeed, the process is often lengthy, frustrating and even painful. The defence mechanisms that define our ordinary everyday way of being in the world emerge in the clinical setting as *resistance*: resistance to self-knowledge and self-reflection. In therapy as in life we resist knowing certain things that our unconsciously controlled mechanisms of mind have deemed it better for us not to know.

If, however, we are so miserable as to not be able to function contentedly and well in our given reality, then we might just have to try to meet and work at our resistance and defences so as to confront those "things". Our dis-ease is telling us that we are no longer in internal balance, or at least not in as good a balance as we might be. Whatever stability we might have achieved in the past, which functioned to enable us to live our lives in a certain fulfilling way, is being threatened as much from the inside as from the outside. Very often it is being threatened because the accommodations among old wishes and desires that we have made in our lives thus far, and the stability we thereby achieved along the way, are no longer adequate. Perhaps conditions have changed (even catastrophically). Perhaps we have new wishes and desires. Perhaps our accommodations weren't ever as stable as we assumed. Perhaps our balance was always precarious and in need of some sort of realignment. Whatever the case, we need to do something to keep the edifice (ourselves) from crumbling. One thing we can do is to examine and renegotiate some of those default positions—those automatic emotional habits that have till now kept us in balance. To do that, however, all sorts of firmly rooted defences against such intrusion need to be confronted and dealt with. Most of us will resist this to the hilt even *now*, when this foray into the realm of our behaviour and feeling is something we have consciously, rationally chosen for ourselves because we are in pain and need help. Even *now* we resist self-clarification. We resist it for the same reasons we always resisted it: because such resistance to self-knowledge isn't a rational, conscious process. Even more importantly, we resist it because our defence mechanisms are still doing some good, honest psychological work that needs to be done. Indeed it's because the defence mechanisms aren't, for whatever reasons, doing their work quite well enough or in the right ways that we are now experiencing distress and dis-ease. In psychotherapy, working through the resistance to self-clarification is a part of a process designed to culminate in different, better functioning, more liberating defence mechanisms.

So let us leave this more theoretical discussion and return to the clinical setting, where the defence mechanisms, in the form of resistance, ultimately provide us with avenues of insight into those unconscious contents of mind that just might need to be interrogated.

CHAPTER THREE

Accepting the gift of therapy: resistance revisited

T hat we have a dynamic unconscious and defence mechanisms that can be engaged and reflected upon in a certain way does *not* prove that psychoanalytic psychotherapy is the best way to address psychological dis-ease. As we've already noted, the opportunity that psychotherapy (like other therapies) affords of talking with another human being about what is troubling you often provides some measure of immediate relief from psychological distress. But, as we've also said, such relief is not the only or often the primary or initial goal of psychoanalytic psychotherapy. Unlike other forms of therapy, psychoanalytic psychotherapy is directed towards helping us to see and reflect on the unconscious processes of mind despite our decided resistances to doing so. It is more than legitimate to ask why one might prefer a form of therapy that very often not only doesn't produce immediate, instant relief, but even adds some considerable measure of frustration of its own.

The claim for the efficacy of psychotherapy is not a claim that any of us ought to take simply on faith. Later in this book we will specify some of the reasons for preferring psychodynamic psychotherapy over other forms of psychotherapeutic interventions. For the moment, however, we wish to return to the subject of resistance in and to therapy and how it works. Even if the arguments in favour of psychotherapeutic intervention are compelling, to take advantage of what psychotherapy has to offer you have to want for yourself the specific things that psychotherapy can give you. Other forms of therapy may well be preferable for individuals who want the benefits that those therapies can offer. Part of the purpose of this book is to specify up front the special offerings psychotherapy promises, even—or especially—for those of us in psychic pain, so as to help you decide whether this is the therapy for you. Getting past that initial resistance to therapy is only one of many hurdles that one has to negotiate in psychotherapy. Since it is the hurdle that determines whether there will be any further hurdles in the future, it is the one we are addressing first.

So let us return to the matter of resistance.

Resistance with a capital R

Like so much else that characterizes the mental life, resistance isn't one thing only; nor is it resistance to this or resistance to that, as if "this" and "that" were completely separate from one another and in some sort of logical relationship or order: first resistance to this and then resistance to that. When we resist something in therapy—when we resist going into therapy—we are resisting many things on many different levels all at once. Nonetheless, it is possible to say that a major and overarching resistance that has to be confronted and worked through (at least in psychoanalytic psychotherapy) before we can confront the many other issues that are the source of our current dis-ease is the resistance to self-knowledge. Since this self-knowledge is the very *raison d'être* of therapy, we can say that a major resistance that has to be challenged, almost before we can go into therapy, is the resistance to therapy itself.

This resistance to therapy may be expressed in any one of a number of ways. It can precede therapy such that therapy never begins. Or it can interrupt the therapeutic process such that therapy is terminated early or the process doesn't achieve its highest goals. The reasons with which we present ourselves for not entering into therapy, or not continuing, or not availing ourselves of the opportunities it presents, will usually appear to us eminently rational and sound. The issue may be money, or time, or having to adhere to a fixed schedule of meetings. And to be sure, time, money and scheduling are all real concerns for all of us in the real world. This problem is exacerbated by the funding agencies, many of which impose time limits and other guidelines for therapy in order for the patient to be reimbursed. But even for those who seek psychotherapy on the private market, certain constraints apply as to how much anyone is willing to invest in the psychotherapeutic process, especially if they are in acute distress. Many potential patients would be better dubbed *im*patients: they are not willing to undergo the kind of intensive process—often more than once a week, often for a period of years—that characterizes psychotherapy. It is more than legitimate for any of us to ask ourselves why we should.

But when we say things like: we don't have time for psychotherapy, when there are for each of us twenty-four hours in every day, what we are really saying is that we would rather use our time for something other than therapy. We are saying that expending our time on therapy seems to us less justifiable than using it for something else. One way or another, what we are saying is that we want therapy less than we want something else. This is true of money as well: in the end, we will all use the money we have available to do one thing or another. If we choose *not* to use it for therapy, it is usually *not* because we absolutely don't have any (though for some people this may be the case) but because other purchases seem more important—for whatever reasons.

We all have the right, even the obligation, to make judicious choices concerning our time, money and energy. Any one of us might be making a wise decision in *not* going into therapy. But the idea of therapy, which is now being dismissed as too costly time-wise or money-wise or in some other way, probably occurred to us for a reason. It probably occurred to us because we weren't feeling well. We were distressed, unhappy, in some sort of emotional pain. When your reasons for not doing something go against your sense of your own self-interest as you yourself have begun to define it, then it is "reasonable" to wonder whether those "reasons" aren't really excuses. How decisions about time, money, scheduling and everything else that gets in the way of our entering or staying with therapy express us will vary for each and every one of us. Somewhere deep down, though, if one "reason" or another is getting in the way of something else you've decided you want for yourself, then you have to consider whether this is reason speaking at all, or just resistance.

One of the reasons for explaining and clarifying the structure of the psychotherapeutic process, especially vis-à-vis resistance, to those who are about to enter therapy is to help circumvent some of these early, virtually unintelligible and largely useless resistances to therapy which can seem to the potential or beginning patient so eminently reasonable and sane as not to need interrogation or investigation at all, and which stand between the potential patient and psychotherapy itself.

The point of our approach, it must be stressed, is *not* to launch the reader into a more cognitive approach to psychological issues. Quite the contrary. Even though this book is a discursive, cognitively organized, informational text, written from outside the process of psychodynamic psychotherapy and at a remove of some years, its intention is not to substitute for or displace the dynamic processes of psychotherapy. It is not intended to bypass or clear away the transference elements on which proper psychotherapy works. Nor is it intended to disarm or neutralize the defence mechanisms or resistances (as if that were either possible or desirable). *Transference* is the life-force, the engine of psychotherapy as it is of psychoanalysis. *Working through the resistances* is its modus operandi. Indeed, one useful definition of psychotherapy (as of psychoanalysis) might be *working through the resistances* to self-understanding and self-reflection.

Such "working through" does not mean (as the phrase sometimes means in our everyday usage) resolving all the difficulties and discomforts we are experiencing in our psychological lives. Rather, it means coming to recognize our defences against hearing our own stories. Indeed, it means recognizing the ways in which those defences actually get caught up in and become a part of our story of self, often in brilliant and fascinating ways. Working through the resistances has to do with engaging and softening the defence mechanisms and our resistance to hearing what the dynamic processes of our mind are saying to us. It means recognizing, grappling with and eventually being able to cope with the mind's defences against inner reflection and self-knowledge. This is one major difference between psychotherapy and other forms of therapeutic intervention. It is a goal that no book can help you achieve outside the psychodynamic process itself.

Our goal is rather to bring the problematical nature of resistance into view so as to help mediate or circumvent some of the *preliminary* resistances to therapy itself. These are the resistances that may prevent the process from getting started or halt it prematurely, before the therapeutic relationship can begin to do its work. And this returns us to the gift-of-the-two-mugs.

Mugging desire

If I had understood and accepted from the start that when my therapist left those two lovely brick red coffee mugs with the blue birds on them on his desk, he was inviting me (quietly but eloquently) to think about myself in all my many facets and dispositions, perhaps I could have taken better advantage of the opportunity that was being afforded me. This was an opportunity that I myself had sought out. It represented a chance to explore, in the safety of the therapeutic setting, the ways in which those mugs were nothing if not an expression of my deepest wishes, needs, fears and desires. They were also an expression of my inability to express at least some of those feelings in some other more useful and self-conscious way. The gift-of-the-mugs, we might say, had to become for me—at least in part—a gift I was giving myself, not the therapist. When all was said and done, this giving-of-the-gift to myself was something I had to come to see also about my gift-giving in general. To be sure, my giving of the gift, even this gift in particular, expressed rather nice things about me: my wish to give other people pleasure, my desire that they know I'd been paying attention and knew what kind of gift they would be likely to appreciate (I'd always registered the smell of freshly ground coffee as I walked in to my therapist's office). *For me,* however, giving a gift *also* sometimes contained some sort of request to receive a gift in return. This is what the unravelling of the gift-of-the-two-mugs eventually came to show me.

Most of the time one is less enacting oneself in the clinical setting (as I was when I literally gave my therapist a gift) than talking about oneself, even though the stories we choose to bring to our therapists very often resonate with the here-and-now of the clinical relationship. Very often they come to relate directly to our relationship with the therapist himself. This is an expression of the *transference*, and we will discuss it shortly. Still and all, the giving of the gift, even though it told a story in and of itself and was *not* (I must confess) the last gift I tried to give my therapist, did not conform to the usual way in which materials are introduced into the clinical setting. The exploration of its meaning, however, did.

Since I wasn't ready, even after a few sessions, to discuss the gift-of-the-mugs when I gave them to my therapist, he thoughtfully put them away. But now and again, gently, almost imperceptibly, he would introduce them into our conversation; or more precisely, he would introduce the idea of giving and receiving something from others. Perhaps I would be telling him about my mother and how angry she was that I had left home and gone to live in another country. My mother was a very stubborn woman, very set in her ways and totally convinced of the rightness of her opinions. She was very little given to being influenced or persuaded by me. In other words it was difficult, he said, for my mother to "accept" things from me. And thus a motif would be established. I would be rambling on in my often interminable lament concerning my mother—not usually having to do with gifts and gift-giving—and my therapist would ask me to clarify something that I'd said. I don't quite understand what you mean, he might say, could you say that again? Or he might wonder out loud, so how do you feel about that? And I might, as in the case of the mugs, simply refuse to respond, or even quarrel with his interrupting me. Often I accused him of trying to get me to say things that I didn't mean but that, I felt, would lend themselves to *his* interpretation. And he would let it go. But later, talking about something else, he might again ask, what about that? What else does it bring to mind? Now perhaps I might venture a comment and he might take the opportunity to recall an earlier moment in our conversation: pertaining, perhaps, to my mother "accepting" something from me, or "giving" me something. I might take the hint or not. I might see connections or not. I might continue to deny such connections as I imagined *he* was proposing. Psychotherapy is that circuitous. It is also that slow. But in going forward, our conversation would also always be sweeping back, right back to the mugs themselves and, of course, to whatever past the mugs were themselves expressing, which had everything to do, it emerged, with giving and receiving gifts in the largest senses of these words.

Seeing a possible relationship between the anger provoked in me in the past by my mother's reluctance to accept my life choices and my different ways of doing things and the anger I expressed when he first suggested that I reflect on the gift-of-the-mugs, he would introduce words like "gift" or "giving" into the restating of my complaints about my mother. These words would, in turn, lead to our exploring together how I wanted or needed something back from my mother, how she wasn't "giving" me something. By having me put my thoughts in these other words, the therapist was helping me (without saying so, of course) travel the course of their various associations to still other words and still other stories. Sometimes he might even reformulate some of my statements for me. He might give me those other words I was having difficulty in finding— words like gifts and giving, but other words as well. I might reject his reformulations (sometimes correctly, sometimes not). I might go with them. I might begin to incorporate new insights into my own revised story-telling.

The part of my past that I came to see rather quickly, once I'd lowered my resistance to having such an insight, was the simple fact that my mother had never been very good at accepting gifts from me. I know lots of mothers who had the same problem (my mother-in-law, for example). I also know lots of people who love to give gifts. Whether they are all the daughters (or sons) of mothers (or fathers) who didn't take kindly to their children's gift-giving, I don't know. Nor do I know why any one of these parents, including my own, was so reluctant to accept gifts. (I have some theories, but they aren't really pertinent here, at least not to understanding *me* and *my* propensity to give gifts.) What I do know is that *my own particular mother* didn't like to receive my gifts; and that *her daughter, me,* likes giving them, and giving them a lot. Entangled in my gift-giving there is, at the very least, the child's disappointment and hurt of gifts not accepted. There is also the desire not simply to give a gift, but also to receive one back—at the very least the gift of her appreciation or acceptance of the gift. For a child this may mean no less a gift than the gift of love. Perhaps I felt I wasn't getting enough love from my mother in my childhood, at least by *my* estimation; someone else—my mother, for example—might well have seen this differently.

There remains, then, in my gift-giving—whether in relation to my mother or others—also a wish to influence, a desire to change, to bring someone more in line with my wishes and needs. This is not the whole of why I give gifts. But it is a part of it. There is also an anger and disappointment attached to the giving of gifts, especially when they are rejected. Concerning this anger and disappointment, the child who also adored her mother and depended on her could only feel tremendous guilt and pain. That child's pain and anger also remained a part of me. They erupted against my therapist when, so much like my mother (in my unconscious internal view of things), he didn't simply, graciously accept my gift-of-the-mugs.

Once I turned my mind to thinking about gift-giving and my mother, numerous memories of my mother's rejection of one or another gift I had tried to give her came tumbling out. These stories went all the way back to my childhood and continued into the present moment of our relationship. They included the other gift-giving moments in my life as well. What I might get back by giving and what I felt I wasn't getting back when my gifts were refused—or, later in life, my advice, my life choices, and so on—was very much to be discovered in the course of my therapy. When I entered psychotherapy I thought I knew everything there was to know about my mother and my relationship with her. I'd certainly discussed her enough over the years with my friends and family. When I finished therapy, I knew I had only scratched the surface of the many facets of our mutual entanglement in the psychodynamics of my mind. But it was enough of an incursion to yield many very important consequences to my psychological being, not primarily in relation to my mother but in relation to all the many aspects of my being.

That process of discovery also had to do with the way in which stories of my mother got mixed up with and triggered other stories. I had no more entered psychotherapy to discuss my mother than I had to discuss coffee cups. In fact, talking about my mother sometimes seemed to me beside the point. Other times it seemed like an easier thing to talk about than other more pressing concerns. That was something else the therapist sometimes pointed out to me: ah, weren't you telling me about x? And now you've mentioned your mother. Again. What I would discover as I journeyed over the slips and slides of my story-telling was the internal resemblance or affinity between the stories I would be telling the therapist and the giving-and-not-being-received motif of my literal gift-giving, both then and now, and in relation to my mother, my therapist, and many, many others—my children, for example.

My two daughters were now on the verge of adulthood and making decisions for themselves (life choices that were in fact taking them far away from me, as once I had taken myself far away from my mother). They were no longer little girls to be thrilled by the little surprises I used to hide away for them under their pillows. And then there was my son. My son had died a few years before I went into therapy, when he was fifteen years old. He had suffered from a number of medical problems. I had therefore functioned not only as his mother but as his occupational therapist, his physical therapist, his teacher, his doctor—he was something of a full time job. Yet when he died, I had eulogized him as a "gift" that had been given into our keeping. I actually called him a gift. I used that very word. And now here I was, this active gift-giver whose mother didn't like to receive her gifts, whose children were no longer little enough to be the happy recipients of her little surprises and presents, and whose son she had eulogized as a gift: here I was, *now* giving a gift to my therapist and taking it very badly when he asked me to reflect on it. I'd have had to be totally unconscious not to begin to perceive the very private and important portrait of self to which the therapist was slowly and carefully drawing me. This was the picture of me as a gift-giver, who was *also* (what was less obvious but equally relevant) a gift-receiver, and who had just *lost* a gift—a very precious and beloved gift—only years earlier. The *lost* gift and the *loss* it betokened would be clues I would later pick up and take in different directions, as we shall see. Sometimes we speak a very metaphorical language indeed. It's worth our while taking our words seriously.

Psychotherapy does not produce simple one-to-one equations. Giving gifts, for example, does not mean x or y or z. It doesn't even mean x plus y plus z, though the addition of meanings is closer to the truth of the psychological life than the series of alternatives. Nonetheless, the addition of meanings produces no simple sum. Rather, as the expressions of the dynamic life of the mind are added up, they also go off in different directions. They produce different equations and formulae and products. Indeed, the motif of gift-giving didn't necessarily have to be the skeleton on which I began to hang my interior narrative. I might well have begun my therapy with another event or story. In that case, the process of self-reflection might have taken another direction entirely. But because we cohere as psychological entities, the different narrative paths our stories take will lead us to the same internal dynamics of self. In my case, as I began to add together my stories and enactments of gift-giving, and as I began to take seriously even the very words in which my stories were told—words like gifts and giving, losing and loss—I could begin to see several "truths" about myself. When all was said and done, these weren't all that difficult to accept, especially since so much of my behaviour had to with the little girl I once had been and no longer was.

By giving a gift to my therapist, to whom I was confiding many things, including my anguish over my son's death, I was also trying to get back the love (itself entangled with the mother-daughter love I felt that I did and didn't get) I felt I had got from my son. My son was for me a "gift" in large part because as a handicapped child he had permitted me to give, endlessly and without stint, the gift of transforming love I so desperately needed to give. To be sure, my husband and daughters were also willing for me to love them. They still are. But, for all the reasons I had to unravel during therapy, I had an excessive need to give a kind of love that exceeded (at least in my own internal view of things) what is appropriate in ordinary family relationships. The desire to love in this way and to have this love accepted (taken as a gift) had in fact not caused me much psychological distress over the years preceding my son's death, precisely because of the way in which my son had served as a willing and even appropriate recipient for that love. And about that I *also* felt a degree of guilt. It felt as if my love for him was tainted because it also served and satisfied me.

It's almost something of a cliché in feminist psychological literature that mothers, in nurturing their children, nurture themselves. Hence the empty nest syndrome: the kids fly the coop and we mothers descend into the doldrums. In clichés are very often contained profound truths, though each and every one of us needs to discover for herself the specificity of that truth for her, in all its manifestations. For me the nest was emptied out with especial cruelty, by anyone's lights. I was quite entitled to my depression. Everyone said so. I felt so myself. But that I was entitled to feel devastated by my son's death didn't quite suffice, psychodynamically, to explain how precisely I was reacting to that death. More to the point, it wasn't helping me to get past my depression and back into my life. Other people's commiseration didn't help. Neither did my own.

The special interior of the nest for me, and the ways in which I nurtured and was thereby nurtured in return—for whatever internal reasons (ethical or unethical, right or wrong) and with whatever psychological consequences—and what then ensued when the chicks (including my son) flew away had to do with *me* and *me alone*. They were not to be explained or cured by some general explanation having to do with mothers and children or with mothers and the death of a child. They went back for me to my own childhood with my own mother and to the many expressions of that childhood as they manifested themselves in all my lived life into the present. That included (albeit not exclusively) my children. It was contained in (but not only in) the giving of gifts.

I did not go into therapy to understand why I give gifts. But analysing why I had given a particular gift to a particular person at a particular moment, especially in the context of the many other (primarily verbal) enactments of myself that were taking place, did enable me to get to important insights about myself. These eventually helped me to reflect on what was ailing me. More importantly perhaps, they led me to think what I might do about it.

I am still an active gift giver. In fact, I think I give even more of them. No amount of psychotherapy is going to "cure" you of being the person you are, in all your default positions. Now, however, I'm a smarter gift-giver. I'm also a happier gift-giver. I can also now see when the gift I want to give is really the expression of a wish to receive a gift instead. Then I can give *myself* what I need in some other more direct and satisfying way—say, by giving myself a gift directly, in the form even of something like therapy itself. In other words, now I have a lot more capacity not simply for giving the best gifts, but for ensuring that my gift-giving and my other modes of self-enactment do the best psychological work *for me*. Psychotherapy, a friend who's a therapist once said to me, isn't about changing who you are; it's about becoming *more* of who you are. And I would add: enabling that *more* to happen on even better, more agreeable terms, *for you*.

But for the gift-of-the-two-mugs to show me something about my gift-giving in general, which is to say to show me something about *me*, I had to get past the wish to decline the invitation to therapy, which the mugs also expressed. I had to come to see the mugs as I see them now: as a gift not to the therapist but to myself. Irving Yalom's guide to beginning therapists is called *The Gift of Therapy*. That gift has everything to do with the way many of us fail to treat ourselves with the same kindness and concern we reserve for others. We give gifts to others. We don't usually give gifts to ourselves. Perhaps we should. Therapy, of course, doesn't come free. But then most gifts cost money. Therapy is a gift we give ourselves. It is part of a whole process of treating ourselves better so that we can also be better (emotionally and ethically as well) in the world.

Reason's reasons; or the rationalization of desire

What psychotherapy sometimes feels like—what it felt like to me in the beginning—is not a gift but a trap. It feels like being arrested and slapped in prison: everything you say and do can and will be used against you in a court of psychological law (including your gifts). No wonder we struggle so hard to avoid or escape it. No wonder we'd prefer to speak to anyone but a therapist—to a friend, say, over a friendly cup of coffee.

The point of telling the little anecdote of the coffee mugs is to help us see the invitation hiding behind what might better be thought of as the trappings, rather than the trap, of psychotherapy. Psychotherapy does not proceed through cognitive process. Rather, it proceeds through the unconscious contents of mind that get caught up and expressed in the stories we tell and live. It also proceeds through the relationship between the patient and the therapist. This is the transference relationship that, as we shall see more clearly later, is also illustrated in my story of the gift-of-the-two-mugs. Nonetheless, knowing consciously how psychotherapy works (seeing the trappings for what they are, which is not a trap) might help some of us enter more fully into the process. It might relieve us of being unduly defensive, especially in relation to what seem to us our best qualities rather than our worst. In our best is also a pattern. Our best also contains a history. It most especially expresses who we are.

By giving my therapist the gift-of-the-mugs, I—in all the unique ways in which I am myself—was saying something about what I needed and wanted to be given. Whatever this something was, I couldn't quite get myself to say it directly. I couldn't say it to the other people with whom I shared my life. Nor could I say it now, to this therapist whom I'd engaged to help me figure out what it was I needed and wanted. I certainly couldn't say it to myself—even with the therapist's subtle prompting.

The insights we arrive at in psychotherapy aren't usually in the nature of sudden revelations. Most often they are arrived at slowly, sometimes painfully, against our resistance to knowing these things at all. Insights slip out of our conscious minds as quickly as they venture to make themselves known to them. They glimmer and flicker and illuminate, only to dim once again, overwhelmed by our settled ways of doing things and by our very conscious interpretations of why we do and feel the things we do and feel. But what happens over the many weeks and months of conversations between you and the therapist, during which you touch upon a whole range of different subjects, both past and present, significant and apparently trivial, is that the patterns that most define us as individual, uniquely differentiated human beings—the patterns which, in my case, the gift-of-the-coffee-mugs contained—achieve a sort of clarity and pervasiveness that is difficult to avoid.

Why, then, didn't the therapist just tell me what the gift-of-the-coffee-mugs meant, since I clearly didn't seem capable of understanding it on my own? Isn't that what I was paying the therapist to do: help me to clarify aspects of my behaviour?

One reason the therapist can't just interpret our behaviour to us, especially at the beginning of the therapy, is that the therapist is no mind reader. He doesn't know our history and experiences. Nor will he ever have as complete recourse to these events as we ourselves do. The therapist can't always interpret our behaviour for the simple reason that it isn't always clear to him, at least not in deep and specific enough ways, what feelings and desires we are expressing through one or another behaviour or statement or gift. My therapist knew that my gift-of-the-mugs meant something. He even had some general sense of what giving gifts to the therapist usually means (after all, I wasn't the first patient to give him a gift). Nonetheless, he couldn't be expected to pin down everything that *my* gift meant—either in the immediate present or as reflecting something about my relationship with people in my past. All of our stories are unique and specific to us. We are the ones who hold the key to their interpretation. For anyone else to interpret us to us would be to lose both our individuality and the potential depths to which our stories can reach.

Just as importantly, however, and even more pertinent to the subject of resistance, he couldn't just attack my resistance head-on for the same reasons that I couldn't see for myself what my behaviour was saying to me. The resistance to self-clarification isn't a conscious process. Furthermore, it is protecting some deeply felt need or desire. For that reason it is very deeply entrenched and well-defended. We have very good "reasons" for our resistances. In fact, these are many of the same reasons that we have come into therapy in the first place. By keeping out of conscious awareness certain internal conflicts and dissatisfactions, the unconscious processes of the mind are protecting us from feelings we cannot tolerate. They are securing our self-esteem. To rip through the resistance to self-exposure would, ironically, be to expose us to just that anxiety, guilt and shame which, despite the resistance to self-knowledge, have begun to leak into our everyday experience. These are feelings of anxiety, guilt and shame for which we are now seeking remediation through therapy.

The psychotherapeutic rule that matches and responds to the obstinacy of resistance is that you can't just challenge it, or try to get past it, or demolish it. Psychotherapy is a way of managing self-revelation so as to preserve, and not puncture or explode, our stability and balance. Just as you wouldn't grab away a crutch before an injured limb is able to bear the body's weight, so you don't just wrench away resistance. Not only would most of us (quite rightly) not willingly just let it go, but we *can't* just willingly let it go. Our resistances constitute a part of the scaffolding on which our psychological integrity has been constructed. The patient has to be ready to see what is right there before her very eyes. It's the therapist's job to help her to be able to look and see.

Even though psychotherapy proceeds through deepening levels of self-clarification, self-clarification is *not* usually why people undergo therapy. People enter therapy to feel better. And it is a wise psychotherapist who knows this. If the therapist had chosen (unwisely) to say to me, way back when I gave him the mugs: ah, I see you are giving me a gift because you want to be in an intimate relationship with me, because you want not a therapist or a doctor but a friend or a parent or a child who will let me take care of him, change him, somehow verify to me that I exist and am important in the world—his statement would not have made any sense to me whatsoever at the time. There is no reason it should have made sense to me, *not* because this statement wouldn't have been true in its own way, but precisely because it *was* true. It was true, however, for reasons and in ways that were anything but straightforward. These were reasons which, in any event, I also needed to protect myself from understanding.

Until I could lessen my resistance to what my gift of the mugs was expressing about me, such interpretations of my behaviour could only threaten me with anxiety or guilt or shame. These were precisely the feelings that my gift was protecting me against uncovering. After all, I was a fully mature professional woman with a loving family: how could I say to myself that I wanted my son's love back? Indeed, how could I, as a good and responsible mother (which by all estimates, including my own, I was), admit to herself or anyone else that what she mourned wasn't only the child's tragic loss of his life but her own loss of what the child gave her back, which she, the mother, needed? And to imagine, further, that in giving the gift-of-the-coffee-mugs I was saying to my therapist not only that I wanted my son's (and/or my mother's) love back, but also that I wanted this love now from him instead: well, please—give me a break! How could I have entertained those thoughts? How could they have made any sense to me whatsoever? They aren't even completely rational to me now, which is, of course, part of the point about all this: feelings aren't rational, even when we rationalize them. How feelings come to make sense to us, and when and in what specific ways they make this sense, are by no means obvious or easy to describe.

Another way of putting this, which goes to the heart of the difference between psychotherapy and other modes of therapy, is that the "truths" about ourselves, which psychotherapy can help us reveal to ourselves, are inseparable from our defences against understanding those "truths". Truth and the resistance to knowing the truth are threaded together. Together they weave the very fabric of our psychological being. It is for this reason that psychotherapy aims at more than articulating, objectively and externally as it were, the contours of one's behaviour. Rather, psychotherapy is geared towards our coming to experience and articulate *for ourselves, in our own words,* the dynamics of our special, unique ways of being in the world.

The problem of understanding certain of our psychological mechanisms isn't simply that we lack the training or vocabulary to understand them. Nor is it the case that psychotherapists are just people who are better informed about such things than we are, who could therefore just enlighten us as to how, psychologically, we are constructed. Rather, the problem is that to reflect on certain of our feelings and behaviours we have to be able to come to see them *as* our feelings and behaviours. To do that, we have to soften those defences or resistances to reflecting on them which have, in the interests of our mental stability, produced those feelings and behaviours in the forms in which they now exist. Certain kinds of intervention on the part of the therapist—such as directly interpreting our behaviour to us—are simply not useful. They would be virtually unintelligible to us. And they would be unintelligible not because the therapist's insights are too complicated for our untrained intellects to grasp, but because they are too painful or compromising or nonsensical for our very sophisticated and well-defended—extremely rational— minds to credit them as being meaningful.

If the therapist is going to make us experience what our statements or enactments are saying, then he is going to have to find some way other than simply defying the resistances to self-knowledge. And that is going to mean helping the patient herself to get to the insight in her own language, in her own way and, just as importantly, in her own time. My therapist couldn't just smash my gift-of-the-two-mugs, either by rejecting them outright or by telling me in so many words what they meant. I would have been offended, hurt, angry and extremely defensive—in even greater measure than I was when they sat there, so beautifully still and unused, on his desk, waiting for me to get ready to reflect on them. To analyse why a friend gives you a gift and, worse, to interpret the gift to your friend is the height of bad manners. And thus I had taken it when the mugs remained there, unclaimed, on the therapist's desk. I was offended, hurt. To analyse a gift in the clinical setting is, however, exactly what is demanded. It is the essence of the psychotherapeutic process, which isn't a chat with a friend over a cup of coffee but a powerful, intimate, working relationship between a story-teller and a story-listener for the sole benefit of the story-teller coming to listen to and hear her own story.[1]

By leaving the coffee mugs on his desk, the therapist was inviting me to reflect on them. He was inviting me to accept the gift of therapy I was giving myself. But in order to accept this gift I had first to get past my resistance to understanding what gift-giving and gift-receiving meant to me.

[1] See Janet Malcolm's discussion of falling in love with the therapist in *The Impossible Profession*, pp. 149-50.

CHAPTER FOUR

The dynamic unconscious speaks

No matter how much psychotherapy or even psychoanalysis we have had, we can never know directly the unconscious contents and processes of mind. We can only come to know the derivatives or precipitates of those contents and processes as they manifest themselves in our behaviour and words, thoughts and feelings. In other words, we come to know of the existence of the dynamic unconscious and what it is communicating to us in the same way that we come to realize that some internal, organic process has ensued when we walk across the room or read a book or even think a thought. We know not because we are conscious of the unconscious processes that produce the action (which are, in the case of walking or eating, physiological processes). Rather, we know because we become aware of the tangible consequences of those processes. In a similar way, even if we do not directly perceive our unconscious wishes and desires, and therefore even if we cannot consciously articulate them, these wishes and desires do manifest themselves in our behaviour, including the words we speak. Let us say that the unconscious contents of mind don't so much speak *to* us (the way our conscious thoughts of this or another subject or feeling do) as they speak *through* us. They manifest themselves and achieve expression in our various behaviours, including our emotional responses and reactions, and often in the words we speak as a part of those behaviours and feelings.

As Freud already understood, we are not conscious of most of our bodily processes; nor do these processes usually produce what we call consciousness. Consciousness seems to be produced by only one of our many bodily organs: namely the brain. It is the brain that produces mind.[1] And it is the mind which is the object of inquiry and treatment in psychotherapy. Indeed, it is Freud who can be credited with thinking of mental processes and mental illnesses as having to do less with the physiology of that organ known as the brain than with the consciousness that the brain produces. That modern research into the brain, even as it provides more and more options for treating mental illness organically (through medication and drugs), nonetheless confirms or complements rather than refutes much of Freud's own theory concerning mental illness says something about Freud's incredible genius. We will return to the very important subject of the relationship between neuroscience and psychoanalysis later in this book. It goes to the heart of why psychotherapy might, at least for many of us, still be the best of all possible therapeutic modes. What concerns us at present is Freud's theory of the dynamic unconscious, which my story of the coffee cups and of my resistance to reflecting on them enacted.

Freud arrived at his theory through his practice as a physician, treating patients who were suffering from what was then called "hysteria". Hysterical symptoms were physical conditions (such as a paralyzed limb, fits and fainting, blindness) which didn't, so far as the medical profession could determine, seem to have origins in any organic disease of the particular body part affected. These illnesses seemed, to the physicians treating these patients, to be conditions produced by some disease of the brain. This was the diagnosis as well for certain obsessive-compulsive behaviours which also didn't seem to have ordinary organic origins. The brain itself, then, became the object of medication and treatment (through such interventions as electric shock or cold baths or simply rest cures). What Freud hypothesized, while treating such hysterical

---

[1] This is not a wholly accurate description of the brain-mind relationship. For the purpose of simplification, however, we will in the following descriptions think of the brain as the physiological organ and the mind (or consciousness) as what the organ called the brain produces. We will provide a more precise description of the mind-body relationship in Chapter Nine.

and obsessive-compulsive patients, was that the physical ailment (the paralyzed limb, for example) didn't originate in an organic disease at all, not even of the brain. Rather, he began to understand that the symptom was a symbolic representation of some idea or feeling in the mind, which the patient could not bear to confront directly. So Freud engaged his patients in conversation, in story-telling, in an effort to get the patient to put into words what she was heretofore expressing as a physical symptom.

What Freud began to see in his patients' narratives (as in the various behaviours those stories recorded and often re-enacted) were certain motifs or themes. These recurrent threads seemed to point to continuities among the patients' otherwise different behaviours and narratives. He also began to see how certain attitudes, behaviours, responses and feelings reflected events that had occurred long before the patients' symptoms emerged, even (and especially) back in their early childhood. He could also perceive a gap between what his patients thought they were doing or saying and what their behaviours and stories seemed to him to be doing and saying.

But Freud did more than examine patients with symptoms. He cast his net wide and investigated the ordinary, everyday, "normal" occurrences of some of the same phenomena he was observing in his clinical practice. Indeed, the more Freud listened and learned from his patients, the more he began to see continuities and patterns among the experiences and narratives of his different patients. In one of his most famous texts, *The Interpretation of Dreams*, Freud put himself into the company of his fellow patients. He examined his own dreams and discovered in their bizarrely disorganized images and events the coding and disguising of rather coherent narratives after all, albeit about matters that Freud realized he would rather not consciously confront. Similarly with jokes and puns and slips of the tongue, and works of art and literature: Freud began to see how everything we say and do as human beings is an expression not only of what we intend to be saying or doing, or even think we are saying or doing, but simultaneously of other currents of thought and feeling of which we do not have conscious awareness. These undercurrents also seemed to reflect common human narratives or dramas concerning our shared experience of being born and assimilated into a world defined by certain natural, biological and societal realities and conventions.

It is useful to remember, in this era when Freud seems of more theoretical (or at very best professional) than ordinary use, that even as he was in the throes of his most creative theorizing, he wrote a book entitled *The Psychopathology of Everyday Life*—the book from which the title of our own book is adapted. Like all medical disciplines, psychoanalysis based many of its theories on the investigation of the abnormal. It is usually when things go wrong with the body or the mind that someone investigates the functioning of this organ or that, one physiological (or psychological) process or another. But those discoveries about the diseased body pertain to the healthy body as well. What psychoanalytic theory, like medicine, is predicated upon is the everyday life of the normal, healthy individual. As in conventional medicine, the purpose of psychotherapy is to restore health where it is absent and to preserve it where it exists. That means recognizing what precisely constitutes such mental health.

Like most doctors, psychotherapists treat patients with serious pathologies. These are patients who require extensive treatment, often involving medication as well as psychotherapy itself. But like most doctors, psychotherapists also treat individuals who are suffering from milder and more prosaic ailments. For a good number of patients in psychotherapy the disease is just that: a feeling of what we have called dis-ease. It is just a rather minor failure to accommodate the pressures, tensions and feelings of everyday life. This is what sometimes makes us feel that psychotherapy is an unnecessary indulgence.

Freud's theory of psychodynamic process is predicated on the idea that in every one of our conscious utterances or actions or responses there are unconscious dimensions which are also being expressed. This is, to reiterate, not a bad thing. It is simply a human thing, and for very good, practical reasons. We simply cannot hold in conscious mind everything we have ever known or thought or felt. And yet to lose the vastness of our experiences would be an impoverishment of our mental resources.

To illustrate how the unconscious speaks, and how its speaking might yield positive rather than negative consequences, let me tell another story. This one isn't about me. Rather, it comes from my ever-increasing collection of grandchildren stories. The benefit of watching how children work psychologically is at least two-fold. Firstly, child-behaviour establishes the comforting fact that even as children, which is to say even before we are old enough to have a lot of complicated and conflicting repressed memories, wishes and desires, we are fitted with a remarkably well-tuned, dynamic unconscious. Secondly, since most children express who they are and what they are feeling quite naturally and spontaneously and without any need for psychotherapeutic intervention, children's stories are generally more non-threatening than adult stories. They are also more engaging. They reassure us that whatever the dynamic unconscious is, it is as often as not on our side.

Even more to the purposes of this book: children telling themselves stories and enacting the dynamic, unconscious contents of their minds—often in play—provide an excellent model of the positive consequences that psychotherapy might produce. Travelling to places of internal conflict and telling ourselves stories about ourselves, without embarrassment or self–censorship, may be an early childhood skill we lose with time. We might do well to recover it. We humans, it seems, are designed to do a good deal of important psychological work all on our own. This is so even if, after a certain point in our lives, we may need some help in re-learning how to do it or in breaching some of the sturdier, more resistant barriers and hurdles of our psychological lives. Interpreting our stories by ourselves may also be a skill that, once reacquired, can be maintained long after psychotherapeutic intervention is over.

So here's my story about one of my grandsons, who will reappear later in this book as well.

Self-expression and the language of the unconscious contents of mind: a child's eye view

Skimming through a book of animals one day with my grandson, then aged six, I asked him what animal he would most like to be. Without hesitation he answered: an elephant. So I asked him why, with no particular ulterior motive, and he explained: because of all the animals the elephant is the best protected. My grandson, on his own, without prompting, and without any external reason that he should have chosen to want to be an elephant as opposed to any of the other animals represented in the book, chose to be this particular animal for this particular reason. This cannot but tell me something about what in going on in my grandson's mind at this moment. To know *exactly* what's going on, in all its depth and complexity, I would need a lot more information. Nonetheless, these are *his* words, no one else's. Even if I've asked a question that he might not have asked himself, and even though that question has perhaps prompted him to think about something he wasn't at that moment thinking about, this is still *his* answer to my question.

As we have already suggested more than once, one major feature of the psychological life, psychodynamically understood, is that everything we say or do expresses us, with the emphasis on *us* and not someone else. We are the origins of our narratives of self in all our broad, verbal as well as non-verbal self-enactments. This is an idea that we often resist, for many reasons. Perhaps knowing that everything we do or say expresses us makes us too conscious of our responsibility for our lives. Perhaps it threatens to make us seem too transparent to ourselves as well as to others. Maybe it seems simply to reduce us somehow to our behaviours or words (and the drives and wishes that power them), as if we were only and simply this quirk or that, the expression of one murky desire or another (I as a mere giver of coffee cups for all the wrong reasons). Yet what could be more obvious than the fact that the words we speak (or the things we do), even when they are responses to outside stimuli, express ideas and feelings in *our* minds, formulated in *our* ways, for *our* reasons? This fact about us is by no means to foreclose *how* our words or behaviours express us. It is never to be assumed or taken for granted what words and behaviours mean. But that they *do* mean, and that they express *us* in all our uniqueness are vital affirmations of our individuality as separate human beings.

If my grandson were an animal, he would want to be an elephant. And being an elephant has something to do, for him, with a sense he has that elephants are well protected. Being well protected is a value for my grandson. It is something he wants or needs. Therefore, whatever else his words do or do not tell me, they do indicate that my grandson, somewhere in his mind, is thinking about the need for protection; he is expressing a feeling of needing to be protected.

To know more than this, I'd need to continue the conversation with my grandson. Like my therapist in relation to my gift-of-the-mugs, I'd need to know more about what he is thinking and feeling. What else does he think about elephants? What other concerns are occupying him at this moment? What events have been going on in his life? Is it his bodily image he's revamping in seeing himself as an elephant? Is his need for protection a local, fleeting anxiety (having to do with school, family, friends) or a more persistent one—the fact, for example, that he lives in a country constantly under threat of war or terrorist attack? A combination of such elements? And if so, in what proportions? More pertinent, perhaps, am I now to rush my grandson into therapy to deal with this?

Absolutely not. My grandson was a perfectly healthy, active, intelligent six-year-old saying and doing all the things a six-year-old says and does. Whatever his inner anxieties, he was coping just fine (and still is today). I might of course, on the basis of this conversation—especially if some very stressful situation were to arise—try to find ways of reassuring him about a multitude of things in rather general, nondescript ways. But then I'd probably do that anyway: as parents and grandparents most of us do try to make our children feel comfortable and safe in the world. Perhaps now, after this conversation, I'd be a bit more conscious of this child's need for reassurance. Of course, were he to begin to manifest real symptoms of distress, I might well want to seek some form of intervention, even homemade. But there's no point in jumping to conclusions, especially about psychologically dynamic and healthy six-year-olds.

Even if my grandson's identification with an elephant were some sort of defence against anxiety or insecurity or, for that matter, gender—it's hard to deny that what is distinctive about elephants is their trunks, which are right up front there, where you can see them and contemplate their sheer hugeness!—there is nothing to be gained by heading directly into this. That is what I would be doing were I to question him, or challenge him, or reinterpret his image to him. It is what my therapist would have been doing had he decided (erroneously), when I gave him the coffee mugs, to say something to me about how they expressed my desire for intimacy with him and how this desire might reflect an earlier desire, which was declined, when I was my mother's and father's little girl. Had the therapist hinted that I was in the least interested in his friendship (or more), I would have found it not only absurd, but completely narcissistic on his part. It would have been so off-putting for me as to make highly questionable whether I should continue in therapy (at least with him). And the same goes for my grandson.

I remember a friend telling me about a conversation she'd had with her son, then about two. He was taking a bath and playing that he was his doll's Mummy. So, fledging psychologist that she was, my friend proclaimed to him, quite abruptly, that his penis would *not* fall off. What her son made of this intervention I do not know. But even if her son were, in his own way, worrying through the issue of gender—what is his relationship to this doll? What does anatomy have to do with the relationship of parents and children? What *is* this piece of equipment I have that Mummy doesn't?—he was dealing with it in his own quite lovely, simple, straightforward manner. His game simply didn't call for any parental intervention. He was asking questions of himself in his own way, through play. He was *not* asking his mother for answers or external reassurances. Indeed, he was perhaps also doing useful psychological work. He was reassuring himself by himself. He was playing being a Mummy and lo and behold, his penis did *not* fall off. Children, we might say, are their own best psychotherapists.

Were these little boys conscious of *why* they were saying what they were saying or playing what they were playing? Not in the least, and that is the point of these stories. By expressing the wish to be an elephant or playing with a little doll in the bathtub, these children were enacting (in words and in actions) wishes, desires, feelings, fantasies, fears, anxieties—a whole range of things which for one reason or another they could best express in these particular ways. Of course in these stories we are talking about children, who hardly have the vocabulary to express what their activities are saying. In the absence of the necessary verbal skills, most children express their thoughts through substitutions, often in play. Adults, as a rule, do have the necessary words and concepts. But then again, what adults need to work through is usually more complicated and has a longer history than what a child is feeling or thinking through. Adults also tend to be more cautious and self-protective when they express themselves, whether in words or in deeds. They've already learned what is appropriate and inappropriate behaviour and speech. So while adults may have better linguistic and conceptual tools available to them, they also have more complex and resistant materials to express. They also have fewer modes of expression available to them. This is why we sometimes need to learn to tell our stories all over again.

In the habit of being who we are

Even though sometimes the exact opposite seems to be the case, what psychoanalytic psychotherapy is really about is preserving our uniqueness as human beings, not dissolving it in the name of someone else's idea of mental or moral good health. In other words, psychotherapy is about what we might want to think of as our *integrity* as human beings. We intentionally use a word with ethical, moral implications in order to describe a psychological condition not because we want to claim that psychotherapy is synonymous with ethics, but rather almost the opposite. We want to challenge the prioritizing of morality over psychological good health. Simultaneously, we want to suggest that psychological good health may be a requirement of the moral life.

If you are being governed in your behaviour by the unconscious forces, processes and contents of mind, the manifestations of which you are having difficulty in recognizing and interpreting in your everyday life, then it is difficult to imagine how much free choice or moral will you have available to you. Psychoanalytic psychotherapy is about increasing our capacity to make decisions on the best and most ample terms possible. It may well be the case, then, that our integrity in an ethical sense depends upon our ability to achieve integrity in the more psychological sense.

For most of us, at least most of the time, our emotional habits aren't in any more need of clarification than our other daily behaviours. But sometimes they are. Take the following very simple, paradigmatic example:

It's Saturday. Your son is sick. Your boss calls: he needs you to come into work. You burst into tears.

Now there is nothing wrong with crying now and again. Sometimes tears are just the right response, and there are even those who claim that an occasional good cry is very healthy and helpful. And probably no one is going to seek psychotherapy because they've burst into tears on occasion. But what if sobbing becomes your default position, your automatic response to frustration? And what if the consequence of that bursting into tears every time you meet frustration of one variety or another is to increase rather than resolve your frustration? Perhaps your boss gets angry or loses confidence in you (fires you or simply doesn't turn to you next time there is a juicy piece of work to be done). Or perhaps your tears make your child hysterical or annoy your spouse.

It must immediately be pointed out that those responses on the part of your boss, your spouse, your child have to do with how they are wired in the same way that your tears have to do with how you are wired. And there is nothing whatsoever that you can do about their responses. It doesn't matter that you think they are being unreasonable and unfair. They think you are being unreasonable and unfair. And their feelings are for them to deal with, not you. One of the hard rules of interpersonal relations, which we learn rather early in life even though we often behave as if we haven't learned this lesson at all, is that it is perilously difficult to change other people.

In psychoanalytic psychotherapy change is always internal. This corresponds to a simple fact about interpersonal relations: that while you can't change others, you can change yourself. You can change how you respond to other people and to the situations in which you find yourself. This is called *taking responsibility for your emotions*. Like the term *integrity*, the phrase *taking responsibility* also hovers on the border between the psychological and the ethical. It suggests the relationship between psychological good health and all of the more intellectual, spiritual categories we generally use to define human behaviour. To take responsibility for your emotions means accepting that whatever external stimulus is provoking your response, your response belongs to you.

In the scenario described above, for example, it doesn't help to say that your feeling tearful is a rational response to frustration. In the first place, feelings are never rational. That is why we call them feelings. This isn't to say that your tears aren't *reasonable* in the sense of *legitimate* or *commensurate* with the situation. Sometimes when people are sad or frustrated or angry they cry. But not everyone responds this way, and not all the time. Therefore it will also not do to *rationalize* your reaction by saying, for example: anyone else would have felt the same way that I did in this situation and reacted the same way—by bursting into tears. That is simply, patently not true, and we don't have to go far for evidence of the fact that it isn't true. You need only to look around you to see that someone else would have dealt with the situation differently. They would have got angry with their boss, or called a babysitter, or simply declined the job, explaining why the request was unfair and calmly telling the boss to turn to them again in the future but today is impossible.

There are countless ways in which, theoretically, we might respond in any given situation. There are usually only one or two ways in which we typically do respond. And those responses have a lot to do with and a lot to say about who we are. We don't necessarily have to interrogate them unless or until they begin to cause us trouble.

So let's carry our story one stage further.

Let's say, in a kind of worse case scenario, that your tears have absolutely the wrong effect on your boss and you get fired for refusing to come into work on a given Saturday when your child is sick. What do you do? Again, there are many responses you could have. You could go in on Monday and plead your case. You could take the boss to court. You could decide that this job, with this boss, is not for you. Or you could, once again, burst into tears. Now jobless, you might indeed become so despondent as to actually need to seek help, at which point you might not only begin to see a pattern here, but to discover that you've been crying a lot lately: that that Saturday with your boss wasn't the first time, in relation either to your job or to other things. Your boss wasn't the first or only person to tip you over the edge. What has happened, you begin to realize, is part of a repeating pattern in which you find yourself having a certain response over and over again.

It might be enough simply to see the contours of the plot: frustration, tears, an inability to take action, more frustration, more tears, and so on—till you are spending a lot more time crying than getting anything done about it. Cognitive therapy, as opposed to psychoanalytic psychotherapy, is focused on perceiving the pattern of our behaviours and then bringing to bear all the powers of the conscious mind in order to change that pattern. But sometimes seeing the pattern isn't enough, at least not for some of us, and/or at least in certain situations. Then it might be necessary or desirable to fill in some of the details, to begin to give more precise names to the events and your reactions. One objective of psychotherapy is to discover the pattern of our typical responses, to show us our emotional habits. Another is to retrieve the psychological story that this pattern is telling—both in the present and, on occasion, as a repetition of a story from the past. How has it come to pass that frustration makes you cry rather than, say, lash out in anger? What job are your tears doing at the moment that you shed them, and not only in relation to what might be gained by them in the outside world but internally, in relation to your own psychodynamic balance? Why is this shedding of tears, in other words, your default position just now, at this moment in your life?

Whatever your emotional responses are, one thing is certain: they are doing some sort of psychological work for you. Sometimes your responses are doing that work very well. Then, even though you might be curious now and again about why you respond to certain things the way you do, there's really no reason to understand your responses in such a way as to change them. Sometimes too much self-consciousness isn't a good thing. One of Einstein's favourite jokes had to do with the centipede which is asked how it manages to coordinate all its 100 legs, at which point it looks back at its legs, tries to figure out how they work, and can't move an inch. If it's not broken, don't fix it, the saying goes; and there's much truth to that.

Sometimes, however, your responses are not doing their work well. Sometimes they were never particularly good modes of reaction to begin with. Sometimes what worked well in the past is suddenly no longer effective. Often our life circumstances have changed. Perhaps *we* have changed. And sometimes those old pathways of response find themselves at loggerheads with other modes of response, with other needs and desires we have and are trying to satisfy. Once upon a time we burst into tears because that was a way we had of getting people to do what we wanted. And it worked. But what we want *now*, we suddenly discover, cannot be gained through that particular strategy. Something has to change, and that something is us—or more precisely, some of our typical patterns of behaviour and response.

We undertake to reflect on our behaviour and feeling when they are getting in the way of our living the lives we want to live.

Transference, integrity and self-expression

The subjects we study, the jobs we choose, the people we fall in love with, the dreams we dream: they all express *us*. *How* the things that express us do so is a different matter altogether. There is no reason whatsoever to be simplistic about how our self-expressions express us—as if everyone who gives a certain gift or lives their life in a certain way or engages in a certain form of behaviour does so for the same reasons, and as if those reasons can now be used to *expose* person *x* for being a particular sort of person: the sort of person who gives gifts for all the wrong reasons, for example. Why one person becomes a teacher is *not* the same reason that another person becomes a teacher. How being a teacher expresses one person's personality— his needs, desires, fantasies—is *not* the same as how being a teacher expresses another person's personality. *How* and *why* we are who we are is something to be discovered, not assumed or taken for granted or deduced from the experience of any other individual.

One great error many of us make in therapy is to leap too quickly to interpretations and to foreclose the possibility of other different, sometimes even overlapping interpretations. My gift-of-the-two-mugs contained worlds—even more worlds than I have already (perhaps rather indiscreetly) put down in print. It expressed so many things, there was no way I could grasp all of them, nor can I today. Towards the end of his career, Freud wrote an essay entitled

Analysis Terminable and Interminable which directly addressed this fact: that there is no end to what we can discover about ourselves. And indeed, professional analysts and therapists themselves often return for analysis or therapy. The point here is simply that there is no exhausting what our self-expressions can tell us about ourselves, if only we'll stay with the images and events long enough, take seriously the fact that they *are* meaningful, and understand that that meaningfulness is concrete and specific and wholly personal. Of course, at some moment most of us do stop therapy. Most of us are not endlessly fascinating, even to ourselves. Nor must everything about us be known. Or said.

As a clinical term, transference has to do with the relationship between the patient and the therapist. But clinical transference is related to the whole natural process of redirection or play or story-telling (as in my children stories), in which we indirectly, unconsciously enact what we are feeling. We transfer, as it were, unconscious feelings and attitudes from one realm to another (from real life into play or from action or feeling into words). Later, as we become older and have more of a history not only of such unsettling feelings and attitudes but of their indirect expression, we continue, unconsciously, to *recycle* our actual experiences (including our relationships to other people) into other, more immediate situations—where sometimes they are effective responses and sometimes not.

One other mode of transference is from feelings, thoughts, wishes, desires, and the resistance to knowing those feelings etc., into language. Since language sits at the very heart of the story-telling-story-listening conversation of psychotherapy, this is a good place to talk about how words themselves work both as expressions of the dynamic unconscious and as ways of intervening when the dynamic unconscious seems to be getting the better of us.

CHAPTER FIVE

Speaking your own mind; or why words matter

Psychotherapy has been around for as long as human beings have been engaged in serious conversation with each other; for essentially that is what psychotherapy is. It is a conversation between two individuals. What is special about this conversation, as we have said, is that it is an asymmetrical story-telling conversation, in which one of the parties to the conversation (the therapist) tries to help the other (the patient) to cope with some sense of dis-ease or dissatisfaction or dysfunction in his or her life. The story-listener (the therapist) also doesn't simply listen to the patient's narrative. Rather, he tries to help the story-teller hear and then re-tell his own story with increasing depth and clarity. The listener (therapist) tells the story back to the patient (highlights features, invites the story-teller to reflect on aspects of the story, asks questions about the story), such that the story-teller can take his story back again with greater self-knowledge and personal understanding, especially of the story's unconscious dimensions.

But before this process of *assisted story-telling* is under way, a simpler, more primary event occurs: you talk. Talking, which is to say putting thoughts and feelings into words, is already of therapeutic value. This is as true inside the clinical relationship as outside it, in our everyday lives. Nonetheless, psychotherapy makes use of talking differently, towards different ends. Psychotherapy is predicated on the psychological value not simply of putting thoughts and feelings into words but of putting them into words that can make a psychological difference. These are words that more and more precisely clarify a thought or feeling and that bring together the story's—indeed the many stories'—multitude of seemingly disparate and unrelated components. So let me tell another one of my grandchildren stories, this one about the value of discovering the word that can help us navigate and negotiate a world of sometimes inexplicable, seemingly unutterable frustration, sadness and confusion.

This story concerns the brother of the would-be elephant. Like his brother, he didn't in the least need psychotherapy. Nonetheless, quite inadvertently and in the ordinary, natural course of things, he received some of a very basic, elementary sort from his grandmother—with definite therapeutic benefit, I am pleased to say.

So here is my story, entitled:

The Fort Da of story-telling

Not so very long ago I was entrusted with calming down my extremely distraught two-year-old grandson. He was weeping in that convulsive, heart-rending way of two-year-olds because his father had suddenly been called away from him, and he was inconsolable. Talking to him was of no avail. No amount of pleading or caressing made the least dent in his sobbing. So in a last-ditch effort to distract him, I rushed him out of doors to engage in an activity that had greatly entertained him the night before: star gazing. In my haste to change the scene I had quite forgotten that it was still early evening and that the stars and moon were not yet out, and so, as we looked up into the dimming but still empty heavens, I said to him softly: all gone, but they'll be back soon. He stared quietly for a while at the empty heavens, still racked by an occasional sob, and then he said, first questioningly and then matter-of-factly: all gone; all gone? All gone; Daddy all gone; back soon—and stopped his weeping.

Feeling bereft, deserted perhaps, maybe even endangered by his father's leaving him (I am, after all, only his grandmother), my grandson burst into tears. He expressed whatever he was feeling physically, by weeping. There was nothing else he could do with those feelings except let them out and let them take their course— which is sometimes exactly what we have to do with strong emotions: let them out. But let them out *how*, and with what benefit or hurt to our psychological well being? My grandson at two years of age said everything that had to be said in his tears. And it was a perfectly age-appropriate behaviour, like playing with a doll in the bathtub. He certainly didn't have access to a sophisticated vocabulary whereby he might explain what he was feeling to others or, more importantly, to himself. He also couldn't somehow redirect his feelings to some other more constructive form of expression than tears. Nor did he need to.

But he was in need of comfort. And my words of reassurance weren't of any use to him when I initially tried to explain to him that his father would soon return. My hugs and kisses weren't any more successful in this regard. So I had to do something, something that might take him beyond or outside his own expression of pain. That was when the something quite unexpected occurred, the something which I hadn't in the least intended, though my reading in Freud was most certainly influencing my behaviour here without my being fully aware of it. This something would initiate him into a whole new stage of his psychological being.

By taking him outside to see the moon and the stars which weren't yet there, I provided him with an external setting that in certain ways evoked his internal emotions. In so doing I acknowledged or confirmed what he was feeling. I also gave him some distance from his immediate pain. I gave him as well, in that non-threatening frame of the night-time sky, some words. These were words he didn't yet know till that moment: *all gone; they'll come back*. And with those words, spoken in that less fraught context, came a concept he also didn't have till then: the idea of loss *and recovery* as something quite natural and non-threatening, a cycle or process he himself could come to cope with, even articulate. He could use those words and that concept to tell himself a story. This story wasn't, like his father's departure, a terrifying enactment of loss. Rather, like the night-time sky itself, it provided distance from his experience and the emotions they were provoking. It also permitted him to add an element to the story of loss. This was the element of recovery from that loss, the recovery back into the life of language and feeling and self-control.

Quite inadvertently I had given my grandson a tool, which he used to do some very important psychological work for himself. Nor were the effects of his small moment of casual "therapeutic intervention" short-lived. Several days later, when his parents set off for a movie and he was once again left alone with his grandmother, he immediately stopped his own weeping with the words *all gone, come back.* Happily he went about his business of playing with his toys, to his grandmother's great relief (and hopefully his own).

Just what was this psychotherapeutic intervention and how did it work?

Anyone familiar with Freud's writings will by now have recognized in the scene of my grandson's coping with the distress of a parent's disappearance another scene, also concerning a grandson, which was sufficiently important to Freud that it forms the centrepiece of one of his most important essays. *Beyond the Pleasure Principle* is extremely complicated and controversial, and there is no need to go into all of its intricacies here. Nor does one have to agree with all of its conclusions in all of their aspects. Nonetheless, a major moment in that text, which figures prominently in the psychological theories of later child analysts and physicians (from D.W. Winnicott to Dr Spock), is Freud's observations concerning his grandson's game when the child's mother, like my son-in-law, goes away for a while. This is Freud:

I have been able, through a chance opportunity which presented itself, to throw some light upon the first game played by a little boy of one and a half and invented by himself. It was more than a mere fleeting observation, for I lived under the same roof as the child and his parents for some weeks, and it was some time before I discovered the meaning of the puzzling activity which he constantly repeated.

The child was not at all precocious in his intellectual development. At the age of one and a half he could say only a few comprehensible words; he could also make use of a number of sounds which expressed a meaning intelligible to those around him. He was, however, on good terms with his parents and their one servant-girl, and tributes were paid to his being a 'good boy'. He did not disturb his parents at night, he conscientiously obeyed orders not to touch certain things or go into certain rooms, and above all he never cried when his mother left him for a few hours. At the same time he was greatly attached to his mother, who had not only fed him herself but had also looked after him without any outside help. This good little boy, however, had an occasional disturbing habit of taking any small objects he could get hold of and throwing them away from him into a corner, under the bed and so on, so that hunting for his toys and picking them up was often quite a business. As he did that he gave vent to a loud, long-drawn-out 'o—o—o—o', accompanied by an expression of interest and satisfaction. His mother and the writer of the present account were agreed in thinking that this was not a mere interjection but represented the German word *fort* ['gone']. I eventually realized that it was a game and that the only use he made of any of his toys was to play 'gone' with them. One day I made an observation which confirmed my view. The child had a wooden reel with a piece of string tied around it. It never occurred to him to pull it along the floor behind him, for instance, and play at its being a carriage. What he did was to hold the reel by the string and very skilfully throw it over the edge of his curtained cot, so that it disappeared into it, at the same time uttering expressive 'o—o—o—o'. He then pulled the reel out of the cot again by the string and hailed its reappearance with a joyful *da* ['there']. This, then, was the complete game—disappearance and return. As a rule one only witnessed its first act, which was repeated untiringly as a game in itself, though there is no doubt that the great pleasure was attached to the second act.

The interpretation of the game then became obvious. It was related to the child's great cultural achievement—the instinctual renunciation (that is, the renunciation of instinctual satisfaction) which he had made in allowing his mother to go away without protesting. He compensated himself for this... by himself staging the disappearance and return of the objects within his reach.[1]

This story, which is sometimes referred to as "*fort-da,*" has proved central to many child psychologists and theorists. It is probably most familiar to most of us, though we might not immediately recognize it

---

[1] What Freud refers to as the child's great cultural achievement is less grandly and more developmentally to be attributed to the toddler's being in the process of acquiring and mastering object constancy: the ability firstly to realize that just because an object is hidden behind some other object which obstructs it, it hasn't simply disappeared; and secondly to begin to comprehend and internalize the emotional fact concerning the people you love, that just because you don't see them doesn't necessarily mean they are gone forever.

there, as incorporated into D.W. Winnicott's theory of the transitional object.[2] The transitional object is that blanket or stuffed animal or other object—even perhaps a spool—that most mothers come to recognize, sometimes to their great distress when they want to wash or clean it, as their child's beloved, inseparable companion. Yet we all tolerate this messy piece of equipment because we intuitively recognize that the transitional object is what permits the child to relinquish her grasp on her mother or father; to permit her parents to disappear, as it were, before they reappear once again.

What is important in Freud's original story is threefold. The first facet has to do with the physical nature of the experience, the way in which the child enacts something in his body. In the game he plays, the child is dramatizing a story physically, bodily. He tosses a spool and retrieves it. Like my elder grandson's wish to be an elephant, that enactment tells us something about what this child is thinking and feeling and wishing. The second aspect has to do with the child's recourse to language: the way in which he begins to tell his story—the same story he was telling with his body—in words: *fort da*. In both of these aspects the child is enacting/telling a story without any self-reflective distance from it. He isn't, in other words, interpreting the story for himself. He's just doing the things and saying the words that express him and which he needs to enact in order to make himself feel better. He is translating raw, potentially overwhelming feelings into more measured, distanced, non-threatening words and actions.

For the child protagonist in this drama, both modes of enactment and telling—the physical and the verbal—are equally valid. In fact, they are more or less equivalent. Indeed, so closely parallel are they to each other that some psychoanalysts (Jacques Lacan chief among them) have argued that the child's physical activities in this game of the spool are not essential to the experience itself. The experience is really primarily about the acquisition of words in which to say things (a wonderful narrative of psychoanalysis is entitled *The Words to Say It*; rumour has it that the author, Marie Cardinal, was one of Lacan's analysands). In my own experience with my grandson there is no physical enactment. There is only a set of words. These words are not even generated by the child himself. Rather, they are given to him by me.

---

[2] *Transitional Objects and Transitional Phenomena.* In: *Playing and Reality.*

Let me stay a while longer with these two aspects of the young child's experience before I get to the third, which, for the purposes of understanding the story-telling conversation of psychotherapy, is an especially important aspect of the *fort da* event. This is a component that comes to the fore in my own story, though not in Freud's.

What, according to Freud, is the child achieving when he plays his game, with or without the accompanying words? There are several ways of understanding what is happening. In the first place, the child is clarifying to himself an event which, as in the case of my own grandson, might otherwise overwhelm him with sadness or fear or distress. He is saying to himself in his own childlike way: my mother is going away. But she will return. And he is saying this not directly but through some mediating distance, which makes the event less threatening. Putting something into words *ipso facto* produces distance: words are not the event itself but its articulation. Saying words also evidences that you have survived the event. You are still there, saying these words about or in re-enactment of an event that had seemed virtually capable of annihilating you.

This shades into another aspect of the experience. A spool rolling away is far less frightening than your mother walking out the door. One might say here that even if the spool didn't return, no catastrophe would ensue. So in playing the game the child is less at risk than in the reality itself. Saying words is less risky than behaving in one way or another, or feeling one way or another. Words can often substitute for feelings, though if we were to remain in this dissociation of words from feelings, other emotional difficulties would present themselves.

Finally, in the game it is the child and not his mother who is in control. He pulls the spool back. He makes it return. The game isn't merely paralleling the events it is imitating. It is producing events of its own. The game, in other words, is its own reassurance.

Words can do that for us. They can do more than speak about a subject (say, the subject of reassurance). Rather, they can create that subject. That is to say words can *be*, in and of themselves, their own form of reassurance. They can validate what we are feeling, which is itself a form a reassurance (it reassures us, for example, that we aren't hallucinating, we aren't feeling what we are feeling for no reason at all). They can also act to exercise authority and control over events: we say and thereby determine what those events are and what they mean. Words can also literally change what we feel by projecting forward a picture or image of what more positive event awaits us in the future. Our mother or father *will* return.

Linguists call certain kinds of words *speech acts*. These are words that perform action in the world, like when you say *I promise* or *I love you*. The words *I promise* or *I love you* aren't *about* the promise or *about* the love. They *are* the promise and the love. They perform the activity of which they speak. In the psychoanalytic context even descriptive or referential words can be understood to be working in a similar way.

Repetition can be a form of neurotic behaviour, in need of intervention and transformation. This is as true of the words we speak as of the actions we take. As an instrument of rational consciousness, language is a critical tool in producing a form of repetition that is not neurotic and that can lead to some form of change. But language is not necessarily, in and of itself, an instrument of such reflection and clarification. Our words may merely repeat what they are describing, perhaps even conspire in producing the unwanted event itself. In Freud's story of *fort-da*, for example, as we have already observed, the words and the actions are virtually synonymous. They are performing the same function vis-à-vis articulating an emotional feeling and controlling it. Action and word here conspire to do positive psychological work—as with the little boy playing at being Mummy in the bathtub. Action and word could, however, conspire to reinforce rather than alleviate the pain. So when we talk about reformulating actions or feelings as words, we mean words of a very special kind.

The physical aspect of the drama that Freud's grandson is enacting is crucial. The mind-body problem is an old conundrum in philosophy, one which has emerged anew in recent discussions of psychodynamic theory. Are we body? Are we mind? And how do we understand the relationship between the two? If the mind is produced by the brain, and the brain is an organ like all the others, a physical entity, then are we human beings simply physiological creatures through and through? Is everything we *think* we think already programmed for us in our genes, wired beforehand to occur one way and not another?

The form of my sentence—everything we *think* we think— already betrays the problem with this line of thought: I can't even express an idea of the mind's being only so much more body without recourse to words which, while tripping over each other (I *think* I think) in order to express my thought, convey also that thinking is possible only because something immaterial is produced by our mental processes. Even if the mind is produced by the body, words, thoughts and feelings are not bits of physical matter. They are not material but immaterial. And if this is the case, isn't it just possible that these non-material entities produced by the embodied mind have their own way of affecting the mind-body that created them in the first place?

Drug intervention, which has become a popular mode of treatment for everything from depression and anxiety to psychosis itself, is based firmly on the idea that the mind is of a piece with the body and can therefore be treated the same way the body can: through chemical means. But if, as research is also discovering, the mind is a part of the body, that is to say if, like the body, it is susceptible to physiological alteration through medication (and this isn't news: we all know what alcohol and drugs do to the human mind), then isn't it more than likely that this same body can be affected by that piece of it called its mind? This shouldn't surprise us. We already know that sad thoughts make us cry, frightening thoughts make us shiver, happy thoughts make us smile, jokes make us laugh. What are tears and trembling and smiles and laughter if not the body's physiological responses to things we think and feel? My grandson felt frightened, disappointed, angry—maybe all these things—and he cried. He told himself a story, looked to the stars, and felt better. We may not know on the biological level precisely *how* this happens (modern science, however, has some clues), but we certainly know from experience that it *does* happen. And it happens a lot, in all sorts of circumstances, to all of us. In fact, it happens as a consequence not only of our own thoughts and feelings but of those of others: we rarely tell ourselves ghost stories and jokes, after all. We read books, go to the movies, enter into conversation with others, and are transformed by those experiences not only intellectually or emotionally but physically: we laugh, cry, jump for joy, quake in terror, run for our lives.

Recent neurobiological research, to which we will return in greater detail in Chapter Nine, has made it very clear that the brain is constructed of a multitude of interconnecting pathways, many of which necessarily converge in the production of any single thought, feeling or action. Nonetheless, the brain's processing of incoming information and outgoing responses to those stimuli is not simply distributed evenly or randomly throughout the brain. Discrete areas of the brain (often infinitesimal in size) are often responsible for different kinds of processes. Thus, for example, cognitive thinking tends to take place in certain areas of the brain rather than others; and similarly with physical perceptions, feelings, and so on. We also tend to produce default routings, such that having already processed a thought or feeling one way, we will tend to route it the same way again.[3]

One of the reasons, for example, that our memories of childhood tend to go back only to age three and no earlier is that the physiological development of those areas of the brain where emotional impressions tend to be stored takes place earlier than the development of those areas responsible for storing more factual sorts of memories. Even our memories, in other words, aren't stored in just one place in the brain; and at least one division between such storage areas has to do with age. This differentiation between kinds of memories and where they are stored doesn't cease with early childhood. Therefore it has very real implications for our psychological lives. It is now standard procedure in many emergency rooms to encourage trauma victims—victims of car accidents, criminal assaults, terror—to start talking immediately about their experiences. The idea is to begin, at the earliest possible moment, the process of linking between memories that are being stored by the brain in its more affective centres and the verbalization and intellectualization of those memories, which are different brain functions. One wants both to facilitate the production of words that can put some distance between the potentially traumatic event and its emotional consequences, and at the same time to maintain the

[3] See Eric Kandell

link between those words and the event as it has been experienced emotionally.[4]

The words we seek in the psychotherapeutic telling of our stories are words of the same type. They are words that can effectively bridge between feeling and intellection and maintain the connection. Through such words we can contain and control potentially overwhelming feelings of dread, terror, pain, loss, and so on, without denying and repressing them and causing them to pop up in other less useful ways (in neurotic habits and behaviours, for example). One need only reflect for a moment on the enormous body of trauma literature—Holocaust survivor memoirs, for example, or first-person stories of illness and dying—to begin to see the validity of this way we humans have of coping with the most horrifying of human experiences by putting them into words. Indeed, it is possible to argue—and some have in fact argued—that the whole of literature is driven by a single impulse: to mediate and contain without repression the potentially incapacitating terror of our own mortality.

The third feature of Freud's narrative, which is important for understanding the relevance of Freud's story to psychotherapy even though it is *not* an aspect developed in Freud's own account, is the position of the audience or listener to the story. Freud remains very much outside his grandson's experience. He is an observer rather than an actor in the story he tells. In my own story, this element of the listener who is not merely an observer but to whom—or even for whom—the story is being told, who may in addition also retell or reframe or contribute to the story, moves to centre stage.

We've already noted how our self-expressions are often constructed in such a way as to conceal from ourselves aspects of what it is we are wishing and feeling and wanting, even as our behaviours and interactions with the world are simultaneously giving expression to just those facets of our needs and desires. In a similar fashion, our actions and reactions are as often as not designed both to communicate to others what we need and wish *and* at the same time to baffle their understanding of these things. In other words, in our interpersonal relations we are always telling our stories *to* someone. At the same time, and for many of the

[4] See Yoram Yovell

same reasons, we are also telling those stories in such a way that our audience—and not only ourselves—is likely *not* to understand what we are saying.

Therapy begins in the being-listened-to because as much as we don't want to share our inner lives with anyone, we also do want to tell our story to someone. We also want that story to be understood—gently, tolerantly, lovingly. Such a reception of our story grants validity to the story, which is to say to the feelings that the story is expressing. It says to us: this is a story that makes sense. Even more importantly, it says to us: this is a story that can be tolerated, even sympathized with.

But the special kind of therapeutic listening that psychotherapy employs does more than convey empathy. The therapist is listening not only in order to hear what the story-teller wants to communicate (*un*consciously as well as consciously). Rather, he is listening in order to help the story-teller himself hear this. This includes all the pains, associations and memories which are not necessarily being consciously acknowledged by the story-teller but which nonetheless feature in the narrative. These feelings, if brought to consciousness, can help to amplify and deepen the story's meaning, not for the outside listener but for the story-teller himself. The therapist, in other words, reframes or retells the story such that the story-teller can become his own best audience.

Assisted story-telling

But I have digressed, and I want to digress further. Before I go on to say how this retelling or reframing of a story might work (which has everything to do with transference and the psychotherapeutic process), let me tell a related story that deals with the somewhat older child (aged three), once again the older brother of the grandson of the stars, who in his later years thought he might like to be an elephant. This story is an expanded, more complex version of the moon-and-stars story. In this story (as in Freud's) the child already has words in which to express himself. But unlike Freud's grandson, whose words were doing good psychological work, my grandson's words were only mirroring his inner turmoil. Therefore his grandmother didn't give him words so much as provide some other words to which he might have recourse. In this way, like the moon-and-stars story, this story also deviates to some significant degree from psychotherapeutic process in that it is the grandmother who retells the story and not the "patient" himself. But a difference between children and adults, even in the professional therapeutic situation, is that children don't quite possess the ability to formulate complex ideas for themselves. Therefore they sometimes need us to give them words or even entire stories. So, noting this difference, here is the story:

My grandson was playing a board game with his mother and me. He lost a round. And he didn't take it well. He refused to continue to play the game; refused, in fact, to play this or any other board game whatsoever again. When he had calmed down somewhat I told him a story about a little boy who was playing a board game with his mother and grandmother and lost. The little boy got very angry. And then, mustering my best dramatic talents, I let loose the stream of words, noises and bodily actions I'd witnessed only moments earlier in my grandson. I also *added* what wasn't in the original enactment—a few words of clarification: I am *so* angry! I *so much* wanted to win. *It isn't fair*. My grandson was enchanted and insisted on hearing the story again and again, till I wished I'd never thought of this story in the first place.

Despite the fact that we see words as marking our progress from childhood to maturity, words—as we have suggested—are not necessarily and *ipso facto* more clarifying and constructive than actions. Words, like deeds, can be hysterical. They can be their own uncontrolled and un-self-knowing enactment of the unconscious life. We've all experienced such words on the part of others. Most of us have manufactured a few of them ourselves. So when we say that substituting words for behaviour represents progress, development, maturation, we mean words that control and clarify and deepen our experience of our thoughts and feelings.

Telling my grandson a story about his behaviour (disguised as the behaviour of an anonymous little boy and his anonymous grandmother) served in the first instance to contain rather than explicate the story. The repetitive retelling made the events more familiar and therefore less frightening. The very fact that we have survived an event, however frightening, makes that event less terrifying than unknown possibilities. Repetition keeps us in a safe, already known place, less terrifying than the future.

In repeating his story back to him I was also acknowledging that I had indeed heard and understood what he was saying to me when he became so upset as to be unable to proceed with the game. I intervened in a similar way with his younger brother when the third brother in the family was born. My star-gazer was hiding under the covers while his mother was nursing the newborn, wailing his mother's first name and asking where she was, and I simply sat down next to him and said calmly and almost matter-of-factly: you know where Mummy is; she's nursing the baby; sometimes it's hard to be the older brother. My grandson simply popped up out of the covers and without another cry engaged me in lively conversation, including not a few requests.

By responding to what I understood my grandson to be acting out through his words (as opposed to what he literally seemed to be saying), as by telling the story back to my older grandson, I was clarifying the story. I was saying to him, as if in his own voice: ah, this is what I am doing and saying; this is what it looks like, this is how it is happening. That picture served to validate the story, to indicate to him that it *did* indeed occur; and more than that, lo and behold: the world (including all its players) survived his less than admirable behaviour intact. The survivability of the world despite our tantrums and ill-will, especially in relation to those in the world we most love, is also something we need to know.[5]

Ultimately what I was doing was giving them (adding to the story) certain words and concepts that were otherwise not available to them: words like *anger* or *disappointment* or *fear* or *frustration* or *older brother*, such that in the future they might be able to *say* in words, rather than enact through tantrums and tears, what was bothering them. By entering into the conceptual space of their minds—that endlessly inventive and creative space—there was also opened up for them, through my story-telling, the possibility for their own rewriting of the story: as when my grandson was able to say *all gone, they'll come back* when his parents went off to the movies.

It took some weeks before my older grandson was willing to play board games, and even then he had to apply to them his

---

[5] D.W. Winnicott, *The Use of an Object and Relating through Identifications.* In: *Playing and Reality.*

new rule, which is still in force today, four years later: there are no winners or losers, the game simply comes to an end and then we start all over again. It may well be that one day he is going to have to retell himself this story one more time, perhaps in another context and with different details, in order to enter into the win or lose aspects of life; or perhaps not: perhaps winning and losing will never be important to him and will never impact on his life in negative ways. He's only seven; it's hard to say. What I do know is that the world is less forgiving about the "rules" than his mother and grandmother, who are quite willing for the game to proceed without winners and losers. So it's quite likely that one day my grandson is going to have to revisit this moment in his childhood and deal with it. Nonetheless, in the immediate present the story did help him overcome a certain barrier. And that permitted him to engage in an activity which had all sorts of benefits it would have been a shame for him to miss, including the interaction with his mother, who happens to love board games.[6]

Intimacy, immediacy and transference

My interaction with my grandsons provided a very intense and intimate arena of story-telling. The story-telling facilitator (me) was an active participant in the story itself. She also had a special relationship with the major protagonists, albeit (significantly) a less critical and fraught relationship than their own mother would probably have had (like Freud, I was only the grandparent). Although there are features of my story-telling intervention that significantly deviate from psychotherapy proper, nonetheless these aspects of the relationship between me and my grandsons' stories—my intimate relationship with them and my actual participation in their stories—do have their correlatives in more formal psychotherapy as well.

Let me say first, lest there be any confusion about this, where my story-telling assistance qualitatively differs from what goes on between the therapist and patient in the formal psychotherapeutic

---

[6] One principle of the psychological organization of self is that we always remain quintessentially who we are. It is likely that my grandson will always struggle with the problem of competition, of winning and losing. His brother, the star-gazer, years after his *fort-da* experience, was once again left alone in my care, when I began to blow up a balloon for still another grandchild for whom I was also babysitting. He immediately expressed his fear of the balloon bursting, which was his way, at age 3½, when it was no longer appropriate to simply burst into tears, of saying that he was feeling anxious about his parents leaving. So I gave him the package of un-inflated balloons, which he quickly proceeded to spread out over the sofa, producing his own patterns and designs. He found a way of exercising control over his fear by exercising control over this object that for him had now come to substitute for his anxiety. And his anxiety was dissipated.

relationship. This has to do with an aspect of the relationship which is actually often very frustrating to the patient: that the psychotherapist generally does not interpret your story for you. And he does not give advice. In my grandchildren stories I enter directly into their value systems and into the choices they are going to make in their lives. I understood my grandsons' troubles with a parent going away and game-playing and sibling rivalry in a certain way: my way. When I gave them back their stories, it was with the intention of helping them to some goal that I, as their grandmother, felt was important. In this way I was contributing a piece of myself—the piece that believes that learning to do without your father for an hour or two or playing board games or being an older brother is a good thing. When I was responding to my grandsons' experience, in other words, I was engaging more as a grandmother than as a psychotherapist—which is OK, since I *am* their grandmother, not their therapist.

Of course there is no way in which, in responding to someone else's story, even with studied neutrality, we aren't going to contribute elements of ourselves that are now gathered up into that story. The very fact that we think the story is worth responding to, or even just listening to (were we to remain completely silent about it) changes the meaning of the story for the story-teller. Furthermore, all of us have interpretive paradigms through which we understand other people's statements and behaviours. If we didn't, we would never be able to understand them. The way experience teaches us how to take in other people's stories pertains even to the practice of professional therapists. Indeed, insofar as professionals actually set about learning certain facts concerning people's typical behaviours and enactments, and since they experience in their practice the overlapping of people's stories, they are probably *more* likely to bring to other people's stories some sense of what they are about than most of us in our ordinary story-listening. In truth, we are paying them to listen to our stories precisely because they possess this particular expertise.

Nonetheless, what the psychotherapist must not do (which even I as my grandsons' grandmother was trying, to some degree at least, not to do) is to violate the integrity of the patient's story. This means first and foremost keeping his needs and desires—even on the *unconscious* level—out of the story. The story the therapist helps the patient to hear and tell has to be the patient's story from beginning to end. It must travel the course of the patient's words. It must culminate in the patient's recognition of his wishes, desires and values, not the therapist's. What the patient then does with this recognition, in the outside world of his real existence, is for the patient to decide.

Nonetheless, in order to help the patient arrive at this place of self-expression and self-empowerment, psychotherapy must employ a feature of the grandmother-grandson exchange, which might seem wholly impossible (not to mention inappropriate) in the professional setting. This is the intimate relationship between the story-teller and story-listener. Strangely, mysteriously, the intimacy between the story-teller and story-listener in the clinical situation takes on many of the qualities of a real-life intimacy (as between a parent and a child or a grandparent and a grandchild). It comes to constitute a *real* intimacy, albeit with an all-important therapeutic difference as well.

To achieve this intimacy-with-a-difference, psychotherapy makes use of several features of the mental life. One is the fact that, as we tried to show in the previous chapter, we all enjoy an integrity of self in which everything we say or do expresses us and only us. Another, which goes back to Freud's *fort-da* narrative which is the subject of this chapter, is the close association of—and yet significant difference between—actions and words. Language gives expression to internal psychological states and in the process transforms them. Finally, as we have also begun to suggest, just as words can refer to events in the real world, so words can themselves become events in the real world—as when you say to another person: I love you, or: I hate you. Speaking words makes things happen, but not in precisely the same way as actions (if, instead of saying to someone: I am angry with you, you were to hit him on the head with a shovel).

In psychotherapy the intimacy of teller and listener and the protected eventfulness of language come together in the transference. Transference is the key to psychotherapeutic process and its life-blood. It is the subject of the next chapter, in which we will also return to the real exchange between the patient and the therapist in the actual clinical setting.

CHAPTER SIX

Transference; or
the performance of your life, Part I
The clinical experience of
psychotherapy: what it feels like, how
it works

The transference relationship between the patient and the therapist is a major component of the psychoanalytic psychotherapeutic process. In large part it is what distinguishes psychotherapy from other kinds of psychological therapies. Despite the terror and comedy that this term sometimes produces, transference really isn't anything more than a particular expression—in the clinical setting—of the way in which all of us tend to have typical responses and reactions to one or another situation. As psychoanalytic theory has begun to acknowledge more and more, transference doesn't involve only the specific unconscious memories of mind. Rather, what are also—and perhaps more importantly—transferred in the clinical relationship are our typical ways of relating and reacting. These ways we have of relating and reacting may largely construct and be constructed by the more autobiographical narratives, but they are not synonymous with those narratives. Nor does the way we have of transferring patterns of behaviour and feeling from one situation or person to another, which characterizes both our everyday lives and the clinical relationship, necessarily doom us endlessly to repeat the same behaviours and responses ad infinitum. To be sure, there are psychological disorders and certain forms of neurotic behaviour in which such repetition is the presenting symptom. Nonetheless, for most of us the ability to transfer thoughts, feelings and reactions from situation to situation and person to person is a necessary tool of survival. It is—or at least might become—the usefully flexible grid on which we plot our past experiences in order to produce new future realities. The film *Groundhog Day* is a perfect illustration of the difference between the unconscious recycling of patterns of thought and feeling, and the accommodations and transformations that insight and reflection can produce. In the movie the protagonist wakes up day after day to the same day and stupidly repeats the same unsatisfying and self-defeating behaviours, until gradually he begins to recognize those behaviours (if not backwards to their past origins, at least as mindless repetitions of each other) and thereby to change them. The protagonist not only comes to learn something significant about himself, he also succeeds in transforming himself in fundamental and useful ways. Conscious awareness of our habitual modes of transference can well yield new mental patterns and new sets of different future possibilities.

In some sense all our relationships are transferences in that they transfer our earliest feelings, wishes and attitudes, with all the subsequent accumulated experiences we have had of love or hate, caring or anger, frustration, loss, and so on, onto new relationships in new situations. There is nothing nonsensical about this idea if you think about it for a moment. Do any of us imagine that we don't build on our past experiences, including prior feelings and reactions? Transference in this sense is no more than a psychological truism concerning the way we work as psychological beings. Right now, as I am writing these words, I am not only expressing the ideas about which I am writing (the intellectual content of this book), I am also expressing who I am as a person. I am by profession a writer. Specifically, I am a person who writes about books. As I write on the subject of psychotherapy and not my usual subject, I am also expressing, in addition to whatever needs and desires my being a writer fulfils for me, the particular needs or desires I have in relation to this particular subject: the field of psychotherapy. Those are fantasies that go right back to the drama of the coffee mugs. In fact they long preceded that drama, which is in part why the drama ensued the way it did and why I had something to gain from reflecting on it. Along with other wishes I was expressing way back then with the gift-of-the-mugs was the wish that I be not the patient but the therapist, or at least his colleague. That wish also had its antecedents.

Our wishes do not generally disappear as we grow older. Rather, they change and adapt, sometimes for the better and sometimes for the worse. As a child I wanted to be the teacher. Today I *am* the teacher. My growth from the child's ambition to the adult's fulfilment happened naturally and without much conscious thinking. The writing of this book is somewhat different. Hopefully it too represents an appropriate improvement on old desires.[1] But it is far more the result of a conscious process, indeed of a process of becoming more and more conscious of old wishes and still present desires. When we explore and confront our dreams and desires in therapy, we can discover improved, more mature and beneficial ways of acting on those wishes. And this leads right into transference in the clinical sense.

For all its connection to transference broadly, non-clinically understood, clinical transference is, of course, also significantly different from the ways in which we generally—and largely unconsciously—reprocess and re-enact (transfer) experiences and aspirations from the past in our everyday lives. To review the basic principles of the dynamic unconscious that make transference not only inevitable in life but of great potential value in therapy:

1) the activity of mental life as such is unconscious (even if it produces something we call consciousness and conscious knowledge);

2) the *dynamic unconscious* is a reservoir of unconscious materials; these materials may well have been conscious at one time; they may still be susceptible to being made conscious once again; but they have been rendered unconscious by various unconscious mental mechanisms whose job it is to defend against certain materials penetrating and becoming a part of our conscious knowledge;

3) these now *unconscious contents of mind* constitute a major, *active* force within human motivation, action and thought;

---

[1] Since much of the following chapter has to do with my own experience of psychotherapy, I will refer to the patient in the feminine and the therapist in the masculine, even where the points made are to be more generally and gender-neutrally understood.

4) human behaviour (whether in action or in speech) expresses or enacts in the present such wishes, needs and conflicts as originate within and now constitute these *unconscious contents of mind*;

5) these wishes, needs and conflicts, which now form the unconscious bases of behaviour, enjoy an historical, developmental relationship to the mental life and the fantasies of childhood; indeed, within the unconscious contents of mind these archaic fantasies remain unchanged even if they are now misinterpreted and misremembered;

6) in every human relationship the individual brings to bear aspects of this archaic self as located in the dynamic unconscious and its adult accommodations;

7) any person can become the object of such projections; and therefore

8) a possibility is opened up in the clinical setting for the *transference*; in the transference the patterns or structures of older fantasies, wishes, needs and feelings remaining from earlier relationships come to be re-experienced and re-enacted—*felt* once again; through the dialogue or conversation that transpires between the patient and the therapist, they become available as materials to be analysed; in this way they are made apprehensible to the conscious mind.

Before we say more about what transference is and how it works, let us try to show you what it looks and feels like. We've already met transference in the story of the two mugs, although what we chose to emphasize in that story was the quality of resistance (specifically the resistance to therapy) that the story also dramatized. So here's another story about my therapy which centres on the transference, though needless to say it also contains its examples of resistance. There is no absolute separation between the facets of our mental lives. My story has a preamble, which leads into the main event.

Shifting into transference, or how to murder your therapist without even trying

I hadn't been in therapy very long when my therapist missed an appointment. More accurately, he arrived late and I had already left.

I had many of my typical responses to this kind of situation. I was a bit baffled as to what had happened. I also suspected that I had made a mistake concerning the time of the appointment. Given the necessity to attribute blame, I tend (or at least I used to) to blame myself. What I didn't feel in the least, and certainly didn't express to the therapist when next we met, was anger. During our next session he asked me, in fact, how I had felt when I arrived and he wasn't there. I answered, quite honestly I think, that I understood that he was a doctor. He might well have had a medical emergency to attend to. Also, traffic being what it is and all the unpredictable variables playing their role, it was quite understandable that he might have been otherwise detained or delayed. I had a list of very valid, very reasonable excuses for his lateness. I didn't reflect on the situation, as in retrospect I can now see he was prompting me to do. Newcomer that I was, I couldn't see any more reason to analyse my response to his being late than I did to analyse my motives for giving him the gift-of-the-two-mugs. And there the issue remained till many months later.

This time I arrived for my appointment to find that not only was the therapist not there, but someone I didn't know was opening the door of the office to me. I maintained sufficient presence of mind to enquire after my therapist, only to be told by this stranger that he had no idea when the doctor was expected. And so I left. And I was furious. Fuming, raging, angry and also, oddly, extremely frightened. What went through my mind almost at once, and which I immediately expressed to my daughter at home, was that this strange man was another patient and that he had murdered my therapist. Being rather sympathetic to my anxieties and fears, and being herself a teen-ager prone to flights of imagination, she thought I should call the police. My older daughter, on hearing the story, was a bit more sceptical of my interpretation. She thought I should simply be angry at being treated so disrespectfully. He could have called from wherever he was to tell me he was going to be late.

The very fact that these two almost identical events, separated by almost a year, should have produced two such different responses in me (a fact brought into focus by my two daughters' very different responses, albeit their responses, of course, have to do with them, not me) suggests how deeply into transference I was. My therapist was, for me, no longer just a doctor who, for any one of a number of very good and perfectly understandable reasons, might have been called away or detained. He was someone who was supposed to be there for me, come hell or high water. I came to my meetings with the therapist with anticipation and expectation and longing. In fact, I came to my therapy sessions a good twenty minutes to a half hour before those sessions were to begin, just so that I wouldn't be late. I would sit in a nearby park, getting ready for our conversations. Given how early I would arrive, it's amazing it didn't feel to me that the therapist was always late!

What I felt when he was truly late, when he simply wasn't there (since I immediately left: I wasn't waiting any longer) was hurt, rejection and profound anxiety. The fact that I quite improbably theorized that he'd been murdered by this other man who, the longer I dwelt on it, was coming to seem to me stranger and more menacing, probably said something about what *I* was at the moment feeling in relation to the therapist. I would have liked to murder him for so disappointing me, for not being there, where he was supposed to be, *for me*. At the same time my worry for him, that something horrible had happened to him, also expressed my fear. This fear contained my genuine anxiety of losing him. It was also, however, a response to my own murderous feelings towards him.

One feature of transference that this story is intended to bring forward is the intensity of feeling that transference produces. The discomfort and dis-ease this intensity produces is often an occasion for getting out of therapy, or at least resisting the terms of the psychotherapeutic conversation (better a cup of coffee in the real world than this). In part it is a consequence of the regressive features of the story-telling situation itself, both in terms of the narcissistic pleasure it provides *and* in terms of the frustration that the therapist's asking you to reflect on that story (and its pleasure) also produces. We will discuss this in a moment. But the discomforting emotional intensity also has to do with the various roles the therapist comes to play in the patient's projection onto the therapist of various scenarios from the patient's past life. Specifically it derives from the emotions evoked in the patient by the therapist's "behaviour" in those roles, whether accidentally, as in the case of the therapist arriving late, or more purposefully, as when the therapist begins more actively to engage the patient's projections. In the transference relationship with the therapist is the re-experiencing of events, situations and emotions from the past, even if what they appear to be in the present seems totally different and unrelated to anything you have ever experienced before.

A thought that had actually been going through my mind that day, when I was on my way to the therapist, was that he might not be there. This, I would eventually come to admit, was not an uncommon thought for me, either concerning him or concerning others in my life. Similarly, a question that also frequently occurred to me, and which accompanied me throughout my therapy (which I could not share with my therapist earlier on but which did eventually become a topic of conversation), was whether my therapist ever thought about me between sessions. One of the patterns of my behaviour that was emerging here, which I began to see when I talked about my inexplicably incommensurate rage with my therapist, is some sort of difficulty I had with believing that the people I loved kept me in mind, or that they would be there for me when I needed them. It was as if somehow I could not keep *them* in mind, or in the world, when we were apart. The fact that my son had recently died didn't help me in this anxiety. It was not, however, its cause.

A story my mother used to tell about me (which my therapist's lateness prompted me to tell) was how, when she was pregnant with my brother, she had felt faint and had asked me to lie down beside her on the bed. I was such a good 3-year-old (this was the point of the story for her) that I was there when she woke up. My earliest childhood memory (which I also found myself telling him) is also connected with my brother's birth. I remember getting lost in the supermarket when my grandmother (whom I didn't know very well) had come to take care of me while my mother was in the hospital. All through my childhood and adolescence I would check up on my mother when she took her afternoon nap to make sure she was still breathing. That my mother was also a woman given to bouts of depression played its role here as well. All of these memories came to the fore as I tried first to justify, later to comprehend, in conversation, my murderous wrath against my therapist.

That old, childish anxiety surrounding my mother's absence, possibly her death, as she lay faint on the bed and then, months later, disappeared for a week to give birth to my brother, and all the subsequent experiences with my mother which then themselves built on these earliest memories of mine, were now thrust into prominence by this little event: my therapist's failure to be there for me at our appointed hour. Indeed, my choosing to tell him these stories about my mother at this juncture in my relationship with him was the key to interpreting my underlying anxieties, not simply concerning my mother then, nor my therapist now, but the other people in my life: my husband, children and friends. I feared for my therapist. I was angry with him. I wanted to kill him. And I was fearful for him because I was angry with him and wanted to kill him.

When I finally told the therapist how I felt, when I eventually came to tell him this story about him and me, I was able, precisely because it was so ridiculous a story, to see in it elements of the little girl who (once in relation to her mother) wasn't quite sure how she felt about her mother's absence and wasn't quite sure what to do with those feelings. (Did I really believe another patient had murdered my therapist in his office? His office was in his flat; didn't I know that other people, not necessarily murderers, might be there, too?) The little girl I once was still inhabited the much older and more mature person I had become. How her presence played out in my ordinary, everyday life outside the clinical setting was what then had to be discovered and dealt with. Perhaps I no longer needed a little girl's way of seeing the world in order to cope with reality. Perhaps I could also now tolerate that child's feelings and confusions which, from my adult perspective, I could see were appropriate to a child's way of being in the world. Perhaps, then, I could even forgive that little girl, then in relation to her mother and now in relation to her therapist, for wishing things she also didn't really want to happen. And perhaps I could begin to relate differently not to my therapist (he was just a prop in this largely internal drama of mine, an occasion for my acting-out) but to my mother and, much more importantly, to the others with whom I shared my life.

How did my conversation with my therapist concerning my desire to kill him produce in me such insights concerning my relationship with my mother in the past and to a whole host of other people (extending far beyond my therapist) in the present? What did he say or do to bring me to inner reflection? We'll return to this scene of therapist-icide later. For the moment, however, let us explain a little bit more about this phenomenon known as transference.

Transference and the turn to therapy

The first act of transference in psychotherapy, which precedes anything as concrete as the above wish to kill the therapist or, for that matter, the gift-of-the-coffee-cups, is our turning to the therapist to begin with. When we turn to someone for help, when we tell them our stories, we are building on a very early, very basic experience of being in a relationship with someone. That someone took care of us (or failed to). He or she protected us (or didn't). He or she listened to us (or not) in all our incomprehensible babblings and spoke back to us; indeed, taught us how to speak. Long ago, when we were feeling sad or hurt or lonely, we turned to someone; or at least we wished to turn to someone (our parents, our caregivers, our siblings) for comfort. If we had good and loving people in our lives (what Winnicott endearingly calls the "good-enough" parent[2]), we discovered that, lo and behold, we could be made to feel better through that interaction. And so most of us, when we are feeling bad, turn to others for comfort. And we speak.

Those of us who did not have this early positive experience of talking and being listened to may need a lot more prodding to turn to someone now. Much of this distrust of turning to another person for comfort and help is likely to come up in the relationship with the therapist, where it can become a subject for reflection. But even if the wish to be listened to wasn't fulfilled in the past, it is probably still there, and we can now transfer this desire onto this new relationship. Therapists, we might say, are one category of

[2] *True and False Self.* In *Maturational Processes.*

individuals to whom we can transfer an early positive experience of care and the genuine joys and benefits of conversation, or at the very least the wish for that care. From this perspective, turning to a therapist for help is actually a sign of psychological health. We believe that we can be helped by other people, in particular by speaking with them, telling them what we feel and what we want.

This speaking with another person, however, even though it is clearly a motive for psychotherapy, is for many people also often an obstacle to entering psychotherapy. Therapy seems merely to duplicate an activity that most of us engage in all the time in the real world with much less fuss and bother, not to mention expense. If psychotherapy were no more than any ordinary conversation, even of a somewhat special, story-telling—story-listening kind, then a compelling objection to professional intervention would be: why pay money, often what seems like a lot of it, to some stranger in order to enter into a process that we enter into every day with friends, family and the other individuals with whom we share our world? After all, we all talk to each other; we all tell each other our stories. And a good many of us get some commentary as well—in the form of good advice—concerning those stories we tell.

Of course, one immediate answer to that objection is that with friends and family we are obliged to listen as well as to speak. We can't quite demand that undivided attention we might occasionally need in order to resolve our own issues. But this isn't quite the case all the time, as most of us also know. Many of us find ourselves often enough in the position of listening to someone else's gripes and sorrows. We know that it is possible for us, too, to share our own grievances in return and very likely receive some valuable listening, all quite for free. In fact we might well feel, quite legitimately, that there is a value to the two-way exchange that some more professional, one-sided conversation can't provide. In recent years, psychotherapy itself has taken on the knowledge that, try as they might, even psychotherapists aren't going to stop being a party to the conversation. One way or another, their responses and reactions (or the lack of them), their needs and desires are going to come to influence the therapeutic relationship, albeit in ways hopefully different from those of a friend.

There is much value to our ordinary everyday exchanges with other people. Conversation is, after all, one of the mind's most important ways of being in the world. One goal of psychotherapy, in fact, is to restore our on-going conversation with the world as much as with ourselves. Helping others and letting ourselves be helped makes the world a friendlier, more nurturing place. Not only is such ordinary everyday conversation not to be disparaged, but it already incorporates some of the major principles of psychotherapy professionally defined. We all need, sometimes, just to be listened to. And that returns us to our initial objection, or resistance, to seeking professional help in order to do what most of us already do in our everyday lives.

Of course, some of us do not have anyone to speak to—for a variety of reasons. The need for pursuing psychotherapeutic intervention would then seem quite obvious and clear-cut and not in need of any further elaboration. Yet almost all of us, at some point or another in our lives, find ourselves in that same position of being cut off from the possibilities of human conversation. Sometimes the issues that pain us are simply too personal or embarrassing to become topics of conversation, even with deeply intimate friends. Perhaps they involve others whose confidences we don't wish to betray. Maybe they concern those very individuals with whom we are in such personal private dialogue—our friends, spouses, lovers, children, parents, and so on.

Nonetheless, the overriding reason for the psychotherapeutic conversation is its relation to the unconscious contents and processes of mind. The internal, *unconscious* origins and components of our emotional conflicts and dis-ease in our feelings are, by definition, not accessible to simple conscious reflection and articulation. They are not the subjects of, nor can they be made subject to, ordinary everyday conversation. They are, in a word, unconscious. Psychotherapy is not simply about telling narratives from the past or about your present life—though this is by and large how the process proceeds. Rather, psychotherapy is about *re-experiencing* the unconscious dimensions of these stories and their affects in very direct, immediate and, most importantly, uncensored ways. It is about re-experiencing these aspects of our interior selves in the here and now of the clinical setting. The unconscious contents of mind, which are inaccessible to ordinary intellectual probing, are awakened in the therapeutic relationship in part by the story-telling situation itself and in part through the patient's coming to experience older feelings, conflicts, wishes, sadnesses and angers in relation to the therapist—as when I became uncontrollably angry and anxious about my caught-in-the-traffic therapist who was barely fifteen minutes late. (The university rule concerning the late arrival of the teacher is that students are obliged to wait at least that long; I'd demanded less of myself than I demanded of students.)

The regressions and pleasures of storytelling

To repeat a qualification or amplification introduced earlier: there are, of course, different kinds of psychotherapist. Some of them are more formal (and Freudian), some of them less so. Therapies (dynamic, non-dynamic, psychotherapy, other forms of therapy) tend to shade into one another. Often they reflect not only different theories but also the different personalities of the individual therapists. Our book primarily concerns psychotherapy of the more strictly psychoanalytic variety. This kind of psychotherapy can be taken as the prototype from which other psychodynamic therapies take their departure.

Psychotherapy (which, for the most part, no longer proceeds along Freud's model of the patient on the couch) is, like psychoanalysis, regressive; and this uninhibited self-indulgent and self-referential, free-associative talking to your therapist (so reminiscent of being tucked in at night and prattling off the day's events to your mother or father) is where the regressive aspect of psychoanalytic psychotherapy begins. In our ordinary everyday relationships and conversations, the feature of our dependency on another person, our need to be listened to, tends to get submerged in or blended with other things. In our regular conversations, when we talk to someone else—even about ourselves—we are also usually listening to that other person as well. As competent, mature adults who can give as well as receive advice and counsel, we are never in the position of the baby small or child who bears no responsibility to hear and listen and attend to what is being said to him.

In our ordinary conversations in the world, then, we cannot as adults permit ourselves the pure, narcissistic luxury of speaking without listening. Equally important, we have already learned to censor certain of our needs and desires and the expression of them. There are some things we almost never say to our friends and family, and never would. This is the case even when we are turning to them for help or comfort. It happens even when we are trying as best we can to be open and honest and undefended. In general, we construct our narratives to keep them, as much as possible, expressions of our conscious rather than our unconscious contents of mind.

Psychotherapy grants us permission to talk only and exclusively about ourselves. If one major trigger of that resistance we've already discussed—both to therapy itself and to the individual insights to which therapy leads us—has to do with this regressive aspect of being permitted to chat on endlessly about oneself, another is the opposite impulse. We resist being reduced once again to children, talking only about ourselves. We also, however, just as strenuously resist the concurrent and antithetical pressure exerted by the therapist to then reflect on what we have said (as in the story of the gift-of-the-two-mugs). Another way that the conversation of psychotherapy (of the more strictly psychoanalytic variety) differs from our other conversations is that the therapist for the most part withholds the responses, satisfactions, even (occasionally) the sympathy we are demanding of him. When we enter into conversation with someone to express a complaint or voice a wish or confess a sorrow, we expect a response in return. Indeed, we often expect a solution to our problems. Sometimes we even fantasize being rescued from our distress, like a princess in a fairy tale, which might account for popularity of fairy tales, especially among young girls, and despite all of contemporary culture's politically correct pressures to the contrary.[3] The therapist refuses us just that fairytale ending—at least within the clinical setting (who knows but some of us may just find such endings in the real world, among our real family and friends). He asks us instead to talk about what we've said, the wishes we've expressed, the memories we've exposed. Such self-reflection takes

---

[3] I recently took my granddaughter, age 3, to a politically correct revision of *Snow White and the Seven Dwarfs* in which the prince does *not* save the princess with a kiss. Rather, they discover they have a lot in common, fall in love, and live happily ever after. During the course of the production, however, Snow White tells the dwarfs the story of *Sleeping Beauty*, in which the prince *does* kiss the princess and save her. My granddaughter quickly forgot the revised ending to *Snow White*. For her the two stories end the same way: the prince's kiss saves the princess.

away the regressive pleasure; and we resist that as energetically as we resisted slipping into regression in the first place.

This is one of the great paradoxes of psychotherapy. Talking about whatever comes to mind, no matter how apparently trivial or unworthy (like coffee cups, for example, or the wish to murder your therapist), might seem too silly for words. So we resist it, in therapy as in life. But once we've yielded to this fantastic idea that we should say whatever is on our minds, and once we've made our deepest wishes and desires explicit, we resist giving up the pleasure. That is in part what I was resisting when I was unwilling to surrender to analysis the good feeling I got by giving my therapist a gift and thereby (in my fantasy of it) making him my friend rather than my doctor. Transference in and of itself triggers resistance—in particular the resistance to giving up the pleasure that the transference itself is now evoking.

Story-telling as transference

The telling of the story, then, already constitutes a mode of transference twice over. First, you are turning to someone for help, which often repeats a childhood situation. Second, you are taking real-life events and transferring them into words. Words are *not* those real-life events. They are a story told. As we have seen, there isn't necessarily any reflective distance between the words and the events, just as there isn't between the spool game and the words *fort da* in Freud's story, or between the desire for protection or strength or power (and the fear that that desire belies) and the wish that is expressed in saying, for instance, as did my grandson, that you want to be an elephant. But there is transference from one realm to another.

In the space between words and events, which it is one of the therapist's jobs to help keep open for you, you can reflect on the meanings of your words, and thereby the meanings of those experiences that your words now recall. And because of the re-enactment of those very same thoughts and feelings in the transference relationship, you can do so without losing altogether the emotional resonance and impact of those past events. You can begin to see more clearly, more fully consciously, the behaviours and feelings that your words are unconsciously expressing and/or recalling. You can begin to recognize the unconscious components within the dramas your stories are relaying. And you can begin to reflect as well on the unconscious elements of the very manner in which you are now telling the story: for *how* you tell the story to the therapist (in what words, with what emotions), and *which* story you choose to tell at any particular moment to this other person (with whom you are also in a relationship, albeit a clinical one), is as much to be reflected on as the contents of the story you tell.

This contextual or structural aspect of your storytelling is also what the therapist is paying special attention to when he listens actively and attentively to your story. In other words, the therapist is listening not only to the plot of your story ("listen to what happened to me, yesterday") or even to the emotions attributed to those events ("I was so angry when my boss called that I cried"). Rather he is also attending to the specific words and images in which the story is being told, especially as they pertain to the here and now of the clinical relationship. For this reason he is also paying attention to how the patient's story and storytelling are making him feel, but we will leave for later the matter of the therapist's responses to the patient and how he utilizes them in the interests of better understanding him or her.

She is giving me a gift, the therapist observes to himself. The gift consists of coffee cups; she gave me these gifts just when our conversation turned to her mother and the death of her son; she refuses to reflect on the giving of this gift. What story is this woman telling me by giving me this gift? And how can I help her to make this into a story that she tells to herself, a story that illuminates aspects of her relationship to her mother and her agonized response to the death of her son. Or: she is furious with me for being late. She thinks someone has murdered me. How does this story hang together, and how does it fit with other stories she's told me? How can I help her to see this, and not only in relation to me, but in relation to her family members and friends?

The details and context of a story always matter. Our job, if we are to understand our stories, is to figure out how and to what end they matter. A gift of a coffee cup is not the same as a gift of a box of candy or a book. It's a particular gift, with specific overtones and implications – less personal than candy, perhaps, more personal than a book. Nor is what the cups look like irrelevant. Or for that matter, when and how they are presented. Even if the patient hasn't chosen the cups herself – say, she herself had received them as a gift and decided to pass them on – that could become a matter for thinking about what it meant that she had chosen to give a gift she hadn't herself selected. And so on and so forth. None of these details might offer a definitive insight into the patient's motivations and feelings. Collectively they might even matter less than other aspects of the storytelling situation. But one way or another they would be expressions of the patient's individual personality: her preferences, her ways of doing things, her associations, her decision-making processes, etc.

The desire to give a gift, like any desire, cannot be reduced to a single, simple thing; nor is the desire likely to remain static, even, perhaps, in the moments of its articulation. It will also change with other features of the storytelling process, which is to say, with other desires, dreams, fears, and so on, which are also getting expressed and repressed in the clinical situation and in the patient's life. And it will change in the being told: the story I tell today is *not* the same as the story I will tell tomorrow, even if it seems identical in all its particulars. The story I tell my therapist will not be the same as the story I tell my best friend or my daughter, not because I am necessarily, on the conscious level, designing different stories to tell (though I might, for whatever reasons, also be doing that), but because I will be expressing different feelings and wishes in relation to the person to whom I am telling the story.

It is in the nature of language always to provide some surplus of meaning. Words are rarely unambiguous. They rarely mean one thing and one thing only. That is a basic principle of literary language and of many jokes. For this reason, perhaps, Freud was so interested in literature and jokes. It is also a basic principle of our self-expressions. We are always saying more than we imagine, more perhaps, than we wish to be saying or wish to be understood to be saying. The psychotherapist is there to hear the surplus. He is there to observe what *else*, perhaps, is being said (sometimes in its being silenced), and to make the storyteller aware of the other possible (usually unconscious) dimensions of his story, including those that pertain to the relationship to the therapist himself.

But that is not all that is happening. In psychotherapy the therapist is also *not* responding to the story in any direct or immediate way. He is, rather, calling attention to one or another of the elements of the story: a particular word or image, for example, or a repeating pattern. This has several effects. The first is that, by not interpreting directly, the therapist preserves the patient's absolute freedom to tell her story in whatever way and with whatever consequences she wishes. Secondly, the therapist's silence forces us, the story-tellers, to do our own probing and clarifying. What the therapist does not do – what this therapist did not do – is to offer his own interpretation. He did not say, ah, you imagined someone murdered me because you wanted to murder me. And that frightened you, because you are frightened by your own aggressive feelings (not those of the unknown man in my office), which is, by the way, why the first time I was late, you didn't respond at all: you buried your anger in interpretations and excuses that, by getting me off the hook, got you off the hook of your anger as well. More than that, these feelings of aggression toward me frighten you because once-upon-time, long ago, you'd felt such feelings of anger toward your mother, whom you also loved and on whom you also depended (as now you depend on me, and also feel affection for me). The therapist resists providing such long rambling narratives because, in the first place, as we've already noted, he can't assume he knows exactly what you are feeling, or which of the many things you might be experiencing at that moment in your internal mental world is more primary, which less. Secondly, and as we've also noted in discussing the resistance to therapy, for him to tell you such a story of your wishes and desires would be for him to imagine that this narrative would make sense to you, which it wouldn't. It would be to head directly into your resistances, and you would (rightly) mount all your psychological forces to defend against it.

This leads into the third and perhaps even more important reason that the therapist does not interpret for the patient. Someone's saying for us what we feel and how we put together our interior worlds is not the same as our saying it for ourselves, which means also: our *experiencing* it for ourselves. The *saying it for ourselves* which is also the *experiencing it for ourselves* goes to the very heart of the transference relationship in dynamic psychotherapy. It is what distinguishes such therapy from other forms of psychological intervention – counselling, for example, in which the counsellor may well provide you with insights and advice. In psychotherapy the therapist tries to remain as neutral as possible. He tries not to interfere. He may assist, prompt, and rephrase, but he does *not* tell you your story for you, even in the form of explicit interpretations, not only for all the aforementioned good reasons, but also, and perhaps even more importantly, because he is a part of the story that is unfolding in the clinical situation. He is a principle player in the transference tale you tell.

Not only do all of our stories (with their themes, words, and images, not to mention their real-life correlatives in the real-life actions they recall) express us, but so does the nature and manner of our-story-telling. The stories we tell (as the behaviours in which we engage) are almost always directed *toward* someone. In psychotherapy (as in my grandchildren stories) we are also in a significant, often intimate relationship with the story-listener. That relationship *also* expresses who we are or wish to be. Indeed, as we have begun to see, as therapy proceeds, the story the patient tells to the therapist very often comes to concern her relationship to the therapist himself. I didn't tell my therapist a story about giving my mother a gift. I gave him a gift. I didn't discuss my anger at my mother, or, for that matter (as we shall now see) my anger at my son. I got angry with him. This is an expression in the here-and-now of the clinical setting of transferring onto the therapist feelings that derived from elsewhere of the patient's real life. In transference you don't come to understand your narratives only or primarily in some sort of intellectual way, from outside the feelings that envelop those stories. This is likely how you would understand them if the therapist interpreted them for you. Rather, you come to understand your personal stories, literally, from within the feelings that produced them in the first place and that they in turn continue to produce, in all of the immediacy and power of those feelings as feelings. This creates for us a deeply personal, internal relationship to our stories – to our wishes, desires, attitudes, feelings, reactions, and the like, which define who we are. For this reason reflecting on the transference feelings becomes a way of coming to reflect on the much more significant and determinative feelings we have in relation to the more "real" others in our lives: in my case, to my mother and my son.

Therapist murder, the child's mother and the mother's child

In Chapter Eight we will specify in more detail what the therapist is doing as he listens to your story—both to its content and to its structure—and as he is listening also to his own hearing of that story: differentiating between his psyche and yours, but also letting his internal responses to your story help clarify the emotions your story is expressing. We've already presented a bit of that process from the patient's (my) perspective in relation to the gift-of-the-coffee-mugs and in relation to my wish to murder my therapist. We want to add a bit more of the murder-your-therapist story here, especially concerning why and how experiencing the emotions associated with a particular thought or feeling enhances our understanding of that thought or feeling.

One of the events from the past that I related to my therapist around the same time that I panicked when he wasn't in his office concerned the panic attacks I used to have the year after my son died. They were so powerful that I would have to hold on to the walls of the university building in which I taught, and I would often find it difficult to find my way back to my office—a place he often used to come after school, since I was still at work when his school day finished. One of the reasons that I went into therapy was that these panic attacks had resumed about two years later.

When once, early on in my therapy, my therapist had arrived late I forgave him and went home. Now when he arrived late I *panicked*. I thought he'd been murdered. Did I have any thoughts, the therapist asked, concerning my feeling of panic? Did it bring anything to mind? In the psychoanalytic view of things, panic is often connected with separation anxieties, hence with loss. My therapist saw this connection. He didn't, however express it. That external, theoretical way of understanding what I was feeling was less pertinent than the process of self-exploration and self-explanation towards which he wanted to guide me. He would have me, by musing on my own words and associations in relation to my panic now, think my way back to the panic I'd felt then, in relation to my son. And back further still: for the panic in relation to my son also had its antecedents, like everything else in my emotional life. These antecedents went back to how I once felt in relation to my mother. That mother's child had, as another child's mother, reprocessed very old feelings, in particular concerning a close affiliation between loss and panic. After all, panic might not have been what I felt in relation to the loss of my son. In fact, it wasn't what other members of my family felt, who had their own very different and equally legitimate (if also psychologically complex and grounded) responses to their son's/brother's death.

The grieving mother's feelings of panic and loss in relation to her son could be illuminated as well by the murderous aspects of the feelings that were also being expressed in the scene of therapisticide.

Murder is a word with strong conotations and implications. I had not simply and vaguely thought that something undefined had happened to my therapist: that he had been in an accident or had fallen ill. I imagined him dead. I also fantasized a particular drama in which a specific person (an unknown man appearing at the door) had killed him, there in his office, where, presumably, his dead body still remained. This is a very precise story beginning to unfold, with a setting and a set of events and a good measure of affect and emotion. What associations come to mind in relation to the word *murder?* the therapist inquires; and the patient either probes the story or not. She either begins (or doesn't) to say what story the word *murder* starts to produce for her that might not be as straightforward or insignificant as she might have assumed, when the story first came to mind, or when she relayed it to her daughters, or when she finally repeated it to the therapist. What about the man in the office? he asks. What about the office itself? The scene of murder in my story is also the scene of my therapy, not to mention that of others. The therapist might not point out this connection directly, but it is there to be discovered and led back to other moments in my life, not in that room and not in relation to therapy.

My feelings of panic opened up one set of meanings in my fantasy of therapisticide. My fear that he was murdered (perhaps by my own hand, though this didn't in the least occur to my conscious mind) opened up others – when I willing to explore them. Both related to my child-self's 'murderous' feelings and panic when my mother went off to have another baby. As hard as it might be to confess this, they also had to do with my anger – and perhaps guilt – in relation to my son. This didn't mean that I didn't love my mother and my son very much. It meant, however, that I felt other things as well.

The untimely death of a cild might well seem like a kind of murder. One might feel oneself guilty in this regard. And one might equally feel like murdering that same beloved child for dying. Shortly after my son died I found his camera, taped together with adhesive tape. My daughter explained that shortly before his death he'd broken it and the two of them together had covered up the scene of the crime. What I felt at that moment was sheer anger, as I would have had he been alive. You don't necessarily stop feeling emotions, even negative ones, in relation to the people you have loved, even after they have died. Personally, I think that's rather a good thing. It helps keep the people we love alive within us. But I don't prescribe this for others. Each of us needs to discover our own ways of coping with death and loss.

Describing to my therapist how I felt about his not being there in his office, telling him I'd thought someone had murdered him and how panicky that had made me, I'd be given time and encouragement to linger on my words: *panic, murder*. He would re-invoke out loud to me, without interpreting them or drawing explicit connections, other stories I had told, both about the present and about the past, some having to do with my mother, some with my son, some with other people in my life, some with the two of us. He would ask me to clarify this or another detail or concept and to put it in "other" words—words which would often themselves begin to produce links to other stories and other feelings. I would then be invited to follow those links, to discover their associations with each other and with the primary narrative I was beginning to tell.

By pausing on a word or image, the therapist would be helping me link my words and stories to each other. He would be encouraging me to plumb the depths of their meanings. Caught up in this process would be many largely innocuous and even, perhaps, fairly irrelevant titbits which might later be dismissed. Or not. Often the conversation between us would include casual, apparently meaningless comments I would pass about him: for example, how hard it was for me to keep to the 45-minute-hour of our sessions, how I needed more time, and so could I schedule double sessions? (One reason I used to arrive early and sit in the park may have been so as to produce more time; this may also be why I always arrive early everywhere I go: perhaps I always feel that there is too little time, or that I am getting too little for my money or my trouble.) You feel that you need us to have more time together, he would say, making me ask myself the question: what *is* this request for more time? Did I feel that he didn't have enough time for me? That he wasn't giving me enough? Did this not-getting-enough have anything whatsoever actually to do with him? For that matter, did it have to do with time at all? An older child certainly might feel, especially after the absence of her mother and her arrival back home with a new and very colicky little brother in arms (and he *was* very colicky, this is not projection), that she wasn't getting enough time or love. And my time with my son had certainly been cut short. Had the love?

My therapist never did say who that man in his office was. But I must confess that when pressed, I had to admit the pang of jealousy I felt when this other person opened the door. This was before the idea of murder entered my thoughts. There *he* was: inside, where I wasn't. *He* was inside the therapist's real world as represented by the rest of the apartment that I was never permitted to see. What child has not wondered what happens behind closed doors, what it is that adults do from which we children are excluded? I seem to have known, even as I was having quite contrary thoughts about him, that this was no murderer but a friend enjoying privileges I did not share. I could have murdered my therapist for that alone. Perhaps I could have murdered his friend as well just for being alive and in this world.

One of my earliest dreams when I started therapy, which now made its way back into our conversation, recalled by the therapist, was one in which I wandered through the apartment where he had his office. What were the spaces and who were the people, I had wanted to know, that filled up his time and place when I wasn't there? What was going on between him and them when I wasn't around? One of the reasons conservative psychotherapists like my co-author do *not* give details of their own lives (why he was late that day, for example, or who that man in his office was) is that it breaks the flow of the patient's thoughts. Permitted to fantasize without any restraints (and also with no obligation to forgive the therapist, which is often what people's words of explanation require of us), I came up with insights and interpretations that told me a lot about myself. This was exactly right, since the point of my psychotherapy was *not* for me to understand (and forgive) my therapist. It was rather to understand (and forgive) myself.

This is also one more reason that psychotherapists do not, as a rule, give us advice. To do so would be to intrude themselves into our psychodynamic processes. These processes are for us, not the therapist, to explore, comprehend and bring to a meaningful conclusion. To give advice would be to put an end to the process of investigation according to the therapist's timetable and values, not ours.

So in dreaming about the therapist and his private life, getting angry with him for being late, pleading with him to give me more time by making an exception to the rules (by giving me a double session rather than by my simply scheduling an additional meeting each week) I was enacting in relation to the therapist wishes and desires, fears and fantasies, needs and their circuitous, self-denying routes of expression in relation to the many people in my life. All of this coming to understand what I was saying to myself, whether through giving a gift of coffee cups or murdering my therapist, and all that these events cycled and recycled (about my mother, about my son), needless to say, took time. It was a slow dawning-of-consciousness. It encountered many frustrations, angers and "resistances" along the way. I wasn't, when I was experiencing my feelings of jealousy, anger, resentment, devastation, whatever, outside those feelings. They were absolutely real for me. They were powerful and determinant emotions. I felt them through and through. Therefore I needed to find ways of transferring the transference feelings into words. I needed to link those words together with other words (which described other feelings both of a transferential and non-transferential nature), and so on and so forth. Then perhaps I could move back from the realm of unconscious feeling to very conscious—rational and intentioned—thought.

The process took time. It also took numerous detours. Some of these detours were productive. Many of them were not. (Few of us live one-issue lives: many things are happening at once.) Some of the subjects that came to displace other subjects were more urgent and necessarily pushed to the fore of our conversations. Sometimes, however, other issues pushed their way forward not because they were more urgent but precisely because they weren't. Sometimes the things we talked about were a way I had of derailing us. They were a way I had of deflecting attention from the genuinely important issues I didn't want to confront. Just as I used to arrive early and sit in the park, so I used to prepare my presentations to the therapist. I made outlines in my head of what I was going to say and why. I worked very hard to keep my conversations with my therapist highly rational and conscious. So sometimes the therapist had to point my attention to how well I'd organized my script. Like little coffee cups, my prepared speeches were saying: let's do anything but talk about what hurts me. I will control this conversation. I will be the giver of the gift. You will be the recipient. Even my attempts to outmanoeuvre my therapist had to become inroads yielding access to the processes of my mental life.

At some moments what I needed to explore was just this resistance in me to accepting that I had an unconscious. Having an unconscious meant that I wasn't, and could never be, in control of everything, not of events in the outside world (my son's death, my mother's failings and foibles), nor of my internal relation to those events. Part of the fear I felt was nothing less than my fear of my unconscious itself and of what would happen if I let myself admit that it existed. More terrifying still, what would happen if I permitted my unconscious thoughts to push to the surface of my conscious mind. Who, then, would I be? Would I even recognize, let alone respect myself?

A lot of things were going on in that room at any one moment and over the several years of my psychotherapy. But in the end, what was being clarified in ever sharper ways, and what was being made available for me to expand the canvas on which I would paint my life, were the materials of that life, including the unconscious dynamic processes of my mind. To have spent that much money to drink a cup of coffee with a friend (even a very good and wise friend) would indeed have been an unreasonable expense. In therapy, however, I was very much getting my money's worth.

CHAPTER SEVEN

Transference; or
the performance of your life, Part II

The analogy often attached to psychoanalysis, and thereby to psychotherapy, is that it is like archaeology. You dig and dig into the unconscious contents of the mind until you find the particular artefacts that give you a picture of the earlier life of that mind. Freud himself was a great collector of antiquities, as any visit to the Freud Museum in London will verify. He himself illustrated the parallel between archaeology and psychoanalysis. But psychoanalysis and psychotherapy are at least as much like gardening as archaeology. The archaeological metaphor preserves the intellectual content of that layer upon layer of accumulated history. But it loses the all-important, equally prominent dynamic, organic quality of the mind's accretions. Transference is the key to this vital, living, transformational quality of the mind. In psychoanalytic psychotherapy you dig down to a living root which is not mummified or petrified or in the least dead. You travel its constantly changing, self-transformational growth, along its length and onto its various branches. You can only travel one of these roots or branches at a time, and even that single branch isn't unified. Each branch itself branches off and is, like the root and all its other branches, also in the process of growing and changing. And then maybe you travel another similarly dynamic branch. And then maybe you look back at the root and see these different branches in relation to each other. But by tomorrow each branch will have changed. The root will have changed. And the overview will have to take into account something that simply wasn't there the day before.

Psychodynamic psychotherapy is just that: dynamic. It deals with the living, changing organism of self, and it deals with that living, changing organism dynamically, through its constantly shifting perceptions, reactions and interpretations—both in the lived life outside the clinical setting and within the clinical setting itself. It is that complicated, but it is also that vital and exciting. Indeed, it is in order to enhance this vitality, the way in which the "truths" of the unconscious life emerge in the present such that we can reflect on them, that transference is the key to dynamic psychotherapeutic process.

So let me tell one more story. This story, which takes place after I'd completed therapy, about two years after I'd "murdered my therapist," serves several purposes. First, it shows how non-clinical transference works in our everyday lives. Second, it suggests how, after we've begun to acquire psychotherapeutic modes of thinking about ourselves and our stories, we can do some good psychotherapy for ourselves on our own. Third, however, and more to the point of this chapter, it also suggests why the presence of an attentive listener, who is prompting you to pay attention to your story and who is provoking in you many of the feelings being expressed elsewhere in your life, can add a crucial element to the experience of hearing ourselves speak. This story illustrates how the therapist produces the difference between the unselfconscious, un-self-knowing enactment of self (whether in word or deed, even by a relatively self-conscious and self-knowing individual) and the transferential engagement that can yield therapeutic change.

The story is called:

Cycling home

I was on study leave in England, doing some writing and research. I was completely on my own for a couple months, no children to worry about, not even my husband in residence. I divided my days judiciously: writing in the morning till lunchtime, then a two-hour bike ride, and then back to work. All of this worked fine until, towards the end of my stay, I started wanting to be a bit more adventurous. I wanted to stay out past my two-hour curfew (this was, after all, a bit of time away from home). What I discovered, to my great chagrin, was that at two hours on the dot, no matter how committed I was to extending the bike ride, I began to feel anxious about getting home. At first I complimented myself on my self-discipline: I wasn't going to waste any of this sabbatical. But even if I wanted to go to the library during my time out of my little cottage, I couldn't get past the two-hour limit. Clearly there was something going on here that wasn't as simple as my being a conscientious, committed scholar.

What I also felt, which prompted me to return home, was anxiety, pure and simple. It felt as if someone were waiting for me, needed me, would be worried if I didn't get there on time. Gradually it began to dawn on me that my two-hour deadline had very little to do with a rational decision I had made concerning the contours of my workday. Nor did it seem to have anything to do with the present moment of my life (though I was in part wrong about this, as we shall see). Rather, somewhere deep inside me, triggered perhaps by my riding a bicycle, which I hadn't done since I was a teenager, was the worry and concern I had always felt concerning my mother. Or more precisely, the worry and concern I felt my mother would experience about me when I wasn't at home. This is also always something to be discovered: whether the feelings we attribute to others, most especially our parents, belong to them or to our projections onto them of something in us.

What I began to realize as I examined my "symptoms" was that, coming home to a home that wasn't at all my home, where none of the people who were a part of my life were in residence, I was reliving old and very unconscious feelings concerning my mother. Now all of this internalized anxiety about my mother, left over from childhood, might not have been worth my bringing to consciousness, were it not for the fact that it was determining my behaviour in very concrete ways. It was making me do something I didn't want to do. Or more precisely, it was preventing my doing something I did want to do. I wanted to take my bike into the countryside and explore to my heart's content. I wanted to ride it to the library in town to do some afternoon research. And I couldn't. As I began to confront what was happening to me, I saw something else as well. This pressure to get home was always with me. It didn't just begin in England. Indeed, the resentment that I sometimes felt at home in relation to my husband and children about getting home on time might have had a lot more to do with my internal needs than with any demands they were actually placing on me. I don't remember my children or husband *ever* reprimanding me for arriving home late. Of course, I never did come home late, so well regulated was I on this score.

Once the existence of the unconscious comes to seem real to us, any number of important insights may follow. What may also follow is the possibility of then transforming one's behaviour—though this part of the process is trickier and harder to attain. To recognize a pattern in our behaviour is not necessarily to be able to do something about that pattern. In this instance, however, it was. As I let my mind drift back over my childhood on my bike, I began to see that at some point I had come to understand, or perhaps only worried, that my mother would become fearful if I were away from home too long. Rather than confront that anxiety about my mother each and every time I rode out on my bicycle or went to visit a friend or whatever, I internalized it. And I did more. In order not to resent my mother's demands on me, especially as I got older and wanted greater freedom for myself, I repressed the way in which the two-hour limit wasn't my own choice. Two hours came to seem enough: I was tired after two hours, or bored, or simply aware of other things that needed doing, and that was it. Home I came, long after such an equation between my needs and my mother's was in the least reasonable. Then, when I had children and a husband, I made them the reason I returned. And so on till I was riding my bike home in the English countryside in an absolute panic that I was going to arrive late—to no one at all!

The problem of repression, we might recall, comes in when—for whatever reason—the wishes and desires that are being resisted become just as important to us as (perhaps even more important than) the wishes and desires that have come to replace them. One reason for this might be that an accommodation we made in the past is suddenly no longer relevant. For example, in my childhood and even in my early motherhood, following some sort of time limit as to how long I might be away continued to serve a useful purpose. Now, at age 50 in England, it didn't. My behaviour had lost any shred of usefulness. It simply imprisoned me against my wishes—or rather, against my *conscious* wishes. Therefore I had to change that behaviour. To do that, I had to come to understand it. This also meant that I had to emotionally experience it as it was way back in its origins in my childhood: a form of protective behaviour. It protected my mother. It protected me. It protected my mother *from* me, and me, from my own unconscious wishes.

By recognizing my rationalization as just that: a rationalization, I was finally able to take long bike rides with only a minimal amount of talking to myself to get myself to extend the two-hour limit. And even after my return home, I was able to maintain a different, more normal relationship to time spent away from home. It's not that I don't sometimes feel a sudden pressure to return home when I've been away from base too long. But I can recognize the pressure as a response to something in the past which I don't need to act on now, in the present. My exercise in self-psychotherapy was successful. The patient was cured of her symptom.

I did not, however, work out all of what was pressing on me there in England. No matter how conscious any of us become, the unconscious is still with us. That is the case whether we sort out our difficulties on our own or in the company of another person. In this particular instance, I was missing a rather glaring dimension of my repression, which suggests how much I had needed to do it.

It was during my sabbatical in England that my mother was diagnosed with cancer. She wanted me to spend the rest of my sabbatical with her, at home—*her* home, which, needless to say, was no longer my home. I did *not* want to take up residence with my mother for several months, a possibility that would not even have arisen if I were then teaching and therefore not free to travel to the States. I was committed to this study leave. I had accepted funding for it. And I knew that spending several months with my mother was not something I was psychologically capable of doing. I'm not proud of this but, for better or for worse I knew it was true of me. I could not go home. My dynamic unconscious, however, wasn't quite as comfortable with this decision as I was. It was very energetically telling me something else: something about my needing and perhaps even wanting to go home to my mother. It was telling me this in such a way that I could not quite hear what my behaviour was saying to me, since my behaviour seemed to have to do with my "home" in England.

From all points of view, my behaviour in England was irrational and pointless. Limiting my bike rides to two hours was of no use to mother in terms of her present wishes. It probably never was. It was also not an adequate response on my part to my internal, unconscious realization of my own ambivalence in relation to those wishes. Even when I was a child, I may not have been giving my mother what she wanted or needed. Perhaps it only fulfilled my imagination of what she wanted and needed. I was the same child who had imagined her dead when she'd fainted; she hadn't said or thought that. I was the same child who fantasized her dead when she left me with my grandmother to give birth to my brother; she knew she was OK and going to come home. Be that as it may, riding my bike in England now, I could not by returning home two hours later give my mother what she *now* wanted, which was for me to come home *now* and not in two hours or two weeks or two months.

In my discomfort concerning bike riding I was experiencing a very real and immediate situation which ultimately had less to do with bike riding than with my mother. Furthermore, in working out one problem I had quite conveniently occluded another, more pressing one. Working out a problem is not the same as working through the resistances to understanding that problem. There were, in England, resistances aplenty standing between me and self-knowledge:

Cycling, recycling and coming home; or: What difference does the therapist make?

As we have already seen more than once, one major dimension of dynamic psychotherapy is to make us conscious of our still active unconscious wishes and desires which, for whatever reasons, our mechanisms of repression are no longer adequately serving. This means two related, albeit somewhat different activities. The first is producing a "picture" of this elusive activity of repression, so that we can *see* what is invisible *except* in its all-too visible and real consequences in our lived experience. The second is tracing the activity of repression back to where it originated. This may be some earlier moment in our adult lives. It may go way back into childhood itself. One of the primary differences between psychoanalysis and psychoanalytic psychotherapy has do with how much immediate, present, day-to-day content seeps into the clinical relationship, and the degree to which that material is directed back out of the present into the past.

Sometimes it is enough to see, in the present moment, the structure of our behaviour. Then we can perceive how our behaviour isn't necessarily being determined by external events but rather by inner qualities and traits that we are bringing to those events. For example, it might have been enough for me to recognize that whenever I left the house (whether in England or at home) my behaviour conformed to a certain pattern. After two hours out I felt the need to return home. I could then see that this pattern didn't make any sense and in fact was causing considerable problems in my life. On the basis of that insight, I might then be able to change my behaviour, without tracing the feelings all the way back to their origin. I might, for example, have taken a tranquillizer to calm me down so that I could endure the anxiety associated with extending my leave beyond what was comfortable for me. Of course, medicating myself in order to be able to take a bike ride might be rather excessive (like giving my two-year-old grandson tranquillizers to calm his crying). It might also have endangered me: some medications do not mix with driving, or even with bike riding. So medicating for anxiety might not, in this instance at least, have made sense.

Behavioural modification, however, might have worked. I might, for example, have lengthened my time out by fifteen minutes each time, lessening the duration of the anxiety and thereby (perhaps) increasing my tolerance for it. Many sorts of phobias and anxieties and simple bad habits are effectively treated through behavioural modification techniques; there is much to be said for them. Or I might have taken a cognitive approach. I might have given myself good reasons for changing my pattern. In this way I might just have been able to convince myself that it was better for me to stay away from home for more than two hours than to return there.

But I might also not have been able to do something as simple as say to myself: this is ridiculous, you are 50 years old and there is no reason to rush home. After all, what I was feeling after my two hours out of the house wasn't in the least rational. It was anxiety, pure and simple. I was feeling fear, and fear isn't an emotion most of us can just put aside. Sometimes it isn't enough simply to recognize a behavioural pattern or to force a change in the behaviour, especially if the behaviour is of long standing and is deeply rooted in the psyche. Additionally, there is the further benefit of understanding a behaviour, knowing its origins in one's personal, private past. Self-knowledge can contribute not only to addressing a particular problem but also to our sense of self-empowerment. Even more importantly, it can also enable insights to proliferate. By discovering the origins of one behaviour, we can often begin to glimpse and start the process of transforming other related behaviours as well. In the particular case of my bike rides through the English countryside, I did see the link between my behaviour now and my childhood experiences. But I needed to take even more seriously the link with my mother. This is the "surplus" that is always contained in the words and images we use (as when his gift-giving mother called her dead son a gift at his funeral). I needed to see as well how my behaviour was telling me to do something very specific in the present: namely to go home to my mother, who might not have been ill and dying in the past but was now.

Ironically, in discovering on my own what in my past was producing a certain form of behaviour in the present, I was missing what in the present was causing me to reflect back on this past in a certain way. Perhaps my taking up bike riding in England (I have *never* ridden a bike in Israel) was my mind's way of putting me in mind of my childhood and the mother who so much wanted and needed me to come home.

In general, psychotherapy of the conservative, psychoanalytically oriented kind I had received does *not* tell you how to decide the life issues it exposes. One reason for this is that there is always more untapped unconscious behind every unconscious wish or desire that we analyse. For the therapist to tell you what to do would, among other things, foreclose the possibility of your reaching the fullest conceivable picture of what your inner life is telling you. This is what I did for myself when I said: aha, I am experiencing bike riding anxieties because of this experience in my past and now I can ride to my heart's delight because I see this. I failed to see what else lay in my unconscious past, perhaps even further back. This had to do with worries for my mother's survival. Those worries were now, with the onset on her present illness, being stirred up into frantic activity. And quite rightly so. There was every reason to worry about my mother's survival, for now indeed she was dying.

Of course, all of us need eventually to act on the insights with which therapy provides us. We need to end therapy and return to life outside the clinical setting. Nonetheless, there is value in letting the therapy linger and ramble. There is a benefit to permitting it to go on long enough to expose as many issues as we can tolerate being brought to the surface of our conscious mind. The longer therapy proceeds, the more it can help us go the further distance to see what *else*, beyond what we may already be able to identify, is also always contained in our stories. Then we can act, or not, on the basis of a much fuller picture of what our internal psychodynamic mind is telling us about ourselves and our motivations.

When we bring our stories into the clinical setting and into the ongoing relationship with the therapist, a number of elements are added. At very least there is one more mind at work, trying to figure out what is going on and why. This other mind, unlike our own, isn't working *against* the decided resistances we are experiencing to clarifying just this "why". One of the great, not-be-underestimated benefits of therapy is that you aren't alone as you go about tackling your unconscious materials. There is someone else there with you. That person can help you not only to soften your resistance to seeing your motives and motivations. He can also help soften the effects of the uncomfortable emotions that are then likely to emerge—the emotions that are producing the need for repression in the first place. The therapist can help you cope.

But the other thing that is happening in the clinical setting, which has been the topic of this and the previous chapters, is that we, being who we are at some very specific moment in our lives, are also entering into a relationship with the therapist on those very same terms. In that therapeutic relationship, as we have already seen, there are inevitably going to be elements of the same personality having problems with bike rides and going home to mother and the anger/fear/worry and whatever else is at work in the dynamic unconscious.

The "murder my therapist" story, as I said, preceded by a couple of years the bike riding experience, which occurred after my therapy had ended. But the earlier psychotherapeutic event already contained the elements that could have helped me illuminate the later event, had I been willing or able to dwell on them. And had I still been in therapy at the time, I might well have re-enacted this scene once again, with a compelling yield of insight into my current situation.

The here-and-now of story-telling and its discontents: transference and the authenticity of feeling

Transference is often one of the most difficult facets of psychotherapy for patients to grasp and ultimately to accept. Life seems complicated enough not to require that we enter into a difficult-to-define and frustrating relationship. It is a relationship that isn't quite real. We're also paying a good deal of money for it.

In point of fact, not all psychotherapies move into the stage of making use of the relationship between the patient and the therapist—at least not in any major or central way. Sometimes the therapist need only be a good listener, or a good explicator of texts. Sometimes it is enough to help a person to clarify his story: to see it in all of its facets and ramifications, its patterns of repetition and the way it merges with other stories and feelings. Such clarification might be sufficient to help that individual shift gears and begin to enact and tell another, better, more satisfying story.

Sometimes, however, more is required. Sometimes the patterns of our enactments in the world require some more immediate, tangible, visible staging—as when I could cure myself of my bike riding time limit but couldn't get myself to see what else was contained in that story, something which was being ignored and defended against in my solution. Sometimes we need a mirror as well as an echo chamber so that we can see as well as hear ourselves speak. We may need vicariously to re-live events or emotions or relationships, albeit in controlled and safe ways. Then we may be able to experience and own them as ours. We may come to be able to identify what they are in all their specificity and nuance, and how they affect us. The relationship between the therapist and us can become this arena in which we narrate ourselves in such as way that the intangibility of our thoughts and feelings can assume the concrete form of a dramatic performance.

In this production of an event, psychotherapeutic story-telling recovers the close association between actions and words that characterizes Freud's original example of *fort-da*. Just as events can become words, so words can take on the character of events. Those events, in the psychotherapeutic setting, become the basis for other verbal events which retell with greater clarity and depth the actual lived events that are now being "re-enacted verbally". Words usually provide some distance from emotions. Words concerning the already distanced and distancing re-performance of self in the clinical setting provide more distance still. My giving my therapist a gift of cups told a story. My refusing to reflect on this gift told another story. My reflecting on this gift would have told another story still. And my reflecting, then, on those words would produce yet another and different story, which I could use to understand me—how *I* enact myself now in the present, not way back when I tried (and failed) to give my mother gifts or to enter into a certain kind of relationship with her. Similarly with regard to my bike riding and the murder of my therapist. With more stories would come greater insight into the larger story, of which coffee mugs and gifts, and worry about (and resentment towards) my therapist, and a host of other phenomena are only the local, temporal, but very vivid, vital re-enactments.

Yet one major hurdle that has to be overcome in psychotherapy is the feeling produced by the transference that your emotions are not being taken seriously by the therapist: that to him they aren't quite "real". This, of course, goes along with the deep suspicion that the therapist's apparent concern for you is similarly make-believe. There is probably no feeling more painful and therefore resisted, in life as well as in therapy, than the thought that the authenticity of your feelings is being questioned; except, perhaps, for the accompanying worry that you aren't really being given care for yourself alone but because of some requirement of the situation: in the case of psychotherapy, because you are paying for that concern. The worry that you aren't being valued and respected for yourself corresponds to something very basic in our real lives as well. So, it turns out, does the suspicion that our emotions aren't being accorded quite the respect we think they deserve. Remember the first time you moved away, or when your best friend found another best friend and your parents told you you'd find new friends, as if your feelings were just childish matters, not nearly as deep and real as adult feelings and purposes?

Most of us, if we are lucky, are born to parents who love us. Their love may not always satisfy in each and every way everything that we want or need from that love. Nonetheless, our parents generally care for us. They give us things. They nurture us. And yet a question that occurs to most of us is whether our parents love us for ourselves or because they have to. Parental love seems written into the contract, and something in us rebels against that idea. We feel hurt and offended by it. Psychotherapy, because of the nature of the relationship between the patient and the therapist, very often forces us to revisit that emotion. Even if that feeling no longer forms an active part of our conscious thinking, it is still there lurking inside us, somewhere in the unconscious contents of mind. It's one of those early basic doubts that, like so many features of the mental life, we sometimes do well to interrogate.

The same is true of the feeling that the therapist doesn't believe your emotions are genuine when you are absolutely sure that they are.

The feelings felt in the transference are certainly as real as any other feelings we human beings experience in our lives. They are what provide a counterweight to the distancing produced by our words. They are what make the experience real in a way that someone else's diagnosis of our problems could not. However, we know that those feelings are also what are being prompted and sustained by the clinical situation itself, as Freud observed early on. This sense of doubleness—that what we are feeling is absolutely real and yet also somehow being staged—also corresponds to a real phenomenon in most of our ordinary lives. D.W. Winnicott speaks in his writings of a "true" self and a "false" self.[1] The "true" self is understood in terms of all those wishes and desires that define you and that (unconsciously) you'd like to express; the "false" self more or less corresponds to the socialized self, the self you present to the world. This is the self that has "decided", in the ways selves decide such matters (which isn't usually consciously) not to ask for, not even any longer to wish for, those things that can't be had or that can only be had at too great a price to the self.

These two selves clearly do not function in total isolation from each other. The "false" self is also a "true" self. In many ways it may even be the truer or truest self, since it is the self by which we are known in the world and through which we interact with that world. Psychological health, then, for Winnicott and others (Alice Miller, for example[2]) does not have to do with getting rid of the so-called "false" self. Rather, it has to do with achieving a reasonable balance between the wishes and needs of the two facets of self. The goal is for the "true" self not to find herself stranded with no means of self-expression and self-gratification within the socialized interactions of the public self.

Becoming acquainted with the doubleness of our self-presentations, the ways in which we are always to some degree or another enacting ourselves in a public way, is one more objective of psychotherapy. But in psychotherapy the positions of the "true" and "false" selves are reversed. It is the "true" self that is being invited to make itself heard and the "false" self that, for the moment

---

[1] *True and false self.* In: *Maturational processes.*
[2] *The drama of the gifted child.*

at least, is being relegated to the secondary position. This has two consequences.

Insofar as it is the "true" self that has got the short end of the stick in our processes of maturation and socialization, this playing at being the "true" self is at the very least a corrective to our former emotional (im)balance. In other words, through discovering this other deeply personal and interior (unconscious) aspect of ourselves, we are adding back what has, through no fault of our own (or any one else's for that matter), perhaps been subtracted too drastically from our living, breathing selves. But something more is going on as well.

We are, when we enter the arena of the clinical setting, already our verbal, intellectual, socialized selves, in an adult relationship with the world and other people (including this man or woman who is our therapist). Therefore we already know that the "true" self, who is giving the performance of her life in the therapist's office—loving, hating, demanding, weeping—isn't going to walk out of that office intact. There are very good reasons the "true" self made its compromises with life. So as we enact our "true" selves, we are also conscious, on some level at least, of the fact that this is indeed a performance. We are conscious, with that observing ego that is also there in the therapist's office with us, that we both do and do *not* love or hate or resent or fear the therapist. In therapy we are ourselves an audience to our self-performance. With our conscious minds we attend diligently to the drama of our unconscious wishes and desires. We observe the fact that we do dramatize, and not only in the therapist's office.[3]

But how do we know that this performance we are giving, which is being prompted by the presence of the therapist in the clinical setting, is an authentic enactment of our own true inner selves? How do we know it is not some sort of hypnotic recitation of an already scripted drama in the therapist's mind? After all, Freud did insist on some very concrete dramas of the psychological life. Most therapists, even if they hotly dispute certain elements of those Freudian stories—the Oedipus complex, for example—do function according to certain paradigms of psychosexual development. Nor are these paradigms to be dismissed. Rather, along with every

[3] Therapists call the kind of regression the patient experiences in the clinical setting, from which the patient then almost immediately recovers his or her mature self, temporary regression in the service of the ego.

other facet of the internal mental life, they are to be analysed and understood.

Take the Oedipus complex. What is important, and largely misunderstood, about Freud's Oedipal model is that it primarily concerns the triangulation of the child's early love relationships, typically in relation to both a mother and a father, but possibly in relation to some other set of caregivers as well. In this triangle of relationships the child competes for the affection of one parent with the other parent. Simultaneously, he or she feels guilty about this competition, since the child also usually loves the other member of the triangle as well. That the competition, whether in relation to parents, caregivers, or even older siblings, involves "sexual" feelings is also pertinent here, though we must keep in mind that sexuality for the young child is not the genitally organized sexuality of the adult. Later in life we censor and inhibit these feelings of childhood such that they come to seem retrospectively (as they are thought back onto our childhoods) somehow indecent. But our adult terminologies and judgments may not adequately or correctly convey what we were feeling as children. Instead, they may have everything to do with how we came to judge and repress those feelings as we began to grow into our adult selves.

Nobody wants to be told that he or she wanted to sleep with his or her father or mother and hated the other parent for having a prior claim on the adored parent. For most of us, that description of our early childhood experience doesn't make any real, meaningful sense. It doesn't correspond to anything recognizable in our memories of our younger selves. Nor does it jive with our feelings about our parents, then or now. But most of us do, in our ordinary everyday lives, experience feelings of jealousy, resentment and competitiveness. We might, therefore, on occasion want to ask where those feelings come from. We might want to consider whether it isn't perhaps possible that from early childhood on (and where, after all, were most of us having our early childhoods if not in the bosom of our families?) we encountered such feelings of jealousy and the like in relation to the people we most loved and who most loved us.

Most of us are born into two-parent families. Many of us also have siblings. So most of us have experienced some form of competition for attention and love. Our jealousy may take the form of feeling displaced if we are older siblings. It may take the form of feeling less loved if we are further on down the road of the family construction. And so on and so forth. Certainly, as family life in the twenty-first century has changed, so have the points of conflict and friction for the young child. But then again, Freud developed his theories of the family in a social context in which children were often being raised not by their mothers but by nannies. It was also a world in which mortality rates meant that not only siblings died but parents died and remarried as well. Freud himself was the child of his father's second marriage and was raised by a nanny. There was variety in the Oedipal drama from its very inception as a psychological paradigm.

Though each of us has a unique and different childhood, nonetheless members of a culture very often do share certain experiences. Until very recently, the structure of family (mother-father-child) was more or less biologically determined. Even if that were not the case, however, family structure is certainly a part of a larger social organization. Parents are themselves produced by society. They rear their children in order to become members of that same society. It makes sense that we'd have things in common with one another.

Nonetheless, however much the drama we enact in the therapist's office corresponds to certain shared models of the psychological life, it is still our own very personal, very private drama. The details are all our own. Nor is our enactment being prompted by some sort of hypnotic suggestion on the part of the therapist. The therapist is not so all-knowing. Nor is he so powerful as to have the ability to completely subdue your rational faculties and make you into an actor of his (rather than your own) script, and a Freudian script at that. Your transference drama is being generated by *you* and *your* experiences. This is one of the reasons that psychotherapy, despite the prominence and power of Freudian theory, may be a more purely personal, individualistic form of therapy than other competing therapies. The insights that matter originate within us. Furthermore, the consequences of those insights are not processed through the therapist's recommendations and wisdom (as in counselling or certain group therapies). Rather, they are returned to us intact, for our edification and decision-making.

The performance of self in the clinical setting, then, is anything but the performance of a role in a play, in which the lines are already written and you need only memorize and deliver them. Rather, it has more in common with what in the world of theatre is called *improvisation*. In improvisational theatre the actors are given in-depth biographies of their characters. Then they are put into relationships with one another in certain settings and with a certain ongoing plot which the director of the play (or movie) also provides. The actors make up their lines and thereby determine the content of the scenes are they go along. (The recent very popular movies of Christopher Guest are examples of this genre.) In psychotherapeutic improvisation, the biographical information to be brought to bear on the here-and-now of the stage set is already contained within the actor as his own autobiographical history. If there is nonetheless still some larger plot in relation to which the individual enactments are being made to function, it is only the vast and amorphous script of Western culture and of the shared condition of being biologically and psychologically constituted human beings, negotiating between inner and outer pressures and demands. This is hardly a restrictive backdrop for the enactment of an individual self.

The stage manager of this personal improvisation is the therapist. His job is not to realize his own conception of the plot. Rather, his job is to help you, the protagonist, realize yours. This stage manager is also, of course, a player in the scene. He does not, however, deliver either memorized lines or even lines coming out of his own wishes and desires. Rather, his lines emerge out of yours and out of the character description projected onto him by you. He then provides the lines (including some hints towards the interpretation of your lines) that are necessary for the central character—you—to continue your improvisation—the self-dramatization which is the transference.

One of the purposes of this transference drama is to enable you to experience, first-hand, your own emotions. It is to immerse you within your own subjectivity. One of the effects of therapy may well be a heightened awareness of subjectivity itself. You re-emerge into the more objectively defined external world in which we all live with a sense of how truly subjective your grasp of the world is. Subjectivity, according to Piet Hein, is like reading a sundial at night with a torch. Sundials depend for their accuracy, of course, on an objective point of reference: the sun. The sun casts its shadow by virtue of where it is vis-à-vis the earth. This has nothing whatsoever to do with us. We do not control the sun. A torch is a man-made, hand-held instrument. We direct its light. The transference drama illuminates how we each cast our own particular light and then, innocently and erroneously, use it as a gauge by which to read the world's reality.

Like every drama, the transference drama is programmed to come to an end. The curtain drops and you are delivered back into the real world again. Even though it is our socialization, not to mention the unyielding resilience of the natural world, which produced that "false" self which we are now cutting down to size by letting the "true" self once again say its piece, still and all we live in a world of intractable matter and of other people as well. We are socialized human beings. We do not control the sun. We cannot continue to function in the world without our socialized selves (even those components of it that are somewhat "false"). Indeed, that mature, conscious socialized self is there with us in therapy, witnessing our dramatic productions. It is sharing the perspective of the therapist (as participant, director and finally also audience), and it knows that it is going to have to walk out of that office to face the noonday sun.

The feelings you feel for or in relation to your therapist in the clinical setting are real feelings. But they are also enactments of those feelings without the censor and censure of the socialized self. This censor and censure are essential to our being mature and responsible adults in the real world. Just as in childhood we had to move from our love of our parents into the love of others, so the point of "falling in love" with the therapist (or enacting murderous rage or fear or disappointment) is to be able to fall in love in the real world (or express anger or anxiety or disappointment) as a responsible, socialized adult.

One of the goals of psychotherapy is to restore us to a good self, less "false" and more "true", but still socialized. It is to make us into our own therapists for life, able to witness, monitor and enact the truest aspects of our being. One way of knowing when to terminate therapy is when you feel, finally, that you can do the therapist's job for yourself—at least most of the time.

Transference love and the truth of countertransference

What, then, of the therapist's feelings? Are they all a sham, especially those responses the patient understands to be expressions of caring, anger, dissatisfaction and the like? If the patient is replacing conscious control with free, uninhibited unconscious expression (without getting rid of consciousness altogether), the therapist is involved in a similar but also somewhat reversed process. The therapist is also permitting himself to feel freely. He does this, however, by putting aside (rather than enacting) his wishes, needs, desires and fantasies as contained in *his* unconscious. In other words, while you are filling the room with your unconscious wishes and desires, including (often) the expectation of fulfilling those wishes and desires, the therapist is emptying it of all and any of his own expectations concerning his own unconscious wishes and needs, even if he is giving those desires free rein in his mind.

The point of the transference in psychotherapy is precisely *not* to gratify the wishes and desires the transference expresses, as simple a solution as that might seem. Two human beings come to understand what one of them wants; what could be more natural than the second person giving the first person what he needs? First of all, if the therapist did gratify the patient's wishes, then there would soon be no more therapists to go around. Each one of them would have to commit himself to the single patient and his desires. He would have to marry the patient, or become the patient's father or mother or best friend or eternal enemy or whatever. Either the play would go on forever or the play would become reality, with those two people forever stuck playing the same (and ultimately boring) role. The point of therapy is to deliver you back into your life so that you can find the solutions to your problems in the real world of other relationships.

The therapist feels what he is feeling, but in the absence of any possibility of enacting or satisfying those feelings. One of the reasons, therefore, that it doesn't make sense to stay in love with your therapist, or remain angry with him, is that what you have *not* experienced in the clinical setting is that part of the therapist's unconscious that in the real outside world has its own demands to make, its own "neuroses" to enact. One might say that the 45- or 50-minute clinical hour is about as long as a human being can go keeping his unconscious in check that way, like taking a deep breath and staying under water: eventually you've got to come up for air. This isn't to say that you weren't alive and kicking while you were under water. It's only to recognize that you can't stay there forever. Remove from the equation of a human being the possibility of acting on and realizing unconscious wishes and desires, and you don't have the wholly engaged psychological entity, only someone holding his breath.

Using his own unconscious only as a guide for the better hearing and interpreting of the patient's unconscious, the therapist gives the patient space in which to enact his unconscious. The therapist permits, indeed encourages the transference. And in that emptied space the therapist himself counter-transfers. He allows himself to be drawn into the drama and to experience reciprocal emotions. Countertransference used to be understood as what the therapist had to avoid. Today it is no longer the bugbear of psychotherapy. Instead, it is in part what provides the therapist with a fuller understanding of the patient, and the therapy with its authenticity.

Since countertransference belongs to the realm of the therapist rather than the patient, it is best discussed in our next chapter, in which the therapist finally gets to speak at last.

CHAPTER EIGHT

The listening cure:
the therapist speaks at last

In psychoanalytic psychotherapy the patient is the dynamic, active agent. He is the one who is telling and retelling his story, transferring feelings onto his therapist and dramatizing the inner psychodynamics of self in the clinical setting. All of this self-enactment will eventually become the materials of the patient's own self-reflections. What, then, is the therapist doing all this time, such that he should get paid for his services? In one of Woody Allen's earliest stand-up routines he confesses rather wryly that it took him six months to realize that his strictly Freudian analyst had died. Sometimes even psychotherapy, which isn't psychoanalysis proper, feels like that: as if there is absolutely no one in the room with you.

But of course there is someone else in that room with you. The very fact that someone is listening to you tell your story and watching you perform yourself is a part of how therapy works. Freud's "talking cure" is as much a "listening cure". As we have already said more than once, sometimes we just need to be heard (and seen) to confirm or validate that we, our feelings and our experiences exist in a world of other people. We need to know that other people can witness these things about us, and that not only can they (like us) survive them, but they can even understand and empathize with us. Sometimes what someone else's silent, listening presence gives us is comfort. It helps us know we are not alone.

But as we have been insisting all along, the psychotherapist is not just your ordinary, casual listener. For starters, he is very often the occasion of the story-telling, which more and more, either directly or obliquely, comes to concern your relationship with him. In other words, without the therapist's presence, your enactment of self simply wouldn't occur—at least not in this dramatic and "self-conscious" way of psychotherapeutic transference. Furthermore, the therapist is the agent of the reflection on and interpretation of your stories, both as they are enacted through the transference and as they are narrated in your stories of events outside the clinical setting (both past and present). Eventually, the job of the therapist is, like a good parent, to withdraw from the scene of listening, transference and interpretation such that you can become your own listening story-teller. But until that moment the therapist has a lot of work to do.

From the start, then, the therapist is a participant in what is going on. Nor is he by any means silent. He may not speak a lot. He may also not speak at the moments when you might imagine or expect or desire he would, or say what you would have him say. Nonetheless, the therapist does contribute something to the story-telling conversation beyond being interested in it. So what exactly does the story-listener contribute, and how? Just as clarifying the theory behind psychotherapy might help to enhance its effectiveness for some of us, so listening in on the therapist's largely silent listening may also help dispel certain misconceptions. It may enable us to take better advantage of the opportunity for self-reflection that psychotherapy is affording us. It may also help us determine whether our own therapist is "doing his job", at least in a psychodynamic venue.

Free-floating listening and free-floating responsiveness[1]

Psychoanalytic psychotherapy depends as much upon the structure of the relationship between the therapist and the patient as upon anything else. Antoine de Saint-Exupéry's *Little Prince* contains

[1] Much of what follows has been translated and adapted from Rudd Abolson, Psychoanalytic Psychotherapy.

a charming little scene that can be read as a vignette of what the therapist-patient relationship looks like if viewed, for a moment, through the optics of whimsy and a bit of good humour. In the story, the little prince wants to befriend the fox, who explains to the little prince that he will have to "tame" him first. "What does that mean—'tame'?" asks the little prince, to which the fox replies: "it is an act too often neglected... It means to establish ties... One only understands the things that one tames." How the fox is tamed and how the friendship is thus established between them is very much to the purpose of understanding the dynamics of the therapist-patient relationship in psychoanalytic psychotherapy. "You must be very patient," the fox tells the little prince. "First, you will sit down at a little distance from me—like that—in the grass. I shall look at you out of the corner of my eye and you will say nothing. Words are the source of misunderstandings. But you will sit a little closer to me every day." They will also meet "at the same hour" every day. "If, for example, you come at four o'clock in the afternoon, then at three o'clock I shall begin to be happy. I shall feel happier and happier as the hour advances. At four o'clock I shall already be worrying and jumping about... But if you come at just any time, I shall never know at what hour my heart is to be ready to greet you." Relationships need "rites", the fox explains, which "make one day different from other days, one hour from other hours".[2]

Like psychoanalysis, from which it is derived, psychotherapy depends on the rites and rituals of the setting—the schedule of fixed regular meeting times, the relative silence of the therapist, and the safe, dependable holding environment created by the therapist's relative distance from the patient. The practice of psychotherapy will differ from therapist to therapist and even, for each therapist, from patient to patient. The nature of the patient's problems, which is to say the amount of his or her psychological strength, will determine the degree to which certain elements of the therapeutic relationship, including the elements of the setting and the kind of listening that the therapist does, are insisted upon or attenuated and compromised.

Initially, Freudian psychoanalysis developed as a way of treating neurotic disorders, the kernel of which was the Oedipus complex. It

[2] pp. 80-84.

focused on the dramatic and passionate struggle of desire, anxiety, guilt and anger, and feelings of exclusion, rivalry, competition and inadequacy as experienced in the mind of the child finding his place in the relationship with his parents—what is known as three-person psychology. Later developments in object relations theory and self-psychology, in tandem with widening knowledge and understanding of the developmental processes occurring in the very earliest years of infant development (the first two years of life, when the child is primarily in relationship with the caregiver), shifted attention to the critical importance of the "pre-Oedipal" phase (two-person psychology). This deepening and widening of the conceptual understanding of development not only profoundly influenced the practice of psychoanalysis, it also shifted the scope of patients for whom psychotherapeutic intervention was appropriate.

Research suggests that there is an optimum level of disturbance fitting for psychoanalytic psychotherapy. Very disturbed patients need large measures of support and are better served by supportive psychotherapy. Those in between—"sick enough to need it, healthy enough to stand it"[3] or "ill enough to merit it, well enough to benefit from it"[4]—are the individuals best helped by psychoanalytic psychotherapy.

There are at least two major groups of patients in psychotherapy, each of which requires different accommodations, emphases and strategies in the way the therapist structures the relationship with the patient and listens to what he or she says. In the first instance, psychotherapy was developed as an alternative mode of treatment for individuals for whom classical psychoanalysis might actually risk leading to further maladaptive behaviour and breakdown. These were, and are today, generally individuals who are suffering from borderline personality or narcissistic conditions and from deficits in early development or ego weakness. Many of them cannot sustain the powerful regressions, transference neuroses and general challenges to the ego that accompany psychoanalysis. A good number of psychotherapy patients suffer from such conditions. They suffer as well as from depressive disorders or prolonged grief reactions, long-lasting and intractable anxiety, or repeated difficulties in interpersonal relationships. In today's environment of

[3] Thoma and Kachele, *Psychoanalytic Practice*.
[4] Batesman and Holmes, *Introduction to Psychotherapy*.

expanding medical intervention into a number of mental illnesses, psychotherapy often also accompanies pharmacological treatment. This includes the psychoses, which Freud explicitly excluded from the province of psychoanalysis.

The other primary group of patients are those who might well be proper candidates for psychoanalysis. For whatever reasons, however they cannot or will not commit the kind of time, money and energy such treatment requires. These are individuals for whom self-reflection and insight are important and sustainable. They can entertain the idea that at least some portion of their psychological problems arises from sources within themselves. They also have some tendency towards introspection and are curious about themselves. Typically, these individuals have experienced long-lasting and basically positive interpersonal relationships in their past, such that they have sufficient ego-strength to endure the regressions and other pressures of the transference relationship.

Keeping in mind that these two different categories of patient will require different kinds of therapeutic relationships, which is to say different degrees of active intervention as opposed to more passive "holding" and supporting, it is possible to provide a general description of the therapist's listening practice, much of which pertains to psychoanalysis as well as psychotherapy.

Freud once remarked concerning psychoanalysis that, like a chess game, one can only describe the opening two or three moves and their variations. One cannot give precise instructions as to how to play the game; nor can one predict the outcome. This holds true for psychotherapy as well. Nonetheless, there are certain rules that govern the game. For patients the one and only rule in psychotherapy is to talk as freely as possible about whatever concerns them. In psychoanalysis this is called free association, and it is clearly not a wholly attainable goal. If the patient could freely associate without descending into psychosis, he would be cured. (It has always been a question whether free association is the instrument or the goal of psychoanalysis.) Nonetheless, free association is a guide to the patient's role in the psychoanalytic setting. In psychotherapy as well the freedom to discuss whatever comes to mind is highly encouraged.

For the therapist the parallel and equally difficult, also largely unachievable rule is *free floating attentiveness* or *free floating listening*.[5] The challenge for the therapist of such free floating attentiveness or free floating listening is doubly two-fold. First, the therapist has to listen to everything that the patient is saying. This means listening not only to the content of the patient's statements but to their structure as well. Secondly, and just as importantly, he has to attend to everything that is going on in his own mind as well—the thoughts, associations and even feelings which are inevitably a part of the therapist's experience of the patient.

This second kind of listening is also composed of two parts. The therapist has to differentiate between two different sets of thoughts and feelings. There are those that have to do with his own psychological interior and that should under no circumstances be brought into the therapeutic relationship. And there are those which are being prompted by the patient's discourse in the "emptied out" space of the therapist's listening mind. These thoughts and feelings have everything to do with the therapeutic situation, especially once a transference relationship has been established with the patient.

One primary job of the therapist is, as Winnicott put it, to "hold" the patient. This is one consequence of listening non-judgmentally, sympathetically, attentively, without breaking the flow or structure of the patient's words.[6] The complement to this even-handed, non-judgmental attentiveness is the readiness and openness it permits to respond mentally to the roles the patient draws the therapist into (in the transference). This has been called "free floating responsiveness."[7]

The patient is encouraged to speak freely. He is encouraged to make the effort to talk about whatever thoughts, feelings and fantasies come to mind and not to dismiss anything, regardless of how meaningless or repulsive it may seem. The therapist does not have this privilege (except in his mind). Therefore, it is a basic rule of psychotherapy that it is the patient who initiates the session. The patient sets the agenda from the moment he enters the door. Everything the patient says or does is an expression of himself at that moment and in relation to the therapist—even the reluctance or inability to begin the conversation. The therapist accepts all of

[5] Bion, *Second Thoughts*.
[6] Winncott, *Holding: A Fragment of an Analysis*.
[7] Joseph Sandler, *Countertransference and Role-responsiveness*.

the patient's communications—verbal as well as non-verbal, vocal as well as silent (silence speaks worlds in the psychotherapeutic setting)—as genuinely meaningful and as legitimate expressions of self. The therapist does not prompt the discussion or otherwise lead the patient into this subject or that. Rather, he allows the patient to speak freely (or not) about what he is thinking or feeling. Listening is itself a goad to the patient's talking. In the unprompted, un-coerced words of the patient, as in his actions, are contained the patient's private, personal truths.

Beginning therapy

The first meeting between the therapist and the patient is equally important to the patient as to the therapist. It is useful for the patient, perhaps, to see it from the therapist's point of view. This initial session is a critical determinant of the future progress of the therapy. It determines whether therapy will even ensue. It is also a microcosm of the process itself. Here the relationship and rapport between the therapist and the patient, through which the bases of the future contact are established, takes its inception. Insofar as the first session already involves the patient's talking about his problems, it is itself therapeutic. It is a part of the process about to unfold.

The therapist, therefore, has a primary responsibility to put the patient at ease so as to make such talking possible. Indeed, the first meeting should seek to facilitate the possibility of the patient's returning for subsequent sessions. However, therapeutic the meeting, little meaningful change can occur in a single interview. The first meeting is an opportunity for the therapist to instil trust in the patient concerning the therapeutic process.

At the same time, this meeting also permits an initial assessment of the patient. This can set the direction for the therapy. The first meeting is an invaluable opportunity for the therapist to collect vital information about the client, through which the future course of the therapy can begin to be mapped; indeed, through which a decision can be made as to whether therapy is even indicated or advisable. Not all people are fit recipients of psychotherapy, and some who would benefit from it nonetheless need to be helped to get into the process.

The psychotherapeutic relationship has to be looked at from two distinct perspectives: that of the patient and that of the therapist. The patient, it is to be recognized, has come to the therapist for help. Feelings of insufficiency or dependency will express themselves directly or indirectly in any number of ways: by over-compensation, by a stance of emphatic independence, through excessive control or aggression, etc. It is therefore incumbent upon the therapist to remember not to take such behaviours at face value. Rather, the therapist must understand such positioning as an expression of compensation for the feelings of childishness or helplessness that often accompany the turn to therapy. *However the patient behaves in the first session, he came seeking help.* It is the therapist's job to understand that need.

The task of the therapist, therefore, is to enable the patient to enter into and continue the process. At the same time that the therapist is putting the patient at ease, he is beginning to assess the patient and interpret (silently, to himself) the material being presented. This means on the one hand taking in the patient's own interpretation of his problems: his understanding of his past history, of his current life situation, of his theories concerning himself and the like. On the other hand it means interpreting (again, silently and to himself) the structure of the patient's responses: how the patient "narrates" himself to the therapist. All of the patient's reactions and responses contain and express everything from the individual's wishes and conflicts to his styles of resistance. From these many things can be gleaned: the individual's capacity or motivation for change, the potential for psychological reflection and emotional response, and the ability to tolerate psychic pain when talking things out. This assessment will as often as not need to be done over some sessions. It should include a tentative diagnosis and a dynamic formulation of the patient's problem. It should be kept in mind that in parallel to the therapist's assessing the patient, the patient is also assessing the therapist and the therapeutic situation, and often resisting them. This should in no way deter the therapist from his task.

Assessment is important because psychotherapy is like a long journey into largely unexplored territory. Even though a map can never substitute for the journey itself, and while there will always be details and shadings that differ between the map and the terrain, nonetheless a map provides points of reference that enable us to see how the parts relate to each other and to the whole. The map helps us bring into focus a meaningful picture. Only the irresponsible embark on such a journey without some sense of the territory and terrain.

In this initial dialogue between therapist and patient, the patient describes aspects of feelings, experiences and behaviour. The therapist responds with gentle and tentative clarifications, reflections or even mild interpretations. The therapist observes whether the patient responds by reflecting on or further elaborating the therapist's comments, or whether he reacts defensively or anxiously. In this way the therapist is able to evaluate whether the patient is a suitable candidate for insight-oriented psychotherapy. If not, the therapist will have to proceed with the utmost caution in order not to provoke disruption of the patient's defensive structure and cause possible disintegration. The therapist must avoid disturbing the patient's defensive responses. Rather, he must provide support until such time as it is possible to help ease the patient into the recognition and revision of these defences.

As we noted earlier, from the moment the patient appears in the therapist's office and begins to tell his story, he has begun to establish a transference relationship. This transference relationship goes back to childhood, when some good supportive (or not) person was willing (or not) to listen to his resentment, fears and sadness. This is also when the individual developed either the satisfaction of or the anxiety concerning being protected and heard. Telling someone your most painful stories *is* regressive. This is why we often avoid it in life and resist it in therapy. The therapist's sympathetic silence helps the patient over the hurdle of his more mature impulses, including his self-consciousness about expressing his innermost fantasies and fears.

Transference and countertransference: the engines of
psychoanalytic psychotherapy

Through his or her active silent listening, the therapist tries to help the patient discover and re-transcribe in his everyday understanding and behaviour the contours of the unconscious contents of his own mind. Since this can best be achieved through the transference, the therapist's silence is also a way of clearing space for the patient to transfer feelings onto the therapist and come to experience and reflect on those feelings.

In this transference relationship the therapist comes to stand for someone whom the patient needs, whether as a love object, a hate object, an object of anger or envy or admiration or whatever. The therapist permits, even encourages this transference. He also consents to the replaying of how that person was used or related to as an object in the past. To the patient, having someone in this role provides a certain necessary satisfaction. Eventually that satisfaction and how it is being obtained will have to be made subject to reflection and thereby made conscious to the patient. In the early stages of therapy, however, the therapist has to accept what is being projected onto him. He has to do this knowing that this "other" is not himself. Yet he must accept this projection without acting on it, so as to give the patient time and space to work out his needs in relation to this person. For this reason a good many things, especially in the initial stages of therapy, need to go unsaid, until it is felt that the patient can tolerate such intervention into his feelings and fantasies.

Because it takes time for the patient to project onto the therapist, time for that relationship to ripen fully, and time for intervention into the patient's fantasies to be tolerated in such a way as to enable new perceptions to replace old ones, psychotherapy is to say the least a time-consuming affair.

Freud saw transference as the main motor of the psychoanalytic relationship. He did not, however, see it as itself a matter for analysis except under certain circumstances. In the same vein he saw countertransference as an obstacle to analysis. Countertransference was understood as the therapist's own desire to act out in relation to the patient. It was therefore what the analyst had to neutralize in the therapeutic relationship. Today therapists deal differently and more directly with the transference. They also distinguish between the kind of countertransference that is simply transference in reverse and a second, legitimate and more useful kind of countertransference. This second kind of countertransference is understood to be a vital part of the transitional overlapping space co-occupied by therapist and patient. It consists of the feelings, responses and associations evoked in the therapist, which are not only his own mental landscape but responses to the patient within the transference relationship being established. Therefore they constitute the therapist's largely unconscious or pre-conscious apprehension of the patient's latent messages to the therapist.

It is important for the therapist to scan and observe and relate to these feelings which are evoked in relation to the patient's transference for two reasons. First, they help the therapist to identify those reactions that do belong to the therapist alone and that therefore must be held in reserve for later analysis and treatment of the therapist, not the patient. Second, the therapist must be able comprehend and analyse those messages that are being communicated by the patient through the transference. The therapist, in other words, must contain—restrain and not act on— his countertransference feelings, and then he must make use of them to further his understanding of the patient.

The therapist's interventions are limited to those which in his judgment will further recognition and understanding of what is being said and (even more) what is being avoided. The therapist never intervenes simply to assert his presence, cleverness, or authority. The therapist's silent, albeit active listening enables the patient to talk and to hear his own talking, to hear his own words. But the attentive and yet non-intrusive listening on the part of the therapist serves additional functions as well. It facilitates the patient's regression and makes possible the contact with his repressed fantasies, desires and fears.

Clarification, confrontation, linking, reflecting, interpreting: the psychotherapeutic interventions

The internal work being done by the therapist when he is listening to the patient, in order to come to the clarity necessary to help the patient with the project of his or her own self-clarification, is compound and multilayered. On the one hand, the therapist has to hear what the patient is telling him about herself in the here and now of her life—in her relationships, feelings, conflicts, wishes and defences in her everyday life. He also has to hear what the patient is communicating about the here and now of the relationship with the therapist, which is also contained in those very same stories. Finally, the therapist must recognize how those wishes, conflicts and defences are crystallizations of other configurations and scenes of wishes, conflicts and defences from the past. At the same time, the therapist also has to be sensitive to his own feelings and associations in relation to what the patient is saying. The therapist's role is *not* to articulate for the patient—to interpret and to give counsel—but rather gently, unobtrusively to assist the patient in articulating for himself. Interpretation is not a spade to dig with. Rather, it a rake to stir up the soil gently, tentatively, so that new impressions and sensations can take root.

For the most part, therefore, what happens in the clinical setting is that the patient talks and the therapist listens. Occasionally the therapist speaks. The major categories of response or intervention on the part of the therapist as he listens to the patient's free-flowing talk can be identified as: *clarification, confrontation, linking, reflection* and *interpretation.* These therapeutic interventions do not necessarily occur consecutively. Nor are they wholly independent of each other. Collectively, interactively, they form the core of the therapist's active work with the patient.

Sometimes helping the patient to *clarify* or *confront* what he is saying means simply asking the patient what he means by this or another thought or narrative. In this way the therapist endeavours to encourage the patient to produce his own greater clarity by bringing an insufficiently clear idea or thought into greater focus and even expanding on it. One should remember that ideas, thoughts, memories, feelings and behaviour that are partial and vague are more difficult to integrate into our conscious knowledge and behaviour. The more clearly something can be verbalized, the more fully it can be made subject to our conscious apprehension and thought.

Sometimes, too, vagueness and lack of clarity are indications of anxiety or resistance. They express the patient's unwillingness or inability to confront or articulate an idea that is more fraught than he realizes. Evidences of resistance—moments of lack of clarity or vagueness, falling silent, refusing to speak—are noted by the therapist. When or if the time is ripe (and this is a place where the differences in patients' ability to sustain inner reflection will produce significant differences in the therapist's practice), they are brought to the attention of the patient. The therapist then confronts the patient with inconsistencies, repetitions and hesitations, and in this way tries to produce clarification of the preconscious and not only the conscious dimensions of the thought or feeling.

Since it is one goal of psychotherapy to reduce feelings of anxiety and guilt, the therapist has to proceed with caution when confronting moments of resistance. Too much anxiety or guilt and the therapy cannot proceed. Too little and there is no reason for it to proceed. In the same vein, if the patient is truly uncomfortable talking about a particular subject but, feeling obliged, talks about it anyway, the therapist has to consider what it means that the patient consents to the therapist's demands (the therapist also has to consider to himself, privately, what it means that he demands such consent).

The therapist also assists the patient in *linking* between different parts of his discourse and between the different meanings and significances that exist within the discourse as a whole. Because patients often experience their lives as meaningless or chaotic, linking helps integrate moments in the present to each other (both in relation to the patient's life outside the therapy and in relation to the therapist and therapy themselves). Ultimately, where possible, the therapist helps link experiences and feelings back to the past of childhood. Naming or giving words to phenomena or feelings is itself a form of linking, producing conscious connections between what otherwise seem disconnected and fragmented events or feelings. Linking provides access into the patterns and structures of the patient's responses such that those patterns and structures can be witnessed by the patient.

Another task of the therapist is to *reflect* back to the patient what he has said, neither adding to nor subtracting from the patient's texts, simply rewording or putting it in other words. "What I hear you saying is…" Reflecting back or rewording the patient's narrative produces an intermediate—transitional and overlapping—space between therapist and patient where the two can explore more deeply the unconscious structures and contents of the patient's mind.

Finally, the therapist helps the patient to *interpret*, to make conscious and give definition to the unconscious structures and contents, the precipitates of which have arisen to view, providing insight and self-knowledge. Such interpretation is never given from the unconscious depths upwards. Rather, it proceeds from the surface (the surrounding environment and the transference) tentatively backwards to childhood. The therapist has to weigh carefully the degree of the patient's anxiety in relation to this regression. The therapist must also resist foreclosing interpretation by jumping in to interpret on behalf of the patient or according to assumed paradigms of behaviour. The therapist must be willing to be as surprised by the patient's associations and insights as the patient himself. Therefore, the therapist must actively resist the tendency to anticipate or prejudge or even, in the first instance, interpret what the patient says. The therapist must permit the patient to transcribe his own narrative for himself. How much the therapist will interpret and how far into the past that interpretation will go differentiates psychoanalysis from psychotherapy and one form of psychotherapy from another.

Encroachments of the real in psychotherapy

In classical psychoanalysis the discipline of the psychoanalytic setting—the use of the couch, the frequency of the encounters between analyst and patient, i.e., analysand (often four to five times a week), the requirement for absolute neutrality and abstinence on the part of the analyst, and the pure, uninhibited free association of the analysand—dominates and thereby to a large degree determines the nature of the process. Psychoanalysis (even of non-Freudian varieties) has been usefully defined as the analysis of the transference relationship (or what is sometimes called the transference neurosis). That is, as the analysis proceeds, the interpretation of the relationship that is being established and enacted between the analyst and the patient comes more and more to dominate the activity of the psychoanalytic session. Nor does this analysis remain in the here-

and-now, adult present of the patient. Psychoanalysis—in large part through the use of the couch, where the patient is out of eye contact with the analyst and where he can also relax into an almost dream-like state—fosters a far greater regression back into childhood emotions and modes of response than occurs in psychotherapy. These earlier childhood contents of the unconscious mind then become matters for the analysis.

In psychotherapy, meetings between the therapist and patient are less frequent than in psychoanalysis (often only once or twice a week). The two partners to the conversation often engage each other face to face. Or they may sit diagonally, thus permitting the patient either to maintain eye contact or not. The patient is therefore better able in psychotherapy than in psychoanalysis to self-regulate the degree of regression that accompanies his or her talking to the therapist. This is a major distinction between psychoanalysis and psychotherapy. Regression is not absent from the psychotherapeutic relationship altogether, but it is attenuated. Therefore, it must be employed differently and to different ends.

This difference in the degree of the patient's regression has implications for how far back into the past psychotherapy will take the clarification and interpretation of the materials brought forth by the patient within the clinical sessions. In dream interpretation, for example, psychotherapy will be less likely to trace the dream's latent meanings all the way back to the archaic, psychosexual conflicts of childhood, which the dreams are probably also expressing. In psychotherapy, the interpretation of the dream, like the interpretation of much else that the patient says, will tend to stay closer to the present. The interpretation will focus more narrowly on the conflicts now being experienced in the patient's life, including, perhaps, the transference relationship to the therapist.

Like psychoanalysis, psychotherapy involves the establishment of such a transference relationship in which there can be a meaningful (regressive) (re)experiencing of the derivatives of the archaic and early childhood conflicts. In point of fact, transference relationships characterize many of the relationships between caregiver and care-recipient (as between teacher and student or doctor and patient). The difference between transference in these other contexts and transference in both the psychoanalytic and the psychotherapeutic setting is that in the latter it becomes a subject for reflection. This is as true in psychotherapy as in psychoanalysis. Yet in psychotherapy, because of the infrequency of meetings and the regulation of the regression, more reality seeps into the therapeutic relationship. This in turn necessitates the therapist's more active intervention in helping the patient perceive and grasp the unconscious—denied, repressed—materials of his or her own behavioural or verbal enactments. For these same reasons, psychotherapy tends to be more goal-oriented than psychoanalysis. There is less demand for free-associative thinking and more focus on the alleviation of symptoms.

Psychotherapy, in other words, remains more here-and-now and goal-oriented. Its main objective is to modify (rather than open-endedly explore and resolve) the patterns of archaic conflicts and their derivatives.

All sorts of apparently trivial matters can become the stuff of psychotherapeutic analysis. For example, even though psychotherapy is not quite as rigorous as psychoanalysis concerning the discipline of setting and scheduling meetings, nonetheless a certain discipline of setting and regularity is generally imposed. This is the case especially concerning the times of session, their frequency, their cost and their duration. There are many reasons for this. By insisting on a regular day and hour for sessions, and by limiting the session to the 45-minute or 50-minute hour, for example, the therapist primes the patient for the therapeutic meeting. He induces him to focus and channel materials into and during the session.

Through establishing regularity in the appointments and insisting on their being paid for whether the patient is present or not, material is also provided for the here-and-now interpretation of the patient. Scheduling contributes to a certain degree of regression. Insisting on payments not only ensures the livelihood of the therapist, it also protects him against becoming hostage to the patient's resistances. Arriving late, cancelling an appointment, quibbling over a fee can all, then, become ways of discussing the patient's relationship with therapy and with the therapist. They all present themselves as events of boundary-crossing or reality-breaking to be observed, understood and interpreted. Similarly, struggling with the time limit set on the session is an opportunity for analysing the patient's relationship to time, separation anxieties, feelings of frustration and the like. This does not mean that alterations cannot be made. By and large, however, they should not be made impulsively or erratically.

For the purposes of psychotherapy, the deeply regressive transference neurosis of psychoanalysis is not only unnecessary, but sometimes it is actually undesirable. Frequently it complicates, obstructs and disturbs the treatment. What makes psychoanalysis and psychoanalytic psychotherapy two distinct, albeit related modes of psychological intervention is this difference between the regressive, childhood-sexuality- and transference-focused elements of psychoanalysis and the more goal-oriented and reality-laden features of psychotherapy.

The dynamics of psychoanalytic psychotherapy have been conceptualized by David Malan as two triangles.[8] One of these triangles is referred to as the triangle of conflict. This triangle represents the inner dynamics of the psychic life of the individual. The other is the triangle of person. It configures the patient's position in relation to the persons and events of his life in the past, in the present and in the transference. In the first of these triangles the individual is defined by three sets of forces or conditions. The first of these is the individual's hidden wishes, needs, desires and fantasies; the second is his anxiety and guilt in relation to those wishes, desires and fantasies; and the third is the defensive accommodation—including repression and denial of the wishes, desires and fantasies—by which he tries to overcome anxiety and guilt. The second triangle consists of the individual in relation to: a) past episodes and relationships in his or her life; b) present events and people in his or her real life outside the therapeutic sessions; and c) the therapist and the therapeutic relationship itself. Every point in the second triangle can be examined in relation to any or all of the points in the first triangle. That is, past episodes and relationships can be examined in relation to a) needs; b) anxieties; and c) defences. The same is true of present relationships and of the transference relationship, such that each point of the second triangle contains a miniature version of the first triangle.

[8] *Individual Psychotherapy.*

As is the case with clarifying, confronting, linking, reflecting and interpreting, no simple one-to-one correspondence between this and that or one single strategy of discovery is ever possible. And yet there is value in occasionally separating out the components of internal and external events and also keeping the external and the internal separate from each other.

For example, the bike riding story told in Chapter Six might be plotted as follows:

One point of the first triangle would be the child's wish to flee her mother, to be independent, free; a second point would be the guilt that this wish occasioned (what would happen to her mother if she were really to stay away too long? And how would her mother feel?); and the third point would be the accommodation: the two-hour limit, which appeases the guilt and yet to some degree realizes the desire for freedom and autonomy.

The second triangle would consist of the relationship to the mother in the past; the present episode in England in which the adult woman, no longer a child, is still riding her bike under the two-hour limit and resenting it; and the relationship to the therapist in which features of the conflict emerge in the transference relationship. Thus, had the patient been in therapy and had something like the fantasy of therapist-icide at that juncture, the fantasy might have been interpreted as resistance to what in the patient's view might seem the inequality and asymmetry of the therapist's demands on the patient (that she appear every week at a certain time and place while the therapist, as she sees it, is free of those demands), which are so like the demands of the mother in the past (as least as the child perceived them). By applying the triangles this resentment could, furthermore, have been seen to contain not only an anger against the mother/therapist but an anxiety for her/his safety as well— both impulses being neatly realized in the fantasy of the murder-of-the-therapist-by-someone-else. And this might well have indicated that what was also pressing on the patient at that moment was her knowledge of her mother's illness and her mother's dying request that she come home.

By examining and reflecting on the wish to murder the therapist, we might have discovered the link to the bike riding story in the present and traced that back to the whole other triangle A, thus discovering the cycle of desire, guilt and accommodation—or, importantly, the lack of it in the transference story. For it is precisely the way in which the transference relationship allows for the possibility that the accommodation will *not* occur, or at least not occur in the same way, that opens up the possibility for insight and reflection and a rerouting of old, default pathways.

To stay for a moment more with this structural or geometrical imagery, we can say that the therapist's function (internally when listening, actively when intervening) is essentially to apply one or more of the points on the second triangle, the triangle of person, so as to help the patient trace the workings of the first triangle in relation to that set of external relations. It is also, when possible, to refer to each other the patterns and structures of the various points of the first triangle as illuminated by the second triangle. The therapist proceeds from the more external materials (and the patterns or structures they suggest) to the more internal, archaic materials. That is, he moves backwards from the present reality of external relationships in relation either to the therapist or to others in the patient's life towards earlier, often childhood experiences. He also moves from the adaptive accommodations back to the wishes and desires and fantasies to which they are responding. And all of this must go at a pace and to a depth determined by the patient's ability to entertain and sustain these increasing levels of insight without doing injury to the patient.

By not aiming at the same degree of radical, structural personality modification which is the goal of psychoanalysis, psychotherapy is able to address more directly the alleviation of the patient's suffering. Yet the objectives of psychotherapy of this sort are wider than direct symptom resolution. Like psychoanalysis, and unlike other forms of therapy (including pharmacological and behavioural-cognitive therapies), psychotherapy focuses on increasing the patient's self-awareness. Through the alleviation of symptoms, such psychotherapeutic intervention intends also to expand the patient's insightfulness and repertoire of available emotional and intellectual responses.

Coming to terms with your life in the clinical setting: the overlapping of the therapist's and the patient's discourse

The therapist and the patient proceed together in the project of psychotherapy. As Winnicott once put it, "just as the transitional object is a joint creation of infant and mother, successful therapy is the joint creation of the patient and the therapist." Or elsewhere: "Psychotherapy takes place in the overlap of two areas of playing, that of the patient and that of the therapist."[9] Together, therapist and patient create a space and a shared language in which the patient comes to experience and understand himself anew through naming and linking, very much as an infant discovers the world and creates his language with and through the mother.

What might this look or sound like?

Reconstructing the psychotherapeutic experience and transcribing it in print necessarily produces a loss of immediacy and intensity. It also tends to produce as an instantaneous moment of revelation what has actually proceeded over months, sometimes even years of long, hard work: working through the resistances, clarifying, linking and interpreting stories, behaviours and the transference, and revising one's very narrative of one's self. But the presentation of the in-clinical exchange will hopefully provide for the reader one more useful encounter with how the psychotherapeutic process works and what it can accomplish.

Patients often enter therapy with no more than a word to guide them as to what they are feeling or why they have come seeking psychotherapeutic help—the word sad, for example, or anxious, or angry, or confused. Sometimes they don't even have that much of a clue: perhaps they are simply crying all the time, or encountering constant confrontations on the job, or having suicidal thoughts. The first thing the therapist tries to do is help the patient give a name to his nameless feelings. He tries to help him towards greater levels of specificity as to what he feels; and then to discover or recover the life-stories and experiences (past and present) that his feelings are recalling. *Clarification, Confrontation, Linking, Reflecting,* and *Interpreting* are the therapist's tools for helping produce for the patient what is largely an internal process of coming to self-knowledge and self-understanding in words.

[9] *Playing and Reality.*

Take the word *lost*, for example, which emerged as a key term in the following therapeutic exchanges, and the stories and finally self-understandings that tumbled out as a consequence of the discovery of that word. This was the word that the former patient—the co-author of this book—used to name what she described in her first sessions as feelings of sadness, weepiness and depression. When invited to *clarify* what she meant by saying she felt sad and weepy and depressed, the word that was said was "lost": she felt "lost".

It was my job, then to have her travel the associative path along the word "lost" that might help her find her way through her own unique psychological landscape as imaged in this word. The question was: what did the word *lost* mean to this particular person that she should describe her feeling of sadness this way? Sadness is not necessarily to be described as being lost. Similarly, the word *lost* carries connotations that do not necessarily have to do with sadness: fear, for example, or anxiety. *Lost* is also a more geographical word than sadness: it locates a feeling in a place and also, perhaps, in a narrative situation. The word *lost* might additionally suggest the fear of getting lost in the clinical relationship: this patient had, she readily confessed at the beginning of her therapy, resisted for many years going into therapy.

Although the therapist must note mentally, to himself, all of these possible connotations of the word *lost*, he must also refrain from articulating his ideas directly, especially in the initial stages of the therapeutic exchange. What are important are the patient's associations to her own word. So, too, is the patient's coming to trust the therapist and developing a sufficiently strong relationship with him to be able to sustain the inquiry inwards into what her words (thoughts, feelings, behaviours) might mean. It was only well into the psychotherapeutic relationship, which ranged over many subjects great and small, that the therapist felt prompted to say, picking up the patient's repeated use of the word *lost*, that what she seemed to be saying is that she feels she has lost her way and that that makes her feel very sad. Does that bring any thoughts to mind?

At this point, the patient might have dismissed the therapist's intervention as wrong or irrelevant, for whatever reasons and whether nor not the intervention was in point of fact "accurate" or not. The therapist might then have concluded (to himself) either that he was on the wrong track, or the opposite: that he was on precisely the right track and that the patient was resisting the awareness that might come through following through on that track. The therapist might then have tried restating the patient's thought in still other, differently inflected or directed words. Or he might have restated them in a less focused and therefore, perhaps, potentially less threatening way, also holding in abeyance confronting the patient with her unwillingness to follow the path that the idea of having lost her way might be laying out for her.

Of course, the patient might just take up the hint of "having lost her way". In this instance, that is precisely what happened. Indeed, she did more than respond to or elaborate on the term. Instead, she remembered a specific incident when she had literally got lost.

The story began with the patient's explaining that she had a very bad sense of direction and therefore getting lost all the time (a typical self-blaming, self-derogatory response, as when—in the earlier of the two incidents already reported in this book—she arrived at the office to find to therapist not in and blamed herself for getting the hour wrong; this connection to other patterns of the patient's behaviour was also noted by the therapist to himself but not, for the moment, articulated or brought to the patient's attention). The association to having a bad sense of direction quickly produced a particular example of this phenomenon, which had occurred several years earlier on the Boston underground. She was on the way to visit friends when she boarded the wrong train and promptly "got lost". What the patient also quickly added was that of course she wasn't really lost, at least not in the real meaning of the term. All she had to do, which she admitted knowing full well at the time, was to hop on a train going in the opposite direction, go back to the place where she'd boarded the wrong train and continue on from there. She could even have taken another line or a cab or phoned her friends for directions.

All of these options, she reported, occurred to her at the time. She was fully conscious of them. And yet what she felt, she said, was intense anguish. In fact, not only was she frightened and anxious, but she felt her eyes brimming over with tears.

What the tears were for she couldn't say; but they were, in her recollection of them, very powerful and very real. She wasn't, she repeated, lost in the sense of not knowing where she was. She simply wasn't where she was supposed to be. She was on her way to friends, and she had made a mistake. And she was reduced to tears.

One easy, obvious link to make had to do with the tears in the story and the tears that had brought her into therapy. She had come into therapy because she was crying a lot and feeling, as she came to put it, "lost", and here she was, describing herself as lost and telling a story about getting lost and crying. As important as the story the patient tells is the particular context in which she tells the story. She is describing crying and feeling lost; and she tells a story about getting lost and crying. One could easily stay with this juncture and ask for further associations. But since this story of getting lost on the underground also came after she'd already told the story of her first childhood memory of getting lost in the supermarket with her grandmother, another intervention presented itself: linking between her Boston story and this other much earlier, childhood tale. What I hear you saying, I suggested, is that when you got lost, you felt a little bit like that little girl who got lost in the supermarket with her grandmother when her mother went off to the hospital to have a new baby. (I could at this juncture just as easily have introduced the possibility, which had also occurred to me earlier, that the fear of getting lost and the story just told about an actual experience of getting lost might be expressing a fear of getting lost in therapy. This anxiety also contained the wish to feel held and guided so as not to get lost. It might well have to do with the gift of the coffee mugs, by which means she might hold on to the therapist as a friend or intimate associate. As earlier, however, it seemed better not to introduce material that might have seemed at that moment an inexplicable intrusion into her thoughts and memories, and which might also have foreclosed her coming on her own to the deepest possible connections between all the pieces of her feelings and associations. Although I felt that she could sustain the regression backwards into the feelings of the young child lost in the supermarket, I did not feel that she could at this juncture tolerate the more immediate and present implication that she was uncomfortable in and had "childish" desires concerning the therapeutic relationship—as evidenced by the gift-of-the-two-mugs).

The decision to *link* the two stories—one from the more recent past, the other from the more distant, childhood past—and the invitation to *reflect* on those stories and their possible interrelations proved effective. It produced an array of interlocking, interconnected memories and associations. These stories, it must be stressed, didn't just pop out. They emerged slowly and often in fragments over many, many months of therapy. They also went in many different directions, not all of which could, of course, be followed at any one moment. All of them, however, had to be noted and kept in mind by me for future possible reference.

Among the many things that emerged over time and in many different ways were general and pervasive feelings of inadequacy and self-blame. These stories about the supermarket and Boston weren't only about getting lost in a geographical sense. They weren't only about having a bad sense of direction and how this was her fault: that she should have known where she was or how to get where she was going. They expressed a lack of self-worth that pertained to many aspects of her everyday life. This included her relationship to therapy, which, she was constantly saying, she felt she was doing wrong. Also caught up in these stories were feelings of embarrassment or shame at having made a mistake. This produced the further association that she was always shy of asking questions: she always had the feeling that other people knew things she didn't but was supposed to know—like, I ventured to intervene at this moment, a child who might want to know where that new baby comes from but is ashamed or embarrassed or frightened to ask; perhaps she thinks she is supposed to know this already; perhaps this evokes earlier kinds of feelings in relation to the parents, about whom she might also feel she is supposed to know something that in point of fact she does not, concerning their relationship with each other.

It was by further reflecting on the childhood story—on why *this* story of getting lost in the supermarket should have remained so prominent in her mind; why indeed it was her *first* real memory from childhood—that the most important association emerged.

This association also served to link the Boston story to the present moment of the patient's life. This was the feeling which was quite prominently displayed in the word "lost" if you knew to look for it, but which was otherwise hidden and out of sight: the word *loss*. The tears in Boston, she began to realize, which she knew even then couldn't be tears of fear or panic even though they felt like that, were not only tears of humiliation and shame. They were also tears of painful *loss*. Being-lost was, we both began to see, in her mind's associative way of thinking inseparable from the much more devastating and tearful feeling of loss itself: the little girl's imagined loss of her mother, who had left her vulnerable to getting lost in the supermarket, but who also, even more terrifyingly, might be perhaps forever lost to her.

There was also, at the centre of all this, the suspicion that somehow she was to blame. Her grandmother (her father's mother) was an immigrant who didn't know the neighbourhood and who also spoke very little English. Had she been told, she wondered, that she should take care of her grandmother? It was certainly a statement she could imagine having been made. She had been told it enough in later life, in relation not only to her grandparents but to her brother as well. She couldn't recall what was actually said to her way back then, when she was three, but the fact that this idea came to mind in this context was more significant for the exploration of her feelings than whether or not the statement had actually been made. And it was worthy of further reflection. Did the feeling that perhaps she'd failed in her responsibility to her grandmother spill over into the fear that she had failed her mother as well? Was it her inadequacy as a child that had prompted her mother to go off and have another baby? Wasn't she enough? Was there something she was supposed to understand or know that she had failed to take in? Had her own ambivalent emotions concerning her mother (including perhaps jealousy, resentment) somehow become visible to her mother?

There are, of course, no answers to these questions. Nor is it important that there be *an* answer, or even several of them. What is important, from the perspective of psychotherapy, is that in asking the questions, in playing out the meanings and associations of the words through which she herself constructed her life's history, certain conflicts come into view. With them also came new ways of looking at her behaviours and feelings. As in dream interpretation, it is less important what the dream means in the sense of some coherent interpretation one might give to it than what the dream triggers in terms of other thoughts and associations to be examined, explored and reflected upon.

Getting lost still resonates for her with that formative moment in childhood when she not only felt lost without her mother but feared that she had lost her mother, perhaps through some fault of her own, perhaps even because of the anger she had felt at her mother for having a new baby. Remember: this is the same person who needed to get back home—no matter where home was—to her mother, whether her mother was there or not, or needed her or not, because in some way she feared that her mother might not be there; that something might have happened to her mother; that her mother might be lost to her. And remember too the other story her mother used to tell her—about how when she was pregnant with her brother and felt faint, she had lain down on the bed and asked her to sit beside her till she woke up, which (good girl that she was) she did. It is not too difficult to imagine what a small child might have felt sitting beside her "sleeping" mother till she woke up. Another memory that emerged in relation to these stories was her image of her mother napping in the afternoon and her need to check in on her sleeping mother several times to make sure she was still breathing. At a much later point in the therapy, when it was felt that she might make use of the couch in order to go deeper into her childhood memories, she popped up after only a few moments to say that the image that came to mind was of her mother "dead" during her afternoon nap. It was at this point that attaching the stories of being lost to stories of suffering loss could be brought into the clinical situation and discussed in relation to the transference itself, including the murderous feelings of anger that emerged when she imagined the therapist dead at the hand of another (sibling) patient.

To put the experience into a larger frame: for this person, a feeling of loss had attached itself to a specific experience, and it was revived (to some degree at least) each time that experience was repeated. But now, in the present moment of her life, there was an interesting reversal. Rather than call into question the earlier pattern, this reversal confirmed it in odd and yet explicable ways. It also made it available for psychotherapeutic use. In the present moment she wasn't lost and for that reason feeling sad. She was sad and feeling lost. She had very recently suffered a genuine loss: the death of her son. And what she felt was lost. The lostness, which contained within it unacknowledged feelings of loss, had become part of a two-way route in which feelings of loss could now trigger or become caught up in the experience of lostness. Feeling lost, one might say, covered over and hid from view (like the word *lost* itself) the far more devastating experience of loss from which there was no easy recovery, no easy route home. In other words, it was easier to confront being lost (especially when she knew she wasn't really lost) than to confront loss itself.

The word *lost*, as a cover for sadness and the fear and pain of loss, was working as a kind of figure of speech. It was articulating a relationship between feelings and the experiences that produced those feelings. The principle behind free association in psychoanalysis proper is that if we let our mind travel randomly over any word or image or memory, it will discover, or rediscover, the connection of that word or image or memory to others in our mental reservoir. Such free association, as Freud knew, also happens to us all the time, even (or especially) when we don't recognize it. Feeling sad, the mind locates a word, which brings together a number of events and feelings associated with sadness that we might not, with our ordinary rational intellects, even begin to imagine have something to do with sadness. And then it launches a narrative that conceals, even while it expresses, what that sadness really is.

Through *interpreting* the nexus of lostness and loss, it became possible to pull into view more than the link between the two words and the two stories (not to mention the many other words and stories which also emerged). It also became possible to explore, reflect on, and finally interpret the many complex emotions that made dealing with the loss of her child so difficult to do. Mourning, as Freud knew so well, is an extremely complex process. It doesn't have to do only with the sadness we feel for the loved one's loss of his or her life. Rather, it also has to do with our sense of deprivation, with the loss to us of what that loved one gives us emotionally, spiritually, psychologically. When we say, following the death of a loved one, that a part of ourselves has died, we are not necessarily speaking in metaphors. A part of us does die: the part that was being uniquely expressed in the relationship with this other person. But to experience that another person is carrying us this way, especially when that other person is a child, can become an occasion for guilt. And so our mourning may come to contain self-loathing alongside the sense of pain and loss. It may not be possible for us to look this grief in the face and see reflected there what is, in our own view of things, our least generous and noble selves.

The perspectives opened up by the word lost and through the narratives that unravelled from it permitted several things to happen. One is that they put some emotional distance between the story-teller and the story being told, such that she was *not*, for the moment, overwhelmed to the point of tears. Another was that the story-teller was nonetheless enabled to experience the emotional affects of her story as both audience and major protagonist. She could cry and know why. She could cry for the right reasons.

In his recent book *Therapeutic Action*, analyst and philosopher Jonathan Lear makes what he calls an "earnest plea for irony". For a mature woman to see herself grieving over her son as might a three-year-old crying in the supermarket could well become an occasion for embarrassment and shame *unless* she could also come to feel a certain compassion and love for that child she once was and for that child's very legitimate and painful feelings of loss, confusion and fear. And that means in some way *feeling* those feelings, experiencing them as genuine and real feelings which a child has every right to feel. That child still clearly resides within her. But she is also by no means the entirety of her present self. And so she might come to see the humour (the irony) in this: the way in which she both is and is not that child. Then what is opened up is the possibility of some new way of finding her way, of getting un-lost. She might develop a more adequate response to the wish not to lose herself, even in grief—as indeed she did when she took her story back and produced it in her own way, as her own life story.

***

E.B. One of my responses, over the years, to feeling sad, which is to say feeling lost, which is to say feeling inadequate (at a loss), has been to find something that helps me recover my sense of competency. This is what I call my three-step solution: I take a walk (which is a way of affirming the forward moving possibilities of life, the fact that I can actually get where I am going), I meet someone else's smile (which helps me remember that I am not alone in the world, that I am not as it were lost and abandoned); and finally, I make a small purchase of a little gift for someone else (which helps me feel in control, competent, and also reassures me of my own capacities for nurture and giving; I failed no one as a child, I was completely adequate to the task of being a daughter and a mother; I am competent now). Notice how the gift-giving has come back into my solution. One more piece of evidence of the way in which I cohere.

If the major motif of my life story as it was being told in my sadnesses and depressions was a sense of lostness which contained within it a sense of inadequacy as well, then the major motif of my life story as I retell it in my three-step solution is of a new-found competence in which I find myself as well. This does not mean that I do not fall prey to sadness and depression. And when I do, I feel lost and incompetent. But at the very least, alongside that very old story of mine is another story that I can also tell, that can displace (even if only temporarily) the story of sadness and loss. What I've noticed over the years is that the new story comes with greater and greater ease and regularity. I've discovered that I don't even need literally to get up and enact my three-step solution. I can just say to myself the word competence for the new story to prevail and for the word lost and its story to retreat. In point of fact, wasn't that little girl who watched over her sleeping mother and did finally come home with her grandmother from the supermarket, that little girl whose mother did in the end return, not fairly competent from the start? When we recover our stories, when we place in a position of prominence the fact of our having survived the stressful events of our lives, what we may well discover is the strength our stories tell about us rather than the weakness.

***

How patients take up their narratives and build on them in their lives—how they come to retell their stories—is for them to determine. For another patient sadness and competence might have nothing to do with one another, and so for someone else this patient's "three-step solution" might be not only irrelevant but slightly absurd. The point of psychotherapy is the discovery of the specificity of the individual story and to put into the patient's hands the power and possibility of that particular personal and private story.

CHAPTER NINE

Neurobiology and the "value" of the talking cure

A lthough there are many different kinds of psychological therapies, the majority of them can be divided into two major camps: the psychodynamic psychotherapies and the non-dynamic therapies. Any reader who has made it this far in reading this book is probably inclined to the project of expanding and deepening self-awareness. This is largely the domain of psychodynamic psychotherapy, specifically of the psychoanalytic variety that has been our primary subject. Psychotherapy of this sort has achieved enough positive results over the years not to need special defending. Recent developments in psycho-neurobiology may help suggest how these results have come about. They enable us to glimpse how on the neurological level (and not only psychologically or cognitively) talking functions materially, literally to change how we think and feel. We do not intend the following foray into the fascinating field of neurobiological and neuro-psychoanalysis to be either exhaustive or deep. Yet even from a non-professional vantage point, looking for a moment at the psychological structures and functions of the brain from a neurological point of view can usefully supplement the more psychological view of the human mind we have heretofore been providing.

As earlier, in trying to define psychoanalytic terms, one must proceed cautiously. In the case of neuroscience as of psychoanalysis, we are dealing with attempts to analyse findings and put into words mental processes that we cannot perceive either directly or objectively—at least not both directly and objectively at one and the same moment. These are processes, therefore, that we can at best only infer and theorize about. In the case of both psychoanalysis and neurobiology there are, to be sure, modes and manners of proof which tend to validate the inferences and theories. And the two theoretical systems of investigation (the one biological and the other psychological), it turns out, tend to validate each other. Nonetheless, describing the mind is a risky venture at best. As in the relationship between the unconscious contents of mind and our conscious thoughts and behaviour in Freudian theory, so in neuroscience what we "see" are only the material, external correlates or precipitates of the largely invisible life of the mind.

With this caution in place, we can nonetheless say that contemporary brain research tends to reinforce rather than refute many of the models Freud himself employed. Indeed, in many instances it tends to restate these models, albeit in different, more scientifically accented vocabularies which are based on technologies that were simply unavailable to Freud and his generation of analysts and neurologists. In other words, neurobiological descriptions or pictures of brain activity are often strikingly similar, in terms of the functions and structures they describe, to the psychoanalytic theories proposed by Freud (who was himself, we should recall, a neurologist). What psychoanalytic theory has described in a terminology focused on "mental" (i.e. non-organic) processes of thinking and feeling, neurobiology has posited in terms of the expression of physiological processes on the intra- and inter-cellular, structural levels of the body and brain. This raises the distinct possibility that neurobiology and psychoanalysis are describing some of the same events. Indeed, it may even be possible to argue that the biological processes are what produce the psychological processes, and—significantly—vice versa; or that biological and psychological processes are the *same* processes viewed differently: the one through external, objective measurements, the other internally, subjectively, through the very same processes of mind that are the object of study.

Therefore, despite the media hype concerning Prozac and other antidepressant and anti-psychotic medications, which seems to suggest that all of our psychological problems are basically chemical and therefore must be treated pharmacologically, the talking cure may still occupy an important place among the psychological interventions. Indeed, it turns out that talking may well be of supreme value to us human beings, not simply on the intellectual or social levels but on the biological level as well. Even where brain pathologies are present and even when drug therapy and/or other sorts of therapy may *also* be indicated, psychotherapy may still have a crucial role to play in our mental health.

What brain research suggests is that, as Freud himself already suspected, our processes of mind are unconscious as well as conscious. In fact the unconscious processes far outnumber the conscious ones. Furthermore, like mental process as Freud conceived it, the brain activities that go into producing consciousness (or mind) as we know it, or that are in fact consciousness or mind, are for any one action, perception, thought or feeling multiple and multiply-determined. Chemical reactions and interactions in the brain, which are the culmination of and cause of other reactions and interactions throughout the body (including the brain), are located in many different places (often simultaneously); they also travel many different routes into and out of and throughout the brain, though over time we tend to develop default routings. Nonetheless, these pathways are enormously flexible. Often, for any one of a number of reasons, they involve themselves in their own self-transformations. Sometimes outside interventions can cause them to change on both the chemical and/or the structural or functional levels.

Of the many components of our everyday experience of and interaction with the world that affect the workings of the brain, conversation, story-telling and other modes of interpersonal communication are as pertinent as any others. Talk, it seems, does nothing less than change the structure of the brain. This means that at the very least, psychoanalysis and psychotherapy are equipped to do the work they are intended to do. In some very real, literal, physiological sense it may well be the case that we change our minds through the thoughts we think and the actions we take.

This fact, however, that talking changes our minds (literally our brain functions) does not tell us if and/or when and/or why psychotherapy might actually be preferred to other modes of intervention (whether drugs or other forms of therapy such as behavioural and cognitive therapy). These non-dynamic therapies, like every other facet of our experience (both internal and external), also produce changes in the circuitry and expression of the brain, which is to say the way in which we perceive, process, and finally act on or enact everything from sense data to internal physiological conditions to thoughts, feelings, wishes, desires, and so on. Given that the goals of psychotherapy often have to do not only with feelings but also with behaviours and relationships, it would seem logical to opt for medication and/or some of the non-dynamic therapies which more directly influence how we feel, act and relate to others.

There are reasons to challenge this logic. At the very least, in cases where self-knowledge and insight are themselves values or goals, psychoanalytic psychotherapy might well be preferred to the non-dynamic therapies or pharmacology. But this need for self-awareness and its value to us as human beings, it emerges, may also turn out to be no less organic than the other features of our mental processes. It may also be a biological rather than a purely philosophical or intellectual value. A "biological value" is a value geared towards maximizing our potential for viability and survival as living organisms. Self-reflection may well be a value of this kind. It may, indeed, be the very basis of consciousness and mind.

The challenge of the non-dynamic therapies

We've said very little concerning the non-dynamic therapies. There are many of them, and many have been proven quite effective, at least with certain individuals. In order to better make the case for psychoanalytic psychotherapy, it is necessary to say a few words about these competing therapeutic modes—not to disparage them, but to indicate how they differ from psychotherapy of the psychoanalytic variety and why some of us might prefer to follow the dynamic route.

Behavioural therapy, for the most part, is modelled on various theories of learning. Behaviours are understood to be not pathologies but the more functional or less functional ways we have of living our lives. As such, they are felt to be treatable through direct address to and remediation of the specific issue or problem itself. Change comes about by learning new coping skills or better modes of communication directly pertinent to the behaviour itself. The approach is practical, pragmatic, geared to developing modes of coping with dysfunctional behaviours or feelings or attitudes— smoking or over-eating, for example, or phobic or aggressive or self-punishing responses to one or another situation. In behavioural therapy, as in cognitive therapy (as well as in many forms of counselling), the therapist takes an active role. He gives advice and otherwise introduces information, insight and observation into the conversation, whether with a single patient or in a group. Indeed, such therapy often takes place in a group setting.

In behavioural therapy it is not necessary to know why a behaviour developed (in relation either to the present or to the distant childhood past). Therefore there is little or no analysis of the unconscious contents of mind. Nor is such therapy concerned with the "value" of a specific behaviour in terms of psychodynamic process—either its primary gain (to the internal world of the individual) or its secondary gain as a mode of manipulating other people's attitudes, responses and behaviours. Change, in short, does not (as it does in psychodynamic psychotherapy) proceed from engagement with—reflection on and interpretation of—dynamic mental process.

Even though behavioural therapy aims chiefly at changing behaviour, nonetheless it almost always also produces a cognitive shift. That is, it alters how we receive and process information, which is also a goal of the dynamic therapies, albeit in different ways and on different terms. In cognitive therapy that cognitive shift becomes the expressed goal of the therapy. Cognitive therapy shares with the dynamic therapies the aim of discovering the continuities of thought and feeling that account for current symptoms. But rather than discover these threads through the repressed, unconscious contents of mind, cognitive therapy proceeds through the conscious mind itself. Cognitive therapy is about changing beliefs and misperceptions. It is a form of reality testing in which unreasonable and irrational conclusions are examined through the collaborative effort of the patient and the therapist. The attempt is made, through intellectual means, to change the emphases or distortions in self-destructive judgments so as to produce more useful and satisfying attitudes, feelings and ways of being in the world. Cognitive therapy utilizes the considerable resources of the conscious mind— our rational faculties, our potential for seeing our strengths as well as our weaknesses, our ability to reinforce our positive experiences in the world—all in the service of transforming ourselves in the here-and-now of our current lives.

Such a direct appeal either to behaviour or to the conscious mind certainly seems to have much to recommend it over the more oblique and circuitous, often frustrating and painful route offered by psychoanalytic psychotherapy. Both behavioural therapy and cognitive therapy have been proven to work. They also tend to be of shorter duration and hence less expensive. They are also often accompanied by drug intervention, which further enhances their effectiveness. Psychotherapy usually shares with the non-dynamic therapies this object of relieving psychological dis-ease. Even if our everyday behaviours and relationships are not the source of such dis-ease, they are as often as not where that dis-ease is manifesting itself. Dealing with our behaviours and relationships through what we know and think about ourselves and our world (i.e. through our conscious knowledge) would seem just that much more efficient than taking the route of the dynamic unconscious and transference. Indeed, even if one grants that there is such a thing as the dynamic unconscious, it is by no means clear how or why might it provide a *better* route to the conscious mind than the conscious mind itself. Perhaps, as with organic diseases of the body, so with the dis-eases of the mind, it might sometimes just be better to opt for the relief of symptoms than for curing the disease; in fact sometimes the relief of symptoms may be all that it is possible to achieve.

The question of when and/or why a direct engagement of the unconscious, which is to say a direct approach to the foundations of our psychological distress and dis-ease, may be preferable to a more symptomatic (behavioural, cognitive, or pharmacological) treatment of them has to do with another question, even more elusive and difficult to answer. That question is not: what is the conscious (as opposed to the unconscious) mind, but: what is *consciousness* itself? That is to say: what is the *mind* (which contains both conscious and unconscious thoughts and processes) and how does it work, that we should imagine psychotherapy as a meaningful intervention—and perhaps more meaningful than others—into the realm of psychological dis-ease? Psychotherapy, it turns out, works in ways very similar to the way in which the brain itself works to produce consciousness—both that "core consciousness" that we humans share with many other creatures of the Earth and that more sophisticated "expanded consciousness" that is the human mind. Insofar as most of us think of ourselves *as* ourselves because of our minds (our memories, thoughts, feelings, ways of being in the world), producing mind for ourselves in the ways in which mind is naturally produced might very well be a way of exercising authority and control over no less a matter than who we are and will become.

Neurobiology, feeling, consciousness and mind

Like the terms *conscious* and *unconscious* in psychoanalytic theory, the word *consciousness* provides any number of difficulties of definition, which certainly does not mean that that something we call consciousness doesn't exist. One of the amazing advances in neurobiological research has been the possibility of actually being able to prod portions of the brain into activity (either through electrodes directly attached to the brain or through stimuli introduced through the various sense organs) and then to register the consequences of this: does a particular stimulus or set of stimuli to a specific region of the brain or to several regions (since brain activity takes place over several areas in the brain) cause the individual to hear or see something, to remember something, or to feel something? Can the individual be said to be "conscious" in the sense of being aware of this? Are the phenomena being produced on the unconscious rather than or as well as on the conscious level? Do the stimuli produce lasting or only fleeting results? And so on and so forth.

What scientists have come to "see" through such research is that consciousness is not synonymous with our intellectual, cognitive knowledge of this or another fact or feeling. Consciousness, in other words, is not synonymous with being *conscious of* some specific content, though the consciousness of something is certainly a part of consciousness as such. Rather, consciousness signals that state of awareness, more neurological than psychological, by which an individual can be said to be awake, alert and thereby, in this sense, "conscious"—as when we say of someone, following an accident or an operation, that she is conscious, or that she didn't lose consciousness. (In line with this definition of the word *consciousness*, one meaning of the word *conscious* can be not to know something but merely to inhabit the state of awareness and alertness we call consciousness.)

To be *conscious of* something is another matter altogether. To *be conscious of* something means to be cognitively, intellectually aware of it, as when we say we know a particular fact, or are conscious of an historical event or of the presence of someone else in the room or even of feeling a certain emotion. To be *conscious of* is only one small component of consciousness, albeit an extremely vital one for our lives as humans.

Most of the components of consciousness of which our minds consist are unconscious—in one of the two senses already defined. Either they are outside the province of what we can consciously know or experience (by far the vaster realm of the unconscious), or they are those contents of mind that are being actively kept out of conscious awareness by various mental mechanisms (the dynamic unconscious in the Freudian sense). This is the kind of unconscious with which psychotherapy is concerned. Psychotherapy, as we have seen, is very much geared towards helping us become *conscious* in the sense of *conscious of*. Such becoming *conscious of* is not, obviously, becoming conscious of all the huge territory of our unconscious organic processes. Rather, it refers to those graspable, perceptible consequences of one portion of the realm of the unconscious: the dynamic unconscious contents of mind. Those are the contents of mind which, even though we are not cognitively, intellectually aware of them (conscious of them) at any given moment, are nonetheless present in our minds and acting to influence our thoughts and behaviours in such a way that their consequences or precipitates *can* become conscious to us.

As Mark Solms and Oliver Turnbull have put it in their book *The Brain and the Inner World*, the question "what exactly *is* the *mind?*" confronts an "ancient mystery" which long precedes Freud and psychoanalysis. This is the mystery of the mind-body relationship, the baffling fact that our "immaterial consciousness—our very sense of existence and identity—emerges from the cell assemblies and other base processes of the brain, whose cells and processes are not fundamentally different from those of other bodily organs."[1]

Immaterial consciousness, in other words, is produced by very material and, one might add, unconscious, physiological processes, such as regulate every other aspect of our bodily functions. The objective of Solms and Turnbull's book is to bring into view how the brain, through such material, biological processes, produces that elusive, immaterial state called consciousness. And their purpose in examining consciousness in this way is to suggest why and how Freud's "talking cure" might, in ways very similar to the everyday, natural functioning of the brain, actually produce changes in consciousness—changes of a particularly useful, therapeutic sort.

The brain, Solms and Turnbull remind us, is an organ like all other organs—even if it is the organ that produces or is associated with that activity or state of mind we call consciousness. Like the stomach or heart or kidneys, it is a concrete, tangible physical entity doing observable, quantifiable biochemical work. What distinguishes the brain from other organs of the body (albeit only in degree) is firstly its purpose or function. The brain is designed as a conduit between two worlds: the world *within* us (which consists of all our other organs and bodily processes) and the world outside us. This external reality includes the physical phenomena of that outer world as well as the other people who inhabit that world.

To manage this mediation between inner and outer worlds, the brain has certain features which also differentiate it, if not in kind

---

[1] *The Brain and the Inner World*, xiii-xiv. The following introduction is adapted from this book.

then at least in degree, from other bodily parts. What is distinctive about the brain on the cellular level is that it enjoys, to a much greater degree than any other organ in the body, the ability to transmit information from cell to cell, both within the brain itself and to other places in the body. Another distinctive feature is that while the brain with which we are born has its own genetic blueprint like all the other organs, it is transformed and individualized more than other organs by environmental factors over the course of our lifetime. Such factors include not only our experiences of internal and external realities but also the memory of those experiences as they are stored and (re)activated in the brain itself.

The brain is a highly plastic organ. It is an agent of its own constant self-transformation. It transforms itself from within its own internal environment of memories, thoughts, wishes, desires, experiences and knowledge. This is to say that we humans are creatures of perpetual self-regulation and self-transformation.

In his book entitled *The Feeling of What Happens*, Antonio Damasio beautifully describes this "confection" we call mind. Consciousness, he writes, is

> the umbrella term for the mental phenomena that permit the strange confection of you as observer or knower of the things observed, of you as owner of thoughts formed in your perspective, of you as potential agent on the scene. Consciousness is a part of your mental process rather than external to it. Individual perspective, individual ownership of thought and individual agency are the critical riches that core consciousness contributes to the mental process now unfolding in your organism. The essence of core consciousness is the very thought of you—the very feeling of you—as an individual being involved in the process of knowing of your own existence and the existence of others.

Consciousness, he goes on, has to do with the relationship of two different entities: the organism and the object with which the organism is involved, which is at that very moment causing a change in the organism.

> Core consciousness occurs when the brain's representation devices generate an imaged, nonverbal account of how the organism's own state is affected by the organism's process of an object, and when this process enhances the image of the causative object, thus placing it saliently in a

space and temporal context... As the brain forms images of an object—such as a face, a melody, a toothache, the memory an event—and as the images of the object affect the state of the organism, yet another level of brain structure creates a swift nonverbal account of the events that are taking place in the varied brain regions activated as a consequence of the object-organism interaction... Looking back, with the licence of metaphor, one might say that the swift, second-order nonverbal account narrates a story: *that of the organism caught in the act of representing its own changing state as it goes about representing something else.* But the astonishing fact is that the knowable entity of the catcher has just been created in the narrative of the catching process."[2]

It is this self-contained self-referentiality of the production of consciousness that makes it so difficult to ascertain from outside the individual mind. It is also the internality of circuitry that provides psychodynamic psychotherapy with a powerful potential relevance to such process, since in psychotherapy you are experiencing your self-reflecting self in a particularly self-conscious way.

What *consciousness* is *for* (biologically) is also very much to the purpose of psychoanalysis and psychotherapy. Quite simply, consciousness is there to tell you how you feel, where by the word feeling must be understood a somatic as well as psychological sense of well-being. As such, consciousness is, like many other components of our mental and physical apparatus, a mechanism of survival. Consciousness (write Solms and Turnbull) is not only "intrinsically introspective", it is also

intrinsically *evaluative*. It imparts *value*. It tells us whether something is 'good' or 'bad' [for us]; and it does that by making things *feel* good or bad (or somewhere in between). That is what consciousness, feeling, is *for*... Consciousness has everything to do with being *embodied*, with awareness of one's bodily state in relation to what is going on around one. Moreover, this mechanism seems to have evolved only because bodies have *needs*. Consciousness is therefore deeply rooted in a set of ancient biological values."[3]

Consciousness—both core consciousness and the more complex consciousness we call mind—is clearly dependent on, indeed produced by, biochemical processes in the brain. Some of these biochemical processes are testable and observable. Similarly,

---

[2] Damasio, *The Feeling of What Happens*, 127, 133, 169-170.
[3] Solms and Turnbull, 91-94; see also Damasio, 50-51.

the consequences of consciousness or mind are perceptible and measurable by others. We can see and hear what other people do and say. We can even, given modern scientific technology, correlate those events with specifiable regions of the brain and with particular brain processes. Much of Solms and Turnbull's book has to do with various clinical conditions and tests which serve to make "visible" to us the largely invisible contours of mental functioning. Nonetheless, consciousness cannot be experienced *directly* as consciousness by anyone except the individual himself.

As Damasio puts it, emotions (which he defines as our bodily responses to this or another stimulus) "play out in the theatre of the body". They are "actions or movements, many of them public, visible to others as they occur in the face, in the voice, in specific behaviours": sweating, for example, or crying, or laughing, or trembling. In contradistinction to this, *feelings* constitute our *relation* to those physiological sensations and expressions. As such they "are always hidden, like all mental images necessarily are, unseen to anyone other than their rightful owner, the most private property of the organism in whose brain they occur." Feelings, in other words, are subjective and internal. They are a private, personal interpretation of the bodily and mental self by itself. They are our way of noting and reflecting on the body's state of well-being or lack of well-being as it is undergoing a particular sensory or mental experience. "Feelings play out in the theatre of the mind."[4] They play out in—produce and are produced by—consciousness.

Consciousness, self-consciousness, and the "talking cure"

It is the realm of consciousness and feeling that returns us from neurobiology to psychoanalytic psychotherapy. Psychoanalysis and psychotherapy are about our feelings—in the largest, most abstract and also most physiological senses of that term. They concern our experiencing of our biologically produced but by no means purely or simply biological selves. In some real sense, consciousness—which might be thought of as the feeling self—is always *self*-consciousness. Even if it is produced by the brain's integration and expression of the various physiological processes and structures that regulate our biological existence; indeed, even if consciousness is identical with the brain's physiological functioning and is just a different, more subjective, mentalized language in which we describe these functions, consciousness is not reducible to physiological functions, at least not for the individual internally experiencing that consciousness as his or her own. Most of the body's processes, as Freud had already pointed out a century ago, are completely unconscious. In fact, the production of consciousness is itself an unconscious process. But consciousness and being conscious of are very real and very vital components of our existence. Consciousness is what occurs when we become "aware" (on some level—since consciousness also contains unconscious elements) of the fact that our bodies are experiencing hunger or fear or joy, or when we register the fact that we are seeing a picture or basking in the sun. Consciousness has to do with feelings. And it is an intra-psychic phenomenon. Indeed, the only mind we can experience directly is our own. All other minds we need to infer from observing the consequences of people's actions, or seeing the results of various medical tests or experiments (which is not to dispute the evidence provided by such means as to how the mind works). Our minds are similarly only to be inferred in this way by others. This is useful to remember when you are feeling vulnerable and exposed. No one knows your own mind (in every sense of this) in the same way that you do.

Drug therapy is one way of addressing feelings by influencing the chemical ingredients whereby such feelings are produced. There is no reason to disparage such interventions. Advances in medications for depression, obsessive-compulsive disorders, delusions, hallucinations, manic states and so on, like treatments for other diseases, have done an immense service in helping human beings to function better in their lives. Because neurobiological research has advanced to a point where chemical and neurological phenomena can actually be monitored and correlated with certain modes of thoughts, feelings, attitudes, etc., doctors can change the body's chemical balances and alter the physiological processes and structures they regulate, so as to modify how we feel and therefore how we will behave.

Nonetheless, the experiening of our feelings is not identical with the neurological and chemical processes and structures that produce and alter them. And as much as our feelings are the result of biochemical events within us, so our feelings (and often the feelings of others, as we take them in and process them) also produce such biochemical events. Drug therapy itself is based on this internal circuitry of physiology and feeling. Modifications in brain chemistry modify feelings which then themselves modify brain chemistry—at least up to a point; since, as we all know, there are unfortunately human beings for whom drug intervention does not suffice or for whom it is at best an inadequate lifelong necessity. This might be one reason why drug therapy alone is not sufficient. Nonetheless, if depression occurs because of a certain set of chemical and neurological processes that can be modified, then modifying those processes can indeed "cure" depression in the sense of making the individual "feel" less depressed.

The same logic pertains to other psychological conditions. The change may be purely symptomatic. Or, insofar as the alteration of mood will produce its own biochemical consequences, it may be at least the starting point for other more systemic changes. For if consciousness, even as it is being produced (in the body) or altered by chemical means (whether naturally or artificially induced), is itself producing such chemically induced transformations as well, then changing consciousness will have its own biological, chemical consequences. These physiological consequences will in turn naturally produce further changes in feeling and consciousness.

Of course if this is so, then we can also conclude that—as we said at the beginning of this chapter—at the very least, the talking cure also promises possibilities for remediation and change, even if in a different way and perhaps with a greater investment of time, effort and money than drugs. But that returns us also to the question: why do through psychotherapy what drugs alone may be able to accomplish?

The word *naturally* in relation to physiological process offers one clue as to why psychodynamic psychotherapy might afford certain advantages over drug therapy. To be sure, inevitably (naturally) drug therapy and the talking cure will both effect changes in consciousness/mind. But the natural way of this, the way it is done *naturally* in our bodies, is for the changes in consciousness to be produced first by our experiences of and interactions with the world, including the world that is ourself. The talking cure mimics nature's own way of producing the self-regulation and self-transformation which is the brain's major activity and the mechanism of our psychological as well as physical survival.

Because talking, even of the everyday kind, can provide relief of psychological symptoms, talking can often be an important accompaniment of drug therapy, even where drugs are vital to the individual's good health. In the first place, many drugs take several weeks to begin to work their effects, so talking is sometimes necessary till the drugs kick in. Even after the medication has taken effect, however, and is the primary mode of treatment, having someone to talk to (which is to say being listened to as well) in an empathetic, tolerant and even psychotherapeutic, self-illuminating way may also be indicated. Even in cases of serious biochemical imbalance (for example manic-depressive conditions, obsessive behaviours, hallucinatory psychoses) where drug intervention is essential, many human beings want to be engaged in this most basic of human experiences: the interaction and conversation with another person. Feelings and words may not be identical with each other. Psychotherapy is, in fact, predicated on the differences between them. Nonetheless, speaking is a normal way that we have of expressing, and thereby discharging, clarifying and otherwise dealing with powerful feelings. It is also often how we get back from other people the support and concern we very often need in order to keep ourselves in mental balance. There is also no reason to suppose that psychotic conditions *necessarily* preclude individuals from desiring and needing to talk and be listened to. It very much depends on the individual.

For all their differences from more ordinary everyday neuroses, psychotic behaviours are also often forms of self-enactment. They are languages. And that means that even where psychotic behaviours seem to be intended to baffle interpretation, they are also almost inevitably addressed *to* a "someone" who might be understood or imagined to understand and somehow respond. Relating to others and being related to are basic human need like eating and sleeping.

And that pertains even more especially to most of us ordinary garden-variety neurotics.

The talking cure responds to a basic feature of our psychological being, whether we have serious psychological ailments and symptoms or only minor complaints and dis-eases. Most of us in our various behaviours, expressions and enactments, are asking to be understood and responded to. The way we behave in the world isn't only about keeping in balance our inner demands and desires. Insofar as behaviour is always an externalization of some internal state, it is also a communication directed outwards towards the world of other people. This communication may be as much designed to conceal from the outside world what we are saying as it is constructed to prevent ourselves from knowing these things about ourselves. And yet, just as we simultaneously do and do not want to know what we are saying to ourselves when we respond one way or another, so (paradoxically) we equally do and do not want our behaviour to be transparent to others.

Of course, it must immediately be added that just as talking is an important supplement to drug therapy, so medication is often an important component within psychotherapy. Sometimes we need an alleviation of symptoms to make available the mental energy necessary for the psychotherapeutic conversation. The point is that medication and psychotherapy do not necessarily contradict one another. The one does not *ipso facto* exclude the other. Medication cannot, however, substitute for what talking provides both in our ordinary everyday conversations and in the special storytelling-listening conversation of psychotherapy. And this returns us to neuroscience and its own special way of looking at the mental life.

In the neurobiological way of looking at feelings, what feelings are for (to adapt Solms and Turnbull's terms) is to impart *value*. They are for telling us whether something is good or bad for us. So if talking makes us "feel" better, it might be a "value" for us human beings, and not simply in some ethical or moral sense. Talking may aid our survival and well-being in the world. Psychotherapy is, at the very least, a form of talking. At the very least it provides an additional benefit drugs alone cannot provide: the interaction and conversation with another human being.

But the talking referred to in the "talking cure" isn't, as we've insisted more than once, simply talking in the ordinary sense of the word. It is also an enactment, a performance, especially once the transference relationship between the therapist and the patient is established. It is a self-staging which may also recover a host of earlier childhood memories and impressions. This self-staging, furthermore, is meant to be witnessed and comprehended as much by the performer as by the audience. It is, in other words, a performance performed as much for the internal audience of self as for any external audience. This self-witnessing might also be a value in the biological sense. It might be likened to the production of consciousness itself, as it is neurologically understood. It is a form of catching oneself in the act of registering, interpreting and comprehending the mental images through which we interact with our world (including the world of other people). In the case of psychotherapeutic transference, the self being caught in the act of registering the mental images is the self not merely interacting with the material world but also reflecting on that very interaction. Psychotherapeutic process is that densely personal, that deeply self-referential. The very materials that produce self and consciousness are the materials that go into producing more self and consciousness.

The "value" of such heightened self-consciousness is, like the value of consciousness itself, to mediate effectively between inner and outer: between the physiological sensations and emotional reactions (as Damasio defines them) which go into producing drives, wishes and desires on the one hand and the external world on the other. This is the world that (in the view of these internal mechanisms—whether they are understood to be primarily biological or mental) may or may not be able at any one moment to satisfy those inner impulses, or able to satisfy them at a cost that our mental mechanisms determine is reasonable for the organism as a whole. In this way our brains (often in largely unconscious ways) "decide" which drives, demands, needs and wishes need to be acted upon. They "decide" which of these forces have to be put on hold or re-routed or denied, such that the organism (we) can survive on the best possible, least stressful terms. This means not only being able to permit certain processes and responses to ensue but, just as vitally, being able to *inhibit* them. Ironically, our freedom and powers of self-determination depend as much upon our powers of inhibition as upon any "positive" freedom of choice we may imagine ourselves to possess. To ensure this freedom, our forces of inhibition (the "defence mechanisms" in the Freudian vocabulary) need to have available to them the fullest, most complete possible range of options and alternatives.[5]

The job of regulating reactions and responses, of mediating between the inner and the outer worlds (which Solms and Turnbull, and also Damasio so deftly describe as the activities of our brains in the process of creating consciousness and feeling) is, we might recall, in the old Freudian terminology the function of the ego. Neurobiology and Freudian theory, as we have already observed, describe very similar processes. We might say, to shift our terms, that the ego is no more and no less than that set of mental processes by which the brain mediates between inner and outer and establishes what an individual organism can or cannot achieve in relation to his needs and desires (both unconsciously and consciously expressed). The ego is not consciousness precisely. But it is a part of consciousness. And it contains both conscious and unconscious contents and features. The ego does its work by shaping the pathways (neurological and/or mental) by which not only are certain events permitted to occur but others are prevented from occurring. It protects us against enactments that are likely to put us at risk or create conditions of dissatisfaction and dis-ease— either physically or psychologically. Given the dependence of our biological selves on such processes of evaluation and judgment, achieving physical and psychological well-being may amount to more or less the same thing.

We tend to think of our human freedom as the range of conscious choices we can make in one or another situation. To increase such freedom we would logically have to expand the range of such choices. And to do that we might want to increase our powers of mind and consciousness. Ironically, it is possible that we can achieve this end only through increasing as well the mind's powers of inhibition—its exclusion of certain possibilities from the range of our actions—in relation to the unconscious as well as the conscious contents of mind. To do that we need to do

[5] Solms and Turnbull, p. 281.

the very thing that psychoanalysis and psychotherapy help us to do. We need to develop skills for attenuating that resistance to self-reflection which prevents us from seeing what materials we are repressing and inhibiting and why.

Remember: in the psychodynamic view of the mind, it is when the forces of repression, which are never perfect to begin with, aren't permitting us sufficient emotional and psychological flexibility (i.e. when they are failing to resolve adequately and comfortably the intra-psychic conflicts that gave rise to them in the first place) that we humans begin to feel psychologically distressed. What the talking cure achieves, by helping us to reflect on our various strategies of self-protection and the materials they are repressing, is an expansion of the field of our knowledge of ourselves. This in turn enables more flexible and more broadly based mechanisms to begin to function. Working through the resistances with the help of the psychotherapeutic conversation is a way of enabling an individual to revisit (in many different ways and on many different levels) and, vicariously at least, to relive some of those moments which were stored in the dynamic unconscious when inhibitory processes first produced certain now ill-fitting or dysfunctional repressions and their consequences.

As Solms and Turnbull so nicely put it, "from the neuroscientific point of view… the essence of 'free will' appears to be the capacity of *inhibition*—the capacity to choose *not* to do something."[6] By bringing into conscious awareness aspects of the unconscious materials that are nonetheless being brought to bear by the mind itself on the decisions we make (the way we behave, the way we feel, the things we choose) we are, according to this way of looking at things, enlarging our possibilities of self-knowledge. And this, it would seem, permits an expansion of self-motivated action and self-agency. Because of the plasticity of the brain (on the biological level) and of the mind (on the psychological level) we can perhaps, through the application of our conscious knowledge of ourselves and of our inner workings, *inhibit* or change some of those default pathways, permitting and encouraging other more satisfying pathways to develop.

The biological picture of this can help us see how such plasticity might work on the psychological or mental level as well. Take,

[6] p. 281.

for example, the way in which memories are stored and accessed in the brain. We tend to think of a memory as a static and rather permanent picture or image, or at best a narrative with a defined beginning, middle and end, like a short story or a film. We therefore also tend to think of memories as being stored in one or other place in the brain, as if our brain cells were so many little drawers or filing cards, each one containing a discrete memory which could be called up at will. Yet what neurobiological research tends to indicate is that any single event is likely to be stored in several different places in the brain. What we call remembering, then, is in fact the coming together of these different components or aspects of the experience in the act of recollection, our calling them (or recalling them) to mind. In other words, bits and pieces of our lived lives, which are stored hither and yon in our brains, travel over various converging and diverging neural highways to reach some moment of (usually) conscious recollection which we call a memory. What is as amazing about this process as its multitude of variable components is its plasticity: which neural pathways are travelled to produce "a" memory are not necessarily always the same pathways; memories, as most of us know experientially, can (unlike the actual events they seem to record) change, often dramatically, from one moment to the next of their recollection.

This plasticity can come in very handy. For example, when a particular area in the brain suffers some sort of injury, often other areas can take over. With time, the brain can "learn" to perform certain functions differently such that skills, memories, knowledge and feelings which were at one time achieved through one set of neurological processes and routings can now be produced through some other such series.[7] This same flexibility, which can serve us on the biological level when some of our default pathways are damaged, can also be understood to help us on the psychological level when our default pathways of feeling and response are, let's say, not so much damaged as for whatever reasons not delivering us to our desired psychological destinations.

Insofar as our highest expressions of our humanness have to do with our being conscious, active agents in control of and determining our own fate, the ability to *inhibit* rather than simply

---

[7] Damasio, Solms and Turnbull, Ramachadran, and Vaughan all discuss this.

to initiate actions and behaviours may be understood to be one of our most important attributes. Doing something necessarily includes not doing something else. And thinking—evaluating, judging, deciding what to do—means *not* doing something for at least as long as it takes you to think that something through in the first place. Language in this sense is inhibitory. Words are what we use instead of acting out or doing something; sometimes instead of feeling something as well. Words can be pretty nasty and aggressive. They can do damage of their own. But they are never the same as actions.

Neurobiology provides potentially valuable physiological pictures of what Freudians describe in psychoanalytic or psychodynamic terms. If one takes, for example, the concept of strengthening the ego, what that might look like in a neurobiological sense is allowing materials (feelings, thoughts, memories, associations, conflicts) that are presently stored unconsciously somewhere and somehow in the brain, outside the range of the ego's conscious operations, to travel the brain's neural highways back into conscious or even preconscious awareness. In this way they can come back into active play within the arena of the self's ego functions. The ego, which functions along conscious as well as unconscious lines, then has available to it the largest possible field of operation. This means also strengthening the ego functions' ability to exercise their inhibitory functions—the possibility of our *not* doing something—in relation to the amplest possible range of our earlier consciously and (just as significantly) now *un*consciously "remembered" experiences. In such an expansion of the ego's inhibitory ability comes an increase in its (our) flexibility, our capacity for making the best possible decisions *for us* and for exercising a maximum of free will. New pathways of feeling and response can be established; new default positions (which may themselves one day need to be reinvestigated and rerouted) can be established; new, more satisfying, more "valuable" forms of behaviour can be enabled to emerge.

Most of us think of self-awareness as a value unto itself. Psychoanalytic psychotherapy, as we've already suggested, is certainly to be preferred to other forms of therapeutic intervention, from drugs to behavioural and cognitive remediation, if self-knowledge is a conscious goal for you. But self-awareness may also be one of our most fundamental *biological* values. It may be nothing less than the foundation for our adaptability (which is to say our survivability) as humans in a complex social (not just physical) world. And therefore the wish for and pursuit of self-knowledge may well be prompted not by our rational processes of decision making but rather, quite naturally, automatically, as a part of our unconscious apparatus.

Psychoanalytic psychotherapy, we might say, is not simply about a shift or transformation in how, on the conscious level, we think, feel, and behave in our lives. Rather, it is about a shift of the contents within consciousness, which produces nothing less than a shift in the internal circuitry of mental process on the unconscious as well as the conscious levels. By expanding the repertoire of our knowledge, of our conscious awareness of thoughts, feelings and patterns of behaviour (including the conditions of their origins, their suitability to our needs, their relationship to our other wishes and desires) psychotherapy doesn't merely cover over feelings. Rather, by activating the unconscious in the pursuit of conscious awareness, it produces new feelings (etc.) which in turn produce new modes of mental accommodation. Enhancing self-reflection and self-knowledge in this way is hard work—the hard work of working through the resistances to such conscious knowledge of ourselves. But it is work of such high and essential *value* (in the biological as well as the moral sense) that if we could come to experience the truth of it within ourselves (or for a moment put enough trust in someone else's report of it to believe them), we might choose it nonetheless *over* our resistance.

The story of your life

The neurological model of the brain offers us a picture or model of how the changes that psychoanalysis or psychotherapy effects may well exceed the transformations in feeling and even consciousness produced by drugs and by the non-dynamic therapies. By entering into that internality and interiority that define the subjective self and through which that subjective self is produced, psychoanalysis and psychotherapy put that subjective self at the centre of the process of producing more of its own very special, uniquely defined subjectivity. They assist feelings in doing what feelings (on the biological level) are meant to do: to monitor and produce the subjectivity (consciousness) whereby we can begin to determine for ourselves (through both conscious and unconscious mechanisms) when and how we feel well. Insofar as there is continuity between the purely unconscious mechanisms of the brain, the dynamic unconscious contents of mind and the conscious mind itself, this means we can begin to say for ourselves when and how we feel well. Such transformations as psychotherapy might produce don't cover over our stories or make them irrelevant, as drug therapy and other therapeutic modes might. Rather, they literally become a part of the production of those stories. They literally become the story of our life. There is more you producing you. And you are in narrative control of the story you are becoming: indeed, you are narrating it (verbally and in the transference) as you are in the process of becoming it.

If our stories are valuable to us, it isn't necessarily for their specific contents, which may or may not be verifiable as truths of our previous histories. Rather, they are important for the way in which they trigger in us thoughts and associations that we can read as indicators of how our minds work. Our stories are like our dreams: they are less important for what they might mean objectively than as ways we have of discovering how we might mean them, i.e. how we might make meaning in and out of our lives. Each and every one of us has his or her stories. Therefore each and every one of us has to find our own creative solutions for the problems that ail us. These solutions can build on our narratives as we come to understand them, and thereby take them in new and more hopeful directions. We can use the internal maps of consciousness to help ourselves get where we want to go.

Psychoanalytic psychotherapy is a site of story-telling in which story-telling must be understood in the fullest sense of the word: as an enactment (emotional as well as intellectual) of who we are (and have been). As almost everyone who has been in such therapy will tell you, the narratives that begin in the therapeutic hour continue to travel their plots and images—cognitively, emotionally, consciously and unconsciously—over the hours and days before the next session. We can ignore these stories we are telling ourselves, just as we can ignore the other forms of our self-expression. We can take them at face value, as meaning only what they seem to mean to our well-defended rational intellects. Or we can begin to explore them. We can begin to ask what a story or dialogue or word might *also* be saying to us, which isn't so obvious or logical or to be assumed.

Plato once said (in *The Republic*) that the unexamined life is not worth living. This is no more to be prescribed for each and every one of us than any other human truth, whether ethical, philosophical or psychological. Nonetheless, for many of us self-reflection is something we value, and not only for cultural or social or ethical reasons. If consciousness is always self-consciousness, then heightening that experience of self-consciousness can be a way for some of us to feel more alive—more competent, more conscious. It can also be a way to uncover what life it is that we are actually living, which hides itself behind our words and images and behaviours and feelings. Then we just might be able to say the words that do not simply describe that life but actually change it, the words that, taken back into our consciousness of ourselves, become the new and better terms of our existence.

CHAPTER TEN

The psychotherapeutic couple: where we are after therapy; an afterword

The "we" in the title of our afterword could be an impersonal first person plural, referring primarily to those of us who have completed the psychotherapeutic process: where do "we" find ourselves psychologically after psychotherapy? To some degree this final chapter does deal with this aspect of the aftermath of therapy. More important, perhaps, than the process itself is where that process takes us for the rest of our lives. But this final chapter has another subject as well. It is an attempt to make good on the unique situation of the co-authorship of a former therapist with his former patient. The "we" in our title, then, is also a personal "we". It also refers to the two individuals who have written this book. This chapter will deal with the transformation in the relationship between the former therapist and the former patient, which occurred when they came together to write this book. In general, the relationship between the therapist and the patient ends with the end of the therapy itself. In the case of this book, that relationship was quite atypically revived some years later in the radically different form of a writing partnership. In this final chapter we want to reflect on the psychotherapeutic process from within that change in our relationship.

The simple fact of the matter is that most patients and therapists do *not* go on to write books together, even when the therapy is long in the past, as this one is. In fact, except for those who are headed into professional careers in the field and whose analysts or therapists may well become their colleagues, most patients never re-establish contact with their analysts or therapists. If they do, it is generally to resume the psychotherapeutic relationship, whether in the long or short term. The psychotherapeutic couple exists for a single, defined purpose: the therapy itself. The relationship ends when the therapy ends.

This is so for several very important reasons. The psychotherapeutic relationship, despite the intimacy it produces, is a relationship deliberately and very carefully set apart from the ordinary everyday world of the two participants. It is defined by all the elements of structure (setting, payment, and the other rules of the game) that we have been discussing in this book. These are the elements that produce, permit and finally protect the very powerful transference and countertransference feelings through which the therapy proceeds. Because of the strong nature of these feelings, and the special kind of intimacy they produce, to move the relationship outside the clinical setting into the real world, without all the safeguards and checks and balances of the therapy in place, would be to risk distortion and exploitation in both directions.

The patient might well continue to use the crutch therapy has provided. She might continue to experience feelings and insights, not in the real world of her life but in the realm of uncensored fantasies and feelings, which have been activated for the purposes of self-reflection in the psychotherapeutic setting. For the therapist there is a similar danger. Even though throughout the relationship his role has been very differently defined and very differently conducted, nonetheless maintaining a relationship with the former patient risks continuing to reside in this same unreal place of the psychotherapeutic bond. This is a place often (though not always) characterized by the patient's over-valuation of the therapist. That over-valuation has, like other projections onto the therapist, been kept in check during the therapy itself by the therapist's understanding of how transference feelings work. After therapy the professional safeguards would necessarily fall away, to the possible endangerment of both parties.

In addition to this, the therapist might well feel that he wants to remain available to the patient, should issues crop up or symptoms recur even years later. Even at a remove of years, a patient may want to return to her therapist for a refresher course, or just to discuss an isolated problem or two. For this reason as well, most therapeutic couples bid their relationship good-bye with the formal end of the therapy as such. Even where the two partners forming the couple do continue some sort of professional relationship, as is sometimes the case among analysts and therapists themselves, they do not usually make their psychoanalytic/therapeutic relationship a continuing topic of conversation between them.

Co-authoring a book on the subject of psychotherapy, like becoming professional colleagues, dramatically transforms the nature of the relationship. In addition, by using as a basis for this now transformed relationship a discussion of the psychotherapeutic relationship itself, as to the best of their recollection it was experienced by the two individuals in that relationship, they have taken that transformation in an even more unusual direction.

What we would like to do in this afterword is to take advantage of the uniqueness of our situation in order to engage in that most primary of psychotherapeutic activities: reflection. What we want to reflect on is not, as in therapy itself, either one of us to the exclusion of the other. Rather, we want to use this new shared space of authorship to reflect on the two of us jointly, looking back on the time when we were a psychotherapeutic couple and contemplating how we have both been changed by that earlier relationship. To say psychotherapy changes the patient is only to claim for psychotherapy what it defines as its major *raison d'être*. But it may well be possible to claim that there can be no successful therapy if the therapist has not also undergone some sort of change—though what that change is, we hasten to add, may be of a very different order and be achieved in radically different ways from the transformation that the patient undergoes. In the case of the relationship between these two co-authors, the change-in-the-therapist had everything to do with his coming to consent to co-author this book. In some sense, the shifts in this psychotherapeutic couple mirrored each other in opposite directions: while she learned to speak, he revisited an interest in writing, so that he had begun to write himself even in advance of his collaboration in the former patient's project.

The intra- and inter-psychic spaces of therapy

The plural—*we, us, ourselves*—which is cropping up with increasing frequency in this afterword already marks the all-important difference between the psychotherapeutic couple (then) and the co-authoring relationship that defines our connection to writing this book (now). Whereas once everything that happened in the relationship was about and *for* one of us, now it is about the two of us, as we each express something about ourselves in the activity not of speaking and listening, one to the other, but of writing together about a shared subject, for an audience beyond ourselves.

As we noted in the chapter entitled "The therapist speaks at last", the relative silence of the therapist throughout the bulk of these pages fairly accurately represents the asymmetries and imbalances of the therapeutic relationship itself. The patient "enacts" her inner life in a variety of ways. She speaks. She "transfers" feelings. She reflects on those feelings. The therapist for the most part listens attentively but quietly. Most of his responses to the patient's stories are internal. Very rarely is the patient made privy to them. Occasionally the therapist makes a comment, asks for a clarification, expresses an internal thought. Sometimes he even offers the rare interpretation. He does not, however—like the patient—enact himself and reap the benefit of someone else's silent, active listening to him.

Of course, in writing this book we have deviated from the actual therapeutic situation of therapy as it is experienced by the patient, by presenting to the reader some of the things that were going on in the therapist's mind while he was sitting there in such apparent detachment. Yet even here, what we have brought forward to public view are only those of the therapist's thoughts, impressions and interpretations (whether expressed or maintained in inner silence) that pertained directly to the therapist's efforts to assist the patient. We did not delve into the cacophony and chaos of the therapist's other more personal thoughts and associations—

his wishes, desires, needs, feelings—all of which were also being evoked by the particular patient to whom he was then listening. These thoughts, sensations and reactions, of course, also helped bring the therapist to just those more patient-oriented conclusions which he does then bring forward for the patient's reflection one way or another. But these thoughts and feelings often exceed their usefulness to the patient. They have to do with the therapist's own wishes and desires for himself. And these thoughts and feelings the therapist precisely does *not* discuss and reflect on with the patient. It is part of the job of the therapist to avoid staging just this inner landscape in the clinical setting.

In other words, within his own mind the therapist is not a neutral backdrop to the patient's enactments. He does not stay outside the patient's words and feelings with a kind of scientific objectivity or detachment. This is the case even if he does not act on or even divulge his own needs and wishes when he does finally intervene in the patient's story. The therapist is always inside the patient's words and actions, living them and experiencing them within the privacy of his own mind. The major difference between the activity of the patient and the activity of the therapist, then, is *not* necessarily what is going on for each one of them personally within what we might think of as their intra-psychic internal landscape of mind. Rather, it is in how each one of them does or does not enter into and enact him- or herself in the inter-personal, inter-psychic space between them.

A useful way, perhaps, of thinking about the psychological arena of the clinical setting is that it is composed of these three psychic spaces: the two separate intra-psychic spheres of the therapist and of the patient and the inter-psychic or interpersonal space they create together, through which the therapy proceeds. Therapists are endowed with the same personal, private, intra-psychic spaces of feelings, impressions, memories, thoughts and so on that we all possess. Therapists, in other words, are no exception to the rules of the dynamic unconscious. The only difference between them and the patient—and it makes all the difference to the psychotherapeutic relationship—is that they do *not* use the therapy in order to stage and reflect on the unconscious contents and processes of mind, at least not in the shared interpersonal space of the psychotherapeutic relationship. Therapy is always and in every way *for* the patient. It is for the benefit of her introspection and gain. It is *never* for the therapist. That is the one inviolable rule of psychotherapy, perhaps of *all* therapies, even of the non-dynamic varieties.

As current theories of psychodynamics (especially within the field of what is called relational psychoanalysis) are stressing more and more, it is never the case that the therapist keeps the inter-personal space totally clear of his own intra-psychic dimension. At some moment the therapist does speak, and what he chooses to say at that moment, however spare, however minimalist, and however directed specifically to the patient's words and feelings, will nonetheless reflect how the therapist understands and puts things together. This pertains not only to how he understands the patient but, at least by inference, to how he relates to the world in general. Patients may not come to know much about their therapist's personal lives in the outside world. They do, however, come to know very well the person their therapist is. They come to see how he thinks and reacts and understands not only them in particular but, by extension, life generally. Yet even as he must necessarily become a feature of the inter-psychic space between himself and the patient, what the therapist does not do is use this space in order to fulfil his own needs (except, perhaps, that need which being a therapist serves for him). The inter-subjective or inter-psychic space between the patient and the therapist must exist *solely* for the benefit of the patient. This commitment on the therapist's part not to use this space for his own benefit is what guarantees this space as a primary, enabling condition of therapy itself for the patient. The patient can be totally uninhibited in her fantasies because she knows beforehand that the therapist will not act either on her fantasies or on his own.

As we shall see in greater depth in a moment, this protection of the inter-psychic space serves to protect the therapist as well. By choosing not to grant himself permission to enter into the inter-psychic space between him and the patient in such a way as to act on his fantasies and desires, the therapist gains within his own intra-psychic space a certain psychological freedom. He can dream his private personal dreams and experience his private personal desires without any need to censor them, because he knows from the start that he will not act on them. One can learn a lot about one's self being a therapist, if one is willing to be self-reflective.

Another way of putting this, which will lead us back to the subject of the present co-authorship of this book, is that in helping to facilitate the patient's writing of her story in the inter-psychic space of therapy, the therapist is also narrating in the privacy of his mind a story of wishes and wants. Yet he is actively refraining from writing that story anywhere but in his own mind. In the present project of co-authorship, the former therapist is telling his story, or more precisely: one particular story, in an external, public way; and he is telling a story that has to do with one of the major motifs of the former patient's story during therapy: her own relationship to writing.

Psychotherapy and the dynamics of professional change

When the idea of writing this book was first broached to the former therapist by the former patient, the idea was met with considerable reluctance. This was the case even though her initial request to him had not been for him to become a co-author. Rather, she had only wanted him to authorize and validate her text (i.e. to make sure the text was accurate and pertinent, backed by professional authority). The therapeutic relationship had ended many years earlier. Nonetheless, the former therapist was still extremely hesitant to enter the inter-personal space of a post-therapy co-authorship, even so minimally defined. This was not unrelated to what is referred to in the profession as the rule of "abstinence"—that basic rule of the psychotherapeutic relationship that we have just been describing, having to do with the therapist's vacating the inter-personal space and keeping it free for the patient. For all the reasons mentioned, even at the remove of many years, this space seemed to him still to belong to the patient.

The potential in psychotherapy for the exploitation of the patient is always great. Therefore the therapist must always be actively resisting it. By exploitation one doesn't need to be referring necessarily to anything as grave as any actual violation of the patient's mind or person. Rather, exploitation might consist simply of finding forms of personal satisfaction in the transference-countertransference relationship. If therapy isn't for the patient absolutely and in every possible way, then it isn't therapy, and it isn't ethical. It's as simple as that. And it seemed that simple still. Yet there is another feature of the psychotherapeutic relationship that is also important and that finally came to weigh in on the side of consenting to the authorial collaboration that in the end produced this book. This is the fact, which we have already begun to broach, that if a therapy is successful, it cannot but change the therapist as well as the patient.

To be sure, the patient and the therapist are going to change differently. The patient's changes are likely to be more obvious, more visible. They are, after all, the ostensible purpose of the therapy. Like everything else that defines the therapist's role in the psychotherapeutic relationship, his internal transformation will not be acted on in the inter-psychic space between them. It will therefore be apparent only to him—if even to him. It will be enacted and reflected upon exclusively within the privacy of his separate psychic space. Nor is it the patient's responsibility that the therapist changes. Like all other responsibilities in the relationship, that one also falls entirely on the therapist. But changes there will probably be.

These changes have fundamentally to do with what it means for the therapist to come to care about the patient, whatever other elements and tensions might also characterize their relationship. Therapists do not necessarily come to like all their patients; and they certainly don't like them all equally. If, however, they don't come at least to care about their patients, it is difficult to imagine how an effective therapy can proceed. Psychotherapy, as much from the therapist's perspective as from the patient's, has everything to do with coming to understand where and how human behaviours (feelings, thoughts, wishes, etc.) originate. It has to do with coming to see such attitudes and ideas from within the intra-psychic space of motivation and satisfaction, hurts and fears, where such criteria as right and wrong, good and bad do not pertain. This means, for the therapist, seeing the patient and his wishes, desires, attitudes, behaviours in some significant *dis-relation* to himself—at least insofar as that other person's being in the world might seem either to fulfil or threaten his own fantasies and needs.

The therapist doesn't dismiss the patient's feelings and attitudes toward him—positive and negative—as untrue or unreal. Nonetheless, he comes to see them as consequences of the transference relationship that the therapy has produced. The patient has cast the therapist in certain roles. The therapist has consented to be the object of the patient's projections. The therapist then, at least ideally, begins to empathize with the patient's experiencing of these emotions which are being directed, he realizes, not so much against him personally as against the person whom he has come to represent for the patient. In order to reach this position of empathetic acceptance of the patient's projections, the therapist often has to tap into his own inner resources of consciousness. He has to discover, or perhaps recover feelings, thoughts, attitudes that do not necessarily define his ordinary, everyday existence in the world. These aspirations and trepidations, memories and beliefs are nonetheless a part of his internal mental landscape.

The therapist's "abstinence" in relation to the inter-psychic space between the therapist and patient, which is intended to provide a safe space for the patient's enactment of her inner life, serves to protect the therapist's internal fantasy life as well. The patient's transference feelings may indeed make the therapist feel uncomfortable in any number of ways. This is one of the reasons that therapists constantly have to be interrogating their own responses to the patient and blocking the direct expression of their own gut reactions to these feelings. But because the therapist is not literally threatened by who the patient reveals herself to be in the inter-personal space (including how the patient feels about the therapist), the therapist can find himself free to respond to the patient with a generosity of spirit that does not usually pertain to our everyday relationships. In our ordinary lives we often do need to protect ourselves from other people's wishes and desires.

Ideally in therapy the therapist gains nothing from the patient's admiration. Nor does he lose anything by the patient's displeasure. Therefore the therapist can be *for* the patient, and on his or her side, in every possible way. That sometimes means being able to permit the patient to evoke in the therapist's unperformed, personal intra-psychic space the therapist's own feelings, wishes and desires. These wishes and desires are safe for the therapist to feel in this protected place of the clinical setting because he knows that he will not allow them to reach articulation, enactment, fulfilment or disappointment.

Generally we make friends, value colleagues, form relationships and fall in love because we have something in common with these other people. We gain as much as we give. Friends, lovers and colleagues satisfy needs in us, just as we satisfy needs in them. In the outside world, when that parity falls away, the relationship dissolves. To develop an intimate relationship with an individual with whom we do not share that reciprocity is a totally different matter. To forge such an alliance, the therapist has to draw on parts of him that are not necessarily the aspects of himself that he usually enacts. He has to discover within himself bases for relating that, for his own personal psychological reasons, may be precisely *not* his default positions. Indeed, they may well be aspects of himself that have, for all the psychological reasons that make all of us (patients and therapists alike) who we are, been placed under the forces of repression. Of course, some of the therapist's patients may well be "like" him. They may be people with whom, under different circumstances, he might well have forged a relationship in the outside world. But there is no depending on this. In therapy the therapist has to plumb the depths of his inner being in order to discover a way of being there for the patient. In this process of self-discovery many an old fantasy may be dislodged. That fantasy may in its own good time, after the therapeutic relationship has ended, have enduring consequences for the therapist. To be there for the writer-patient who is the co-author of this book, the silent, active listening therapist had to enter into a relationship to the written word that was not only unusual for him but that actually sat on an earlier, more hopeful, wishful relationship to writing. As the writer-patient was learning to speak, the listening therapist was reflecting on what it meant for her, and by extension for himself, to write.

The writer learns to speak in the intra-psychic space, or how the therapist came to be a writer as well as a listener

R.A. When my co-author first approached me with her idea for writing a book, I was reluctant to be involved in any way. She was still, from my point of view, a patient, albeit a former patient. All the old cautions and guidelines warned me away from renewing the connection with her in this way. Nonetheless, she had a clear idea in mind, which I thought a rather good idea at that. She had already taken the fruits of her therapy into her writing as well as into the conduct of her personal life: she was in many perceivable ways quite transformed from the person who had presented herself to me so many years ago.

In the initial conversations between us she spoke and I listened: a familiar pattern for me and for us. I was to act as a consultant, no more. The idea was for her to e-mail me what she had written (she'd already written a considerable number of pages), for me to read it, and then for us to meet occasionally to discuss and correct her ideas, for her to revise, write some more, send it on, and so on and so forth. But as the pages began to grow into a book and as I began to see my own ideas getting caught up and incorporated into the text, I experienced a sense of change in my relation to the project. I could hear my own voice speaking through hers until it wasn't always clear to me which portion of the text was hers and which was mine. I felt myself becoming less a consultant and more a co-author. And as I began to feel more and more comfortable in this give-and-take between us, I began to re-examine my reasons for not agreeing to become a fully fledged co-author of this text. This brought me back to reflections on the former patient (the predecessor of this current co-author) and what her psychotherapy had perhaps changed in me, not only in her. Might not the venture of writing about psychotherapy represent a new space for both of us?

My worry concerning co-authoring the book had to do with the ways in which the project might, despite her protestations to the contrary, be for her either a veiled repetition or a continuation of our previous psychotherapeutic relationship, now on the highly dubious grounds of professional collaboration. One of the reasons for "professional abstinence", i.e. for not permitting oneself to use the inter-personal space of the therapeutic relationship either for one's own gratification or, for that matter, for the patient's, is to prevent the patient from making good on her fantasy wishes and desires within the non-real place of therapy. Wishes and fantasies are to be reflected upon in therapy, not satisfied. There might well be fulfilment of such desires in the patient's real life outside therapy: what the patient does with the insights gained during therapy is for her to determine. But in therapy itself, fulfilment is never an immediate realization, certainly not within the psychotherapeutic relationship. The possibility that co-authoring a book with me (or even using me as a consultant on her own book project) might be a delayed playback of earlier wishes and fantasies was especially troubling because of the role writing had itself played in her therapy, even though it was that role that had also produced something of a change in me, which I was now inclining not to want to dismiss.

Like all therapists and analysts, I had had the experience of establishing a new and different kind of relationship with former patients who had gone on to become therapists themselves. Though it is likely that, to some degree at least, the earlier special quality of the relationship between therapist and patient necessarily continues to resonate, however tentatively, in the newer relationship of colleagues, nonetheless that special quality, I knew, does recede over time. Professional concerns come to replace earlier personal issues. And that change is aided by the fact that the earlier relationship no longer remains a topic of conversation between us. This was a different situation entirely. This former patient was not a professional therapist, although (and this only made matters worse) she clearly had aspirations (expressed during the therapy itself) to be a therapist, at least her own. Furthermore, what she was proposing was a project in which the subject was still going to be her therapy, even if now it was to become a more rational, intellectual, conscious topic of conversation rather than one handled through the transference and countertransference between us. There were many causes for caution and concern here. And even now, after my decision to come on board the project, they cannot all be dismissed out of hand.

And yet, even though she had hardly entered the field of psychotherapy in a professional way, she had made psychoanalysis into a subject of her academic work. She was writing and publishing about psychoanalysis and literature. She was utilizing these materials in the courses she was teaching. She was also involved in another book project, on a different subject, with another psychotherapist. If hers had indeed been, as she claimed, a successful therapy (and I had no reason to doubt that it was), then couldn't I acknowledge and accept that difference between her then and now? For that matter, couldn't I act on changes within myself as well, changes that had to do with my own relationship to writing? So I went back into my own memory of her therapy in order to discover what changes might have occurred in me, which I might not want now to dismiss so quickly.

One of the first things I had noticed about the patient when she first entered therapy was that she could discourse eloquently and intelligently about everything and anything except herself. She also, whenever tensions developed in the psychotherapeutic relationship, refused to discuss these tensions. Instead, she wrote me a letter. Indeed, she virtually bombarded me with written materials: essays and books she had written, essays and books written by others that seemed relevant to one or another topic we were discussing, and most especially the letters—long, convoluted, densely packed letters expressing what she was feeling; or more precisely: the feelings she was avoiding expressing in spoken words and in the clinical setting. Her letters were more eloquent than the coffee mugs, but they served much the same purpose. They were a substitute for a more direct articulation, in spoken words, of what she was wishing, wanting and needing. Whatever she thought those letters were expressing, they were certainly also expressing her resistance to therapy.

Like the coffee mugs, the letters contained a goodly amount of positive transference: indeed erotic transference. They weren't love letters exactly, but they were efforts at intimacy. They endeavoured to produce a shared space outside the professional relationship, such as drinking a cup of coffee together might also have produced. But the gift-of-the-letters was not a gift outright. The letters demanded a lot more of me in terms of my private space and time. In this way they were also a much more direct plea for help to which I needed to respond somehow. But the letters were also a much more direct assault on me. The letters, like the gift-of-the-mugs, also contained a goodly amount of negative transference. They were a demand and an aggression—such as she expressed in one of her dream-narratives, when she found herself in the office with both me and my family: in the dream she became one of my family. (The patient also thought I was much older than I really was, placing me firmly in the father position.) Like the cups, and like the dream, the letters also constituted an attempt to invade or otherwise intrude into the private spaces of my personal life outside the clinical relationship. They were also invasions into the personal space of my mind, which is, after all, where reading takes place. It was as if she would control not only what I would do and say but what I would think as well, and not only within the space of our professional relationship.

Even more than the cups, then, the letters were also an expression of negative and not only positive transference. Though she would hardly have accepted this description of them then, the letters were also acts of aggression. She would dazzle me with her verbal arts, and not only to win me over. She was also telling me how inadequate I was as a listener, which is to say as a therapist, but also as a wielder of words. My silence might well have seemed to her to express my lack of language. Probably the fact that although my spoken English is good, I am not a native speaker of English fed into this fantasy. In any case, her letters insisted that she was going to have the last word in every conversation, including this one of psychotherapy, in which she had everything to lose by not listening to someone else; indeed, by not listening to herself.

Negative transference is internally registered and interpreted by the therapist in the same way as the positive transference: to the therapist it may feel less comfortable to be the object of hostility rather than of worship, but still and all, that is what therapists are trained to deal with: the negative transference feelings which, like the positive transference feelings, don't really have to do with him per se but with who he is at that moment representing in the patient's inner world. I heard the assault—or rather, read it—with my professional ear, as an expression of her resistances and defences, her wishes and desires, her need not only in the clinic but in her life to avoid saying and doing by writing down her thoughts and feelings instead.

Letter-writing, like gift-giving, became a nexus around which to organize incursions into the sources and meanings of her various behaviours. Indeed, in many ways letters are like gifts. As in gift-giving, letters may carry the weight of things that cannot be broached directly and in so many words. Despite all the words of which a letter consists, there may be a great deal a letter does not say, especially about what kind of letter you'd like written in return. One benefit of a letter over a gift is that it is usually read; indeed, you often don't know not to read the letter or to ignore its contents till after you've read it. You can't return a letter once you've read it the way you can return or refuse a gift. In this way a letter is a gift that insists on being received by the recipient. And for her that made letters both a successful strategy of ensuring the acceptance of her gift (and the wishes and fantasies and complaints it unconsciously expressed) and also a woefully inadequate one.

One important feature of the psychological life is that whatever accommodations we have made, and however good they are, they will always carry with them to some degree the conditions of their origination. When this writer wrote—even her professional articles and books—she experienced that sense of a failure-of-communication, the failure of the giving and receiving of the gift (in both directions) which her letters to me also conveyed. And so there was sometimes in her professional writing as well a slightly needy, melodramatic edge, as if the writing were carrying the burden of something beyond itself.

I tried to use the letters to therapeutic ends, to open them up to reflection on her part, and to help her to see for herself the complicated personal stories letter writing itself (and not any particular letter) was telling. Hopefully, to some degree I succeeded in this. The letters did stop coming, first so fast and furiously and finally altogether. She had also ended her therapy in what we both felt to be a good psychological place, which included a good amount of self-knowledge concerning her reasons for writing. Had this not been a successful therapy, I would never have consented to advising her in the writing this book, let alone agree to become a co-author myself.

But writing this book also had to do with another aspect of my relationship to her writing, which had primarily to do with me and not with her. Needless to say, this aspect did not make its way into our clinical conversations—at least not directly—because I did not forbear to express my appreciation, even admiration of her writing talents. In truth, however, I was slightly dazzled by the letters and the other bits of writing she put into my hand. I could not help but be amazed at her persistence in assaulting me this way, and I could not help but marvel at the cogency of her written texts. If she wanted to make me feel inadequate, to some degree she succeeded—not in the face of coffee mugs or dreams, but before these very well constructed epistles of assault, which I did permit myself to read, outside office hours, in the private spaces both of my non-clinical hours and of my own mind—a concession not in keeping with my otherwise more disciplined, abstinent psychotherapeutic approach. In fact, when I once registered my ambivalence and even anxieties concerning all that letter writing—which of course I did not share with her directly—and she offered to pay me for the time I spent reading them, I refused the offer—though in retrospect I wonder whether I might not have got her into conversation and out of letter writing earlier had I taken her up on it. There are rarely sure calls in psychotherapy: often it's hard to know which route to take.

More to the point of this chapter, however, the therapist—who was the audience to this writer's drama of writing rather than speaking, and who had many ideas about what this might mean and how he might get her to reflect on the story being told by her refusal to put that story into anything but the written word—also had his own relationship to the written word, which her assault-by-letter brought into focus for him.

I had always wanted to write. In fact, unbeknown to the patient, during the early stages of her therapy I was on a partial sabbatical leave from my regular job. (In retrospect I wonder: did she intuit this? Did I let drop any clues that might have led her to understand this about me? Such self-scrutiny is imperative for the therapist even when the results of the therapy are positive, as they were in this case.) Ostensibly I was going to use that time to write. I valued good writing. But I had deliberately refused in my own life to become a writer, even a therapist-writer. To say the least, I had a complicated, perhaps even conflicted relationship to this barrage of written materials I was receiving from her, part of which had to do (I find myself confessing) with feelings of competitiveness, jealousy even, and some degree of failure—both because she was busy writing away, which she was not supposed to be doing in therapy (or at least *as* therapy), and also because she was doing this thing I would have liked to do so well myself. So well, in fact, was she producing the written word that she was succeeding in co-opting my private time and space, which I should not have permitted. To make matters worse, I was enjoying the invasion. I didn't say any of this to her. More problematically, however, I only partly said it to myself.

Of course, what the therapist does during the therapeutic relationship is to interrogate such responses on his part. This is what is meant by the therapist dealing with the countertransference, which is just as inevitably a part of the therapeutic relationship as is the transference itself. As has already been said more than once in this book, the only difference—which is nonetheless a major, definitive difference—between the transference and the countertransference is how they are implemented (or not) in the clinical setting. The therapist uses his countertransference in order to get a better understanding of the patient, and in order to better enable her to reflect on herself, including her transference onto the therapist.

But the fact of what the therapist feels—the feelings that the countertransference produces in him—do not necessarily simply disappear just because he utilizes them on the patient's behalf rather than his own. It is not as if, as these reactions are put into the service of the patient's self-dramatization of herself, they are self-consumed, such that they simply dissolve into the therapeutic work. They may well continue to dwell within the therapist. They may also become the bases for his further self-reflection, both during therapy and long afterwards.

This is what happened to me. The countertransference relationship to the writer and her writing continued to reverberate long after the patient had come to learn to speak, and in speaking to find other more useful ways to express her needs and wishes in relation to her family and friends and the world outside the clinical setting. What, I asked myself, is my own relationship to writing? Why had I never entered into that aspect of the profession? Perhaps the reason that this question landed so hard was the fact that while I had taken a sabbatical to write, I hadn't done all that much writing. And here had been this patient, writing away.

Many therapists are, of course, both listeners and writers. They write up case studies for admission into psychoanalytic institutes. They publish articles in academic journals and books with scholarly presses, especially if they are teaching academics. They write for the popular market. But I had *not* chosen the publishing route in my own career. I had been the head of a major clinic, had run a private practice, taught scores of students, been a member of a number of institutional teams throughout Israel. But, except on rare occasions, I had not published.

Part of the therapist's coming to care for the patient has to do with his respect for the way in which the patient is able to make the therapist privy to thoughts and feelings and wishes and fears that he or she would never directly express or expose to anyone else. That self-exposure eventually becomes self-conscious; that is, the patient comes to *consent* directly to clarifying, in words, what she is thinking or feeling and often obliquely expressing through other means, like coffee cups and letters. This is, in large measure, the goal of therapy. But until that time, the therapist is entrusted with a self-disclosure of which the patient herself is not necessarily aware. The patient's letters seemed to me acts of courage of this kind. Even if they were also acts of resistance, which intended to avoid saying certain things in a certain way, they did express and expose much of her private, personal, deeply inner life. I couldn't help but respect that willingness to put herself out there that way, to risk committing to the enduring shelf life of a written document (rather than the fleeting moment of the uttered word) what someone else might find trivial or foolish or even wrong. In coming to value her brave letters to me, not to mention her other writings, I couldn't help but become cognizant of the degree to which I myself was less brave in this regard, both in terms of such self-exposure as the written word inevitably carries with it and in terms of believing myself capable of writing something worth someone else's reading of it.

The former patient had made good on what psychotherapy had had to offer her. I felt I could make good on changes that had come about in me as well, especially now in relation to a project that seemed to me inherently valuable and the kind of project I would like to undertake. What finally prevailed over the quite legitimate worries I had concerning the resumption of the connection with a former patient *and* my more personal hesitations in relation to writing in general was the feeling that this was a project that was worth my while.

E.B. Words express us. Words also conceal us. When they do the one and when the other is very much to the point of psychotherapy. Writing about literary texts, the literary critic hides behind another writer's words. Writing a literary text, an author hides behind the words of characters, narrators, plot and the like. And yet hidden in the text is the author herself. In concealing the author, the text also exposes the author. It reveals what the writer would also not like to say. No matter who the protagonist of the story or what its subject is, or how much a particular writer tries to take him- or herself out of a given work, writing a story, like telling a story, is an enactment of the writer's inner life. This is as true of literary criticism and psychoanalytic writing as of any other kind of more transparently autobiographical text.

I hope that it has been fairly clear throughout this book how writing it has made good on certain of the writer-patient's fantasies concerning her relation to the field of psychoanalysis and psychotherapy. These fantasies preceded therapy. Indeed, in retrospect I wonder whether I didn't catapult the crises that sent me into psychotherapy because I so much wanted this experience which so many of my colleagues and friends had had and which, I hadn't been willing to "indulge in" for myself. Psychoanalytic literary criticism was also a field that attracted me. I wanted to try out that special and, to my mind, very exciting and satisfying way of reading and writing about literary texts. And I didn't quite know how to do it. Whatever my reasons for going into therapy, mixed in with them were the early professional decisions that made writing into my career and determined that I had written about literary texts in a certain intellectual and philosophical way. My hopes and aspirations in relation to my academic writing were not usually the central topics of my therapy. But they hovered around it. They were there in my wish to become a therapist, or at least an interpreter of my own stories: my therapist's colleague and not his patient.

One of the more productive consequences of the therapy for me was the definition of a new scholarly direction for my academic work. I could now, within my own professional expertise, further my acquaintance with the psychoanalytic literature I'd begun to read during therapy. I could also begin to use it, in the form of psychoanalytic literary criticism, in my own writing and teaching. By becoming acquainted with psychoanalytic strategies of literary criticism I was suddenly enabled also to look at a group of texts that had heretofore not formed the focus of my academic work, even though they had always been (for a variety of reasons I finally came to see) intensely interesting to me. Through my psychotherapy I came to understand *why* I'd chosen to become a teacher of literature in the first place. I came to remember why as I child I'd loved to read, and I began to understand how reading continued to meet some of my deepest psychological needs. The work of therapy, in other words, continued on for me in my private and professional life outside therapy, until finally writing a book *about* therapy itself seemed a logical and productive next step. Psychotherapy isn't intended to cure us of the fantasies that define our inner worlds. It is designed to help us discover what those fantasies are, and to find more useful, more satisfactory ways of expressing them in our lives.

In learning how to speak my thoughts and feelings and in coming to experience them from the depths outwards, from their unconscious contents to their very conscious expressions, I had also learned how to write again, in ways I experienced as much more meaningful, exciting and finally satisfying. Just as I learned when to give a gift to myself, so I learned how to write myself a letter—even if it seemed for all the world addressed to someone else, perhaps to the world itself.

I thought I had come into therapy with a particularly bad case of the "empty nest" syndrome: I was no longer defined by my role as mother; the grandchildren had not yet been born so grandmothering was not then an option; and I couldn't, for some reason, see myself only as a full-time academic and wife. What I could not see was that writing did the emotional work of excluding from my life certain feelings and emotions that had been expressed in my relationships with my husband and children, including my son who had died. Until writing came to include rather than substitute for those wishes and desires, I could not find writing satisfying. I couldn't find it satisfying because it wasn't satisfying: it wasn't satisfying my deepest emotional and psychological needs. I needed to access those needs. I needed to come to experience them and to discover how to "speak" them. In other words, I needed to learn to "speak" again in order to learn to "write" again. And when I did, the writing followed as naturally as thought from feeling.

Psychoanalytic psychotherapy and the uniqueness of self

The end of the psychotherapeutic relationship is not easy for either partner in the relationship—another reason why the temptation to maintain the relationship, and the need to resist that temptation, are both essential features of the psychotherapeutic contract. To lose such an intimate tie with another human being cannot but feel like what it is: a loss. This is one reason why, towards the culmination of the therapy, some time and attention are usually brought to bear on the patient's feelings about its termination. Although the therapist might seem (if only because of the sheer number of patients they are likely to encounter over a professional lifetime) immune to such a sense of sadness or loss, the professional person also often suffers from similar feelings at the termination of therapy. Even if they are a *therapeutic* couple, the patient and the therapist are nonetheless, in the deepest sense of the word, a *couple*. Despite those external circumstances that structure psychotherapy (time and money, for example) and despite the transference and countertransference feelings through which the therapy proceeds, they function in partnership with each other. In fact, it is largely because of these factors that they are a couple in the first place. When one thinks about relationships in the outside world, they too are often defined by the structures in which they exist (family, friendship, the workplace). They too carry forward feelings from the past into the present. Indeed, it is because of this similarity between "life" and "psychotherapy" that psychotherapy can work.

In co-authoring this book, two individuals who enjoyed that very unique atypical, asymmetrical relationship of psychotherapy moved into the much more normative run-of-the-mill sharing of inter-psychic terrain. The former therapist permitted himself to enter into this space with the former patient. And the former patient, who had once been granted exclusive use of that space, learned to make room there for the former therapist. For the patient-writer this has meant discovering an essential truth of writing and speaking, which is perhaps also an essential truth about psychoanalytic psychotherapy as a theory and a practice; namely that writing and speaking, reading and listening aren't about holding on to meanings, or holding them in. They aren't about possessing meanings and controlling them, or using them to possess and control others. Rather, writing and speaking, reading and listening are always about sharing: about taking in and giving out what belongs neither to the speaker/writer nor to the reader/listener but to them both. This making space in our lived lives for others is also true in relation to our own inner others—those dynamic unconscious contents of mind that contain the multitude of our other selves, our wishes, desires, memories, fantasies and dreams.

Psychotherapy is about coming to live our lives on the best possible terms for us. This means two things. It means coming to understand what those best terms are, which means coming to access the unconscious contents of our minds. It also means employing our rational intellects not only in analysing those contents but in discovering their relationship to the wishes, desires, wants and needs of other similarly constituted psychological beings. If what propels psychoanalytic psychotherapy forward is the curiosity it generates concerning who we are and what we wish for ourselves, the gift we gain in the end is an appreciation of the very special uniqueness of each and every one of us, not only ourselves. Co-authoring this book has been a very special experience. It has enabled both of us once again to appreciate psychoanalytic psychotherapy not only as a mode of psychological intervention, which aims at and hopefully achieves a specific objective, but as an enduring reminder of how extraordinary each and every one of our human lives really is.

Selected readings in psychotherapy, neurobiology and related matters

Albert, G. (1995). *The Other Side of the Couch: The Healing Bond in Psychiatry*. Faber & Faber.

Cardinal, M. (1984). *The Words to Say it: An Autobiographical Novel*. P. Goodheart (Trans.). London: Pan Books.

H.D. [Hilda Doolittle]. (1984). *Tribute to Freud: Writing on the Wall*. New York: New Directions.

Damasio, A. (1994). *Descartes' Error: Emotion, Reason, and the Human Brain*. New York: Avon Books.

Damasio, A. (1999). *The Feeling of What Happens: Body and Emotion in the Making of Consciousness*. New York: Harcourt Brace.

Damasio, A. (2003). *Looking for Spinoza: Joy, Sorrow, and the Feeling Brain*. New York: Harcourt.

Greenberg, J. (1989). *I Never Promised You a Rose Garden*. Signet.

Kramer, P. (1999). *Should You Leave?* Penguin.

Lear, J. (1998). *Open Minded: Working out the Logic of the Soul*. Harvard University Press.

Lear, J. (2003). *Therapeutic Action: An Earnest Plea for Irony*. New York: Other Press.

Luepnitz, D.A. (2002). *Schopenhauer's Porcupines: Intimacy and Its Dilemmas*. New York: Basic Books.

Malcolm, J. (1980). *Psychoanalysis: The Impossible Profession*. London: Picador.

Miller, A. (1981). *The Drama of the Gifted Child: The Search for the True Self*. New York: Basic Books.

Rabinowitz, Ilana (ed.) (1998). *Inside Therapy: Illuminating Writings about Therapists, Patients, and Psychotherapy*. New York: St Martin's Griffin.

Phillips, A. (1999). *The Beast in the Nursery: On Curiosity and Other Appetites*. New York: Vintage.

Phillips, A. (1993). *On Kissing, Tickling, and Being Bored: Psychoanalytic Essays on the Unexamined Life*. Harvard University Press.

Phillips, A. (1988). *Winnicott*. Harvard University Press.

Pinker, S. (2002). *The Blank Slate: The Modern Denial of Human Nature*. London: Allen Lane.

Pinker, S. (1997). *How the Mind Works*. New York: Norton.

Ramachandran, V.S. & Blakeslee, S. (1998). *Phantoms in the Brain: Probing the Mysteries of the Human Mind*. New York: William Morrow.

Vaughan, S.C. (1998). *The Talking Cure: Why Traditional Talking Therapy Offers a Better Chance for Long-Term Relief than any Drug*. New York: Henry Holt.

Weinberg, G. (1990). *The Taboo Scarf and Other Tales*. New York: St Martin's Press.

Winnicott, D.W. (1977). *The Piggle: An Account of the Psychoanalytic Treatment of a Little Girl*. New York: International Universities Press.

Yalom, I.D. & Elkin, G. (1974). *Every Day Gets a Little Closer: A Twice-Told Therapy*. New York: Basic Books.

Yalom, I.D. (2002). *The Gift of Therapy: An Open Letter to a New Generation of Therapists and their Patients*. New York: HarperCollins.

Yalom, I.D. (2000). *Love's Executioner*. Perennial Classics.

Yalom, I.D. (1999). *Momma and the Meaning of Life: Tales of Psychotherapy*. London, Piatkus.

Yalom, I.D. (2005). *The Schopenhauer Cure*. New York: HarperCollins.

Yovell, Y. (2001). *Sa'arat Nefesh* [Mindstorm] Tel Aviv: Keshet. [Hebrew]

Bibliography

All quotations from Freud's works are from the *Standard Edition*.

Aronzon, R. (2003). Psychoanalytic Psychotherapy. In: J. Hatav (Ed.), *Psychoanalysis: Theory and Practice* (pp. 323-341). Tel Aviv University Press. [Hebrew]

Batesman, A. & Holmes, J. (1995). *Introduction to Psychoanalysis: Contemporary Theory and Practice*. London: Routledge.

Benjamin, J. (1988). *The Bonds of Love: Psychoanalysis, Feminism, and the Problem of Domination*. New York: Pantheon.

Corsini, R.J. & Wedding, D. (Eds.) (1995). *Current Psychotherapies*. Fifth Edition. Itasca: F.E. Peacock Publishers, Inc.

Damasio, A. (1994). *Descartes' Error: Emotion, Reason, and the Human Brain*. New York: Avon Books.

Damasio, A. (1999). *The Feeling of What Happens: Body and Emotion in the Making of Consciousness*. New York: Harcourt Brace.

Damasio, A. (2003). *Looking for Spinoza: Joy, Sorrow, and the Feeling Brain*. New York: Harcourt.

De Saint-Exupéry, A. (1943). *The Little Prince*. K. Woods (Trans.). New York: Harcourt, Brace & World.

Kandel, E. (1999). Biology and the Future of Psychoanalysis: A New Intellectual Framework for Psychiatry Revisited. *American Journal of Psychiatry, 156*: 505-524.

Khan, M.M.R. (1972). Introduction. In: Winnicott, D.W., *Holding and Interpretation: Fragment of an Analysis*. New York: Grove Press.

Laplanche, J. & Pontalis, J.-B. (1973). *The Language of Psychoanalysis*. London: Hogarth.

Malan, D.H. (1979). *Individual Psychotherapy and the Science of Psychodynamics*. London: Butterworth.

Mitchell S.A. & Black, M.J. (1995). *Freud and Beyond: A History of Modern Psychoanalytic Thought*. New York: Basic Books.

Moore, B.E. & Fine, B.D. (1968). *Glossary of Psychoanalytic Terms and Concepts*. The American Psychoanalytic Association.

Ramachandran, V.S. & Blakeslee, S. (1998). *Phantoms in the Brain: Probing the Mysteries of the Human Mind*. New York: William Morrow.

Sandler, J. (1976). Countertransference and Role Responsiveness. *International Review of Psychoanalysis, 3*: 43-47.

Sandler, J., Dare, C. & Holder, A. (1992). *The Patient and the Analyst*. London: Karnac.

Solms, K.K. & Solms, M. (2000). *Clinical Studies in Neuro-Psychoanalysis: Introduction to a Depth Neuropsychology*. London: Karnac.

Solms, M. & Turnbull, O. (2002). *The Brain and the Inner World*. London: Karnac.

Solms, M. (1997). What is Consciousness? *Journal of the American Psychiatric Association, 45/3*: 681-704.

Thomä, H. & Kachele, H. (1987). *Psychoanalytic Practice*. New York: Springer.

Vaughan, S.C. (1998). *The Talking Cure: Why Traditional Talking Therapy Offers a Better Chance for Long-Term Relief than any Drug*. New York: Henry Holt.

Winnicott, D.W. (1965). *The Maturational Processes and the Facilitating Environment*. New York: International Universities Press.

Winnicott, D.W. (1971). *Playing and Reality*. New York: Basic Books.

Yovell, Y. (2002). From Hysteria to Posttraumatic Stress Disorder: Psychoanalysis and the Neurobiology of Traumatic Memories. *Neuro-Psychoanalysis, 2*:171-181.

Index

actions, 81, 186
actors, 132
advice, 23, 89, 113
Allen, Woody, 136
Analysis Terminable and Interminable (Sigmund Freud), 73
anger, 49, 107, 108, 111
animals, 64–5
antidepressants, 26, 168
anxiety
    childhood, 66
    everyday experience and, 57
    hidden wishes and, 152
    interpretations of behaviour and, 58
    mechanisms against, 32, 37, 38
    mothers and, 119
    routine and, 118, 122, 123
    therapy and, 148
archaeology, 116
assessment, 143–4
authenticity, 127

babies, 34–5
balance, 41
behaviour
    anxiety and, 58
    clarification of, 56
    as communication, 181
    dynamic unconscious and, 60–1
    modification of, 123
    principles of, 94
    problems with, 39
    protective, 120
    repetitious, 91–2
    structure of, 122
    unconscious and, 68
behavioural therapy, 27, 170–1
Beyond the Pleasure Principle (Sigmund Freud), 77
blame, 40, 94
boundaries, 36
brain, 166–9, 174–80
    decisions made by, 182
    Freud and, 61, 167–8
    injuries to, 185
    memory and, 83
    mind and, 81
    neurological model, 187
Brain and the Inner World, The (Mark Solms and Oliver Turnbull), 174, 176

Cardinal, Marie, 79
censoring
    childhood feelings, 130
    learning to, 103
    a mature response, 133
    superego's function, 36
    of wishes and desires, 19
change
    capacity for, 143
    discovering, 72
    learning and, 170
    other people, 69
    purpose of therapy, 27–8
    for therapist, 192
child within, 163
childhood
    adult behaviour and, 62, 94
    anxiety, 66

conflict from, 39, 64, 150
exclusion by adults, 112
experiences from, 148, 154
fairy tales, 103
memories of, 83
regression into, 150
relationship with family,
    130–1, 139
children, 64, 76–7, 79, 86–7
clarification, 147–8
cognition, 55
cognitive therapy, 28, 31, 71,
    170–1
communication, 181
competence, 164
compromise, 32
conflict
    childhood and, 39, 64, 150
    different levels, 32
    on entering therapy, 22
consciousness, 34, 172–9, 182,
    187
consequences, 31
control, 22
conversation, 9–12, 23, 31, 74,
    100–3- see also talking
coping mechanisms, 37
countertransference, 135, 145,
    146, 206- see also transference
crying, 68, 70–1, 75–6, 157–8
curiosity, 25

Damasio, Antonio, 175, 177, 182
defense mechanisms, 24, 37–9,
    41–3
depression, 53, 164, 179
desire, 38, 65, 106
development, 139

discrepancies, 4
dis-ease, 25–6, 28–9, 32, 41, 44
dreams, 62, 113, 150, 161
drugs, 82, 140, 168, 179–80
dynamic unconscious, 28–32
    basic principles of, 93–4
    benefits of psychotherapy
    and, 43
    discovering, 60
    Freud's theory of, 28, 61
introduction, 24
living on better terms with, 40
words and, 73

ego, 33–7, 39–40, 183, 186
Einstein, Albert, 71
elephants, 64–6
empty-nest syndrome, 53,
    209–10
enactment
    self-knowledge and, 18
    story-telling as, 41, 79, 188
    talking cure as, 182
experiencing, 108
exploitation, 196–7
expression, 17, 68
external objects, 34

fairy tales, 103
fantasies
    childhood, 94
    discovering, 209
    therapist's, 199
    therapy the place for, 113, 201
fathers, 76–7
fear, 123
Feeling of What Happens, The
    (Antonio Damasio), 175, 177

feelings, 127–8, 177–9
  old feelings, 102
  function of, 188
  neurobiology and, 181, 183
  patient's for therapist, 133
  therapist's, 9, 19–20, 103, 105,
      134–5, 147, 194
  transferring, 193
feminism, 53
fort-da, 78–81, 126
free association
  Freud's rule, 17
  initial bewilderment over, 23
  principle behind, 162
  therapist's reaction to, 149
  vital role of, 140
free floating, 141
Freud, Sigmund
  brain and, 61, 167–8
  differences in approach
    compared to, 2
  dynamic unconscious and,
      28, 61
  feelings prompted by
    analysis, 128
  free association, 17, 162
  id, 36
  mind-orientated views of, 26
  model of mind, 5
  nannies, 131
  neurobiology and, 186
  as observer, 84
  opening moves in analysis,
      140
  perceptions of today, 3
  psychosis, 140
  story-telling, 62
  talking cure, 136, 174
  terminology, 29

  three part division of psyche,
      33
  transference the main
    driving force, 145
  unconsciousness of body's
    processes, 178
Freud Museum London, 116
funding agencies, 45

gender, 11, 67
gift giving, 15–24, 47–56
  differing gifts, 105–6
  letters as, 204
  as a story, 126
Gift of Therapy, The (Irving
  Yalom), 54
Groundhog Day, 92
Guest, Christopher, 132
guilt
  everyday experience and, 57
  hidden wishes and, 152
  interpretations of behaviour
    and, 58
  loss of a child and, 111
  mechanisms against, 32, 37,
      58
  mourning and, 162–3
  therapy and, 148

hunger, 34
hysteria, 61–2, 86

id, 36
immaterial consciousness, 174–
  see also consciousness
impatience, 45
improvisation, 132
inhibition, 184–6
insight

acting on, 124
conflict and, 22
consequences of, 131
development of, 99
fantasy as route to, 113
not sudden revelations, 55
self-knowledge and, 123
of therapist, 59
instability, 39
instinct, 33, 35, 38
integrity, 68, 69, 90
interest, 25
interpretation, 16, 56, 89, 107–8,
  149–50
Interpretation of Dreams, The
  (Sigmund Freud), 62
intervention, 59, 146, 149, 151
intimacy, 90

jealousy, 131
jokes, 82, 106

Lacan, Jacques, 79
language- *see also* words
  children, 79
  expression by, 23, 90
  a major tool, 20
  repetition and, 81
  story-telling's heart, 73
  surplus of meaning, 106
Lear, Jonathan, 163
letters, 202–5
light, 133
linking, 112, 148
listening, 85, 109, 137, 141–2,
  146- *see also* story-listening
Little Prince (Antoine de Sainte-
  Exupéry), 137–8

loss, 76–7, 160, 161–2
love, 35–6, 52–3, 58, 127

Malan, David, 152
meaning, 20, 106
meaningfulness, 4, 73
medicine, 63
memory, 30, 83, 185
mental health, 36–7
mentalization, 33, 34
Miller, Alice, 128
mind
  attempting to define, 172
  brain and, 81
  defences of, 47
  dynamic unconscious and,
    29–30
  ego and, 33
  Freud and, 5
  other people's, 178
  unconscious and, 28
mind and body, 81, 82, 174
money, 45
mothers, 48–51, 78, 97–9, 110,
  118–21
mourning, 162–3
murder, 110–11

narrative- *see also* story-telling
  Freud's observations, 62
  reactions and, 91
  self and, 52
  solutions and, 188
  therapist and, 74
needs, 33–4
neurobiology
  complementing Freud, 186
  feelings observed from, 181,
    183

research developments in 166–7, 178

nurture, 53

object constancy, 78
obsessive-compulsive
    behaviour, 61–2
Oedipus, 129–31, 138

pain, 18, 45
panic, 109–11
parents, 127, 130–1, 139
patients
    anger, 108
    childhood experiences, 148, 154
    choices of, 12, 105–6, 165
    conversation in therapy, 74, 100
    end of relationship with
        therapist, 9
    exploitation, dangers of, 196
    feelings for therapist, 133
    first meeting with therapist, 142
    free association by, 17, 140
    frequency of meetings, 150–2
    Freud's, 62
    helped to cope, 125
    impatience of, 45
    insight gained, 55, 99, 124, 131
    lack of advice for, 23
    need for therapist, 145
    old feelings located, 102
    performance of, 129
    projection on to therapist, 96–7, 145
    purpose of talking, 11
    resistance by, 15
    self-disclosure, 207
    a set-apart relationship, 191, 194, 198
    specificity issues, 155
    story-telling, 12, 31, 48, 90
    suspicion of therapist, 127
    therapy is for the patient, 195
    transference and, 73, 90–1, 144
    trusting the therapist, 156
    types of, 63
performance, 129, 182, 183
pictures, 5, 35, 122
Plato, 189
post-therapy, 10
projection, 37, 96–7, 145, 198
protection, 64–6
Prozac, 26, 168
Psychopathology of Everyday Life,
    The (Sigmund Freud), 63
psychosis, 140, 180

rationalization, 120
reaction formation, 37
reality, 35
reassurance, 80
reciprocity, 199
recovery, 76–7
recycling, 73, 113
re-experiencing, 101
regression, 150
relief, 4
repetition, 81, 86–7, 91–2, 125
repression, 37–9, 120, 122, 184
Republic, The (Plato), 189
resistance, 41–7

centrality of, 3, 10
choice patient has made and,
    21–2
reflection and, 14–15, 103
to self-clarification, 56
to self-knowledge, 22, 24, 41,
    47, 57
to self-reflection, 22, 41, 46
therapist softens, 124–5
understanding and, 59
vagueness signifying, 147
respect, 127
re-telling, 13
rites, 138
rituals, 138

sadness, 156
Sainte-Exupéry, Antoine de, 137
scheduling, 151
self, 128–9, 132, 133–4, 182
self-awareness, 154, 169, 186–7
self-clarification, 42, 56, 57
self-consciousness, 10, 71, 182,
    189- *see also* consciousness
self-empowerment, 123
self-esteem, 57
self-exposure, 57, 207
self-knowledge
    enlarging the possibilities,
        184
    insight and, 123
    resistance to, 10, 22, 24, 41,
        47, 57
self-reflection
    defining, 17
    different possible paths, 52
    permitting oneself, 20
    resistance to, 22, 41, 46

self-revelation, 57
self-worth, 159
sessions, 151–2
sexuality, 130
shame, 32, 37, 38, 57, 58
sharing, 211
silence, 142
Sleeping Beauty, 103
Snow White and the Seven Dwarfs,
    103
socialization, 133
Solms, Mark, 174, 176, 183, 184
speech acts, 81
Spock, Dr, 77
stage managers, 132
story-listening- *see also* listening
    a conversation, 31
    helping the story-teller, 85
    intimacy of, 59, 90
    a patient's terms for, 21
    re-telling and, 74
    story-telling and, 13, 117
    therapist and patient, 12
    therapist's responses to, 109
story-telling, 104–8
    actions and words, 126
    assisted, 74
    by children, 64, 76–7, 87
    choice in, 52
    context in, 105
    deciphering, 31
    defence mechanisms against,
        41
    different stories, 106
    discovering new stories, 48
    as expression, 108
    a feature of psychotherapy, 7,
        12–13, 21

Freud and, 62
as indicators of our minds,
    188–9
intimacy with listener, 59, 90
language in, 73
listening to your own story,
    59
other people's stories, 14
patient's, 12, 31, 48, 90
recovering of, 164
reflected in therapist, 137
sharing one's inner life, 84–5
specificity of, 165
structural aspects, 105
transference and, 12, 73, 104
unconscious and, 12
subjectivity, 133
sundials, 133
superego, 36
symptoms, 39

talking, 11, 74–5, 168–9, 180- see
    also conversation
talking cure, 136, 174, 179, 181–2
terminology, 6, 29
Therapeutic Action (Jonathan
    Lear), 163
therapists
    'abstinence' of, 196, 198, 200
    advice and, 113
    assessment by, 143–4
    calmness, 15
    conversation with patient,
        74, 100
    coping strategies for patients,
        125
    countertransference, 206
    dangers for, 191–2

end of relationship, 9, 190,
    192, 210
feelings of, 9, 19–20, 103, 105,
    134–5, 147, 194
first meeting with, 142
gratification of patient, 134
interpretation by, 56, 89,
    107–8, 149
intervention by, 59, 146, 149
links made by, 112, 148
listening functions, 85, 109,
    137, 141–2, 146
neutrality of, 108
only there for the patient,
    195, 197
patient's need for respect
    from, 127
patient's resistance, 15
privacy for, 113
projection by patient, 96–7,
    145
resistance encountered, 148
role of, 136–7
selection by,107
silence of, 13, 107, 138, 193
space between words and
    events and, 104
stage manager as, 132
story-telling relationship
    with patient, 31, 48, 90
structure of relationship, 191
surplus of meaning and, 106
task of, 143
transference and, 73, 90–1,
    144, 203
thinking, 81–2
three person pyschology,139
time, 45, 112

toys, 78
tranquillizers, 122
transference, 90–6
    as basis for psychotherapy,
        149
    as clinical term, 73
    difficulties in understanding,
        125
    as drama, 132–3
    feelings in, 128
    first act of, 99
    Freud and, 145
    from first encounter with
        therapist, 144
    key to therapy, 90, 117
    letters as means of, 202–5
    lifeforce of psychotherapy, 46
    mini-staging of one's life, 40
    on to therapist, 145
    relationship with therapist,
        48, 55
    story telling and, 12, 73, 104
    therapist encourages, 134
    transformation of mind, 116
    words in, 104, 114
transitional objects, 79
trauma, 84
truths, 58, 117
Turnbull, Oliver, 164, 169, 183,
    184

unconscious
    behaviour and, 68
    consciousness and, 172–3
    consequences of accepting,
        119
    dimension of in everything,
        63
    emotional conflict from, 101
    Freud, 29
    length of time one can spend
        in, 135
    mind and, 28
    processes of, 60
    processes outnumbering
        conscious ones, 168
    psychotherapy proceeding
        through, 55
    resistance to accepting, 114
    story-telling and, 12
subjectivity required, 188
of therapist, 134
wishes and desires, 104, 122

value, 181, 187

winners and losers, 88
Winnicott, D. W., 25, 77, 79, 99,
    128
wish, 93
words, 80–1- see also language
    actions and, 126, 186
    ambiguity in, 106
    as a bridge, 84
    dynamic unconscious and,
        73
    events and, 90, 104
    expression and concealment,
        208
    hysteria in, 86
    stories and, 104
    transference and, 104, 114
writing, 208–10
'working through', 46

Yalom, Irving, 54